DATE DUE

GAYLORD			PRINTED IN U.S.A.

Perfect Justice

Also by Don Lasseter

PERFECT JUSTICE

A True Crime book

Don Lasseter

SEVEN LOCKS PRESS

Santa Ana, California

Seven Locks Press,

P.O. Box 25689

Santa Ana, CA 92799

800-354-5348

Printed in the United States of America

ISBN1-931643-48-2

Library of Congress Cataloging-in-Publication Data

available on request.

Cover and interior design: Richard E. Cheverton/ Waypoint

TABLE OF CONTENTS

Author's Note

OUTRAGE GRIPPED JUDGE DONALD A. McCARTIN when he opened his morning newspaper on Saturday, June 28, 2003. He felt as if he been kicked in the stomach. The stunning headlines trumpeted an incomprehensible act by the U.S. 9th Circuit Court of Appeals.

How could they have done it? This time they had gone too far; throwing out the entire verdict and death penalty for Rodney J. Alcala. The condemned inmate had been found guilty TWICE of savagely murdering a 12-year-old girl in Huntington Beach, California, and spent twenty three years on death row for the bloodthirsty crime.

Not only had the court nullified what two juries had spent torturous months hearing and deliberating, but it had also accused McCartin of judicial errors!

"Hogwash!" the retired judge shouted, and picked up his telephone.

NO STRANGER TO TRUE-CRIME READERS, Superior Court Judge McCartin sent nine convicted killers, including Alcala, to death row from Orange County, California.

Trials he conducted have been chronicled in three books and a motion picture made for television:

If You Really Loved Me (Simon and Schuster, 1991), by Ann Rule, tells the story of David Arnold Brown who persuaded his fourteen-year-old daughter, Cinnamon, to murder Linda Brown, her own step-mother. Brown was sentenced to life imprisonment by McCartin. The daughter served several years in a juvenile facility.

Love, Lies and Murder, a television movie about the same case, was shown on NBC.

Angel of Darkness (Warner Books, 1991), by Dennis McDougal, chronicles one of the most prolific serial killers in the United States, Randy Steven Kraft, who was tried and sentenced to death by McCartin.

Property of the Folsom Wolf (Pinnacle Books, 1995), by Don Lasseter, describes a rape-murder spree perpetrated by a couple, James Gregory Marlow and Cynthia Lynn Coffman. Judge McCartin tried Marlow and sentenced him to death. Coffman received the same penalty in a San Bernardino County trial.

BEFORE NOON ON THAT SAME SATURDAY, I answered my telephone and heard an old pal, Don McCartin, seething with fury. "Let's write a book about this," he said. I had read the *Los Angeles Times* account of the shocking reversal, and immediately agreed to collaborate with him.

In researching the project, I found both the crime and the judicial labyrinth gripping. Something else, though, riveted me as well. During my visit with the judge at his Bass Lake home, he filled me in on his personal history. His narrative was loaded with famous names, remarkable events, and salty humor. So, this book will tell three stories:

1) Rodney Alcala's convictions for the murder of a beautiful child, and the system of justice that lifted him from the confines of death row twice to face yet a third trial.

2) The personal memoirs of one of the most colorful judges ever

appointed to the bench, and regarded by many as a Solomon with a sense of humor, but by others as Roy Bean reincarnated.

3) Tales of eight other killers convicted in McCartin's court and sentenced to death by him.

The 9th Circuit Court is notorious for frequent reversals and rebukes by the U.S. Supreme Court. Critics accuse 9th Circuit justices of being too liberal and willing to strike down death penalty cases in accordance with their personal or political agendas.

McCartin voiced his opinion in stronger terms. "Seventy percent of death penalty cases are overturned by the 9th Circuit Court, a bunch of hacks who have never tried a case themselves. They expose their own political biases. Too many of these federal judges don't have trial court experience. It's like reviewing a book without reading it. They need to understand that trial judges can see the demeanor of witnesses and observe expressions on their faces. In the sterile world of high courts, they only read the dry words in transcripts. You can reverse any case if you give undue weight to minor, harmless issues. They want perfect justice, and that's like wanting utopia. There is no such thing."

Perfect justice?

You decide.

Foreword

Word ricocheted from cell to cell, through the exercise yards, and along the cold concrete-steel halls of death row. It spread from the iron-grated entry, over which someone long ago had painted Old English letters reading "Condemned Row." The buzz filtered to the sixth-floor north segregation housing unit regarded as the penthouse by inmates; to the multitiered cells of the crowded east block where birds flit from nests clinging to upper beams and deliver songs that can sometimes be heard over the incessant bedlam of human noise. For some, the amazing news came with breakfast delivered from hot rolling carts to men cramped in endless rows of ancient five-by-nine-foot cells. When their barred doors clanged open to allow exercise, they relayed the word from man to man. In whispers and shouts, it even moved on to the "AC," the adjustment center where "badasses" land after violating rules.

Within a day, more than six hundred condemned men inside California's aging fortress of San Quentin prison had heard about Rodney Alcala. Many of them knew him personally, while others had heard of him only in passing.

As the remarkable information worked its way through the grapevine, its impact varied among the men. Some reacted with raised eyebrows or soft curses of envy. Others speculated about Alcala's future.

Eight inmates, among the forty–seven men convicted in California's Orange County Superior court, probably took particular notice. They had something in common with Alcala—all nine had been tried, convicted, and sentenced by the same judge, Donald A. McCartin.

RANDY KRAFT, CONDEMNED TO DEATH IN 1989 for murdering sixteen male victims, very likely showed no emotion, preferring to concentrate on the daily game of bridge that occupied much of his time. Richard Boyer, bespectacled, balding, arms covered with tattoos, and probably envious, had once said he'd rather die in the gas chamber than rot in prison for life, but had occupied death row nearly ten years. Martin Kipp, a former U.S. Marine, born and raised on a Blackfoot Indian reservation, kept the impassive expression he showed during his 1987 trial. James Marlow, buffed, burly, with a howling wolf tattooed on his side, may have shown his extraordinary sense of humor and joked about it. Richard Ramirez, sometimes mistaken for the notorious "Night Stalker" of Los Angeles County who occupied a cell elsewhere on death row, wondered if his own appeals would ever help him. Bill Payton, blue-eyed, blond, good looking, facing his fiftieth birthday in a few months, may have said, "God bless him." Payton had lived on the row twenty–one years. Robert Thompson, a twenty-year resident, most likely leveled his piercing brown-eyed stare at the news carrier and scoffed. Thompson's writs had been rejected by the appeals justices. Gregory Sturm, 33, had been in San Quentin nearly one-third of his life. The news may have given him some hope.

A worrisome statistic might also have piqued interest by these men. About seven per-cent of the row's total population had been sent there from Orange County. Only ten convicted killers, from thirty–seven counties throughout California, had been executed in San Quentin since reestablishment of the death penalty in 1978. Three of the ten, or a lop-sided thirty percent, had been tried and sentenced in Orange County.

RODNEY JAMES ALCALA HAD ENTERED the dreary routine of death row in June 1980 and, with time out for a repeat of his murder trial in 1986, remained a resident until June 2003. Twenty–three long, miserable years. The 9th Circuit Court decision came on June 27, 2003, just two months before Alcala's sixtieth birthday. When he had first arrived at San Quentin, only a few dozen men occupied the cells in the north segregation housing unit, the original section designated as death row. He watched the population gradually swell to nearly 650 convicted killers, overcrowding the facilities to the straining point. In April 1992, he had seen Robert Alton Harris go to the gas chamber and become the first California inmate put to death in more than twenty–five years. After Harris, between 1992 and January 2002, nine more had been executed, most by lethal injection. Alcala had repeatedly endured the nerve-straining anxiety of knowing that men scheduled to die were sweating out their final days of life. More than a few convicts facing execution had been close to entering the death chamber before receiving last-minute reprieves from the courts. During Alcala's long stretch on the row, thirteen men had committed suicide, exceeding the number executed. Twenty–two had died from other causes.

Like many other condemned men, and the dozen women in a separate facility, Alcala doggedly held out hope that his legal appeals would eventually win his freedom. When the California Supreme Court overturned his conviction in 1984, his optimism soared. He was sent back to Orange County in Southern California, where he faced trial in Judge McCartin's court. Once again, though, a jury found him guilty of first-degree murder and recommended a sentence of death.

In 2001, a federal district court examined the trial, ruled that constitutional errors had been made, and issued a grant of habeas corpus relief. The decision was appealed to the U.S. 9th Circuit Court of Appeals.

Now, in June 2003, the 9th Circuit Court had granted Alcala's wish by affirming the district court's reversal of the 1986 conviction.

While Alcala celebrated and waited to see what his future held, at least two other people reacted in horror.

In Norco, more than five hundred miles south of San Quentin, Marianne Connelly (formerly Frazier) felt her life turning upside down again. She had suffered unspeakable horror in 1979 when her beautiful young daughter had vanished. After more than a week of desperate heartbreak, she heard that her child's battered remains had been found in a remote mountain ravine. Rodney Alcala's arrest, trial, conviction, and death sentence didn't bring closure, but provided a sense of relief. It was much too brief. The pain ripped through Connelly once more when California's Supreme Court overturned the conviction five years after Robin's death, generating a repeat of the whole process. The distraught mother had attended every hearing and each day of both trials. Once more, Alcala had been sent to death row. Now, Connelly wondered if the nightmare would ever end. A third trial loomed on the dark horizon.

In Bass Lake, a retired judge fumed in outrage. After Donald McCartin had presided over Alcala's second trial, he firmly believed that justice had been properly administered. But black-robed members of the federal court had pointed fingers directly at McCartin, accusing him of judicial errors. They were wrong, insisted the former judge. "Alcala was as guilty as anyone who has ever entered my court."

Officials in Orange County pondered the dilemma. In both of Alcala's trials, prosecutors had presented a case based primarily on circumstantial evidence. The district attorney realized that much of the evidence previously used would be unavailable as a result of the federal courts' rulings.

With the passage of nearly a quarter-century, would it be possible to convict Alcala a third time?

That question also made the rounds in San Quentin's death row.

"Didja hear about Alcala?"

"What about him?"

"Ninth Circuit Court overturned his conviction and penalty!"

"Man, that's unbelievable. That dude's been here more than twenty years."

"Yeah. And this is the second time his rap's been overturned. That California Supreme Court broad cleared him back in eighty–four. He got convicted again in eighty–six. Been here ever since."

"Maybe he didn't do the crime. If the courts overturned it twice, maybe he's gonna skate for good."

"Maybe."

PART I

THE CRIME

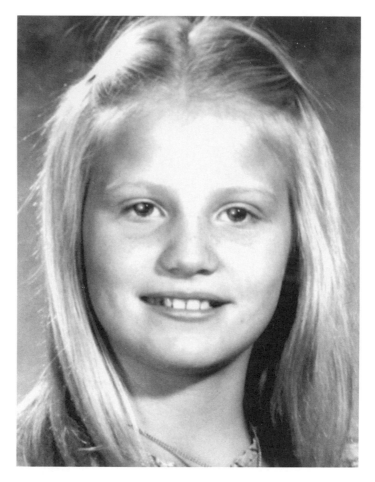

Robin Samsoe
Murder victim

Death of an Angel

O N THE FINAL DAY OF HER LIFE, 12-year-old Robin Christine Samsoe and her best friend raced across Pacific Coast Highway toward the ocean. They scouted for a good place on the cliffs to sit and watch throngs of sunbathers below. A few blocks to their left, they could see strollers and fishermen on Huntington Beach's historic pier. In both directions, thousands of bikini-clad women and bronzed young men sprawled on multicolored towels, juxtapositioned in irregular patterns along the wide stretch of hot sand. The breeze carried music blaring from portable radios, mostly tunes by the Bee Gees. Swimmers frolicked in foamy saltwater rushing and retreating while in the distance, surfers bobbed on sparkling swells, waiting for the perfect wave.

At about two–fifteen on that clear, breezy, sunny afternoon, Robin and Bridgett Wilvert, also twelve, found a spot on the cliff top and sat down to catch some rays. They planned to stay no more than half an hour so Robin could keep her five o'clock ballet class appointment at Beverly Fleming's Dance Studio.

Both girls lived in apartments, separated by a few blocks, each within walking distance of the shore in "Surf City." Huntington Beach had adopted that title from the popular 1960s hit song by Jan and Dean.

With its eight miles of inviting sand, spectacular blue waves curling and crashing into the sand, and a pier jutting nearly two thousand feet out to sea, the community attracted hordes of surfers, sun worshipers, fishing buffs, and vacationers. The crowds peaked in summer months, but continued coming even on balmy winter days. Officials took pride in the city's low crime rate, but with thousands of people playing on the beach, a few among them certainly had something on their minds other than tanning and swimming.

In the early part of the twentieth century, the sleepy seaside village, first known as Shell Beach, then Pacific City, had been renamed after railroad magnate Henry E. Huntington. The great pier, first built in 1903, had been ripped and battered over the decades by stormy waves sometimes towering more than twenty feet. It had been repaired, extended, and reinforced several times. By Wednesday, June 20, 1979, when Robin and Bridgett soaked up the sun nearby, the pier seemed invulnerable to the gently rolling water underneath. But, like frail and tenuous human life, it would be destroyed again and again by terrible forces.

Not long after they arrived, the two young girls glanced at one another and giggled when a slim man holding a camera approached them. He stood a little under six feet tall and had dark, curly, shoulder-length hair. With a smile, he asked if he could take their pictures. He said he was enrolled in a photography class and would like to enter snapshots of them in a contest. His charm was hard to resist, so they agreed to pose. The stranger first photographed them together, then asked Robin to pose alone with her foot up on a ledge.

The session was interrupted when a woman acquainted with Bridgett's family walked over, thinking the young blond girl was her niece. She was mistaken about the relative, but recognized Bridgett as a neighbor. With a smile, Jackelyn "Jackye" Young asked. "What are you two young ladies doing?" Her presence apparently alarmed the photographer. Without a word, he spun around and headed quickly toward the pier, glancing back toward them several times.

AT ABOUT THREE O'CLOCK, Robin suggested they should leave so she would have plenty of time to keep her appointment at the dance studio. Robin would help answer telephones from four to five o'clock, after which her lessons would begin. Someday, she had promised herself and her mother, she was going to be a ballerina. She eagerly anticipated the upcoming session because, for the first time, she would advance to the use of "toe shoes."

Robin pulled on white shorts over her black swim suit, and retied her blue and yellow canvas tennis shoes. If anyone had looked closely at the footwear, they would have seen little secret hints of puppy love she had hand-printed on the sides. She donned a red T-shirt imprinted with the words "Here Comes Trouble." Tiny gold-colored balls attached to her earlobes reflected sunlight while golden rays glanced from the light blond hair cascading past her shoulders. A glow of angelic innocence reflected from the child's soft brown eyes.

On this bright day full of wonder and joy for the two friends, accompanied by Jackye Young, they walked among the tide of people crowding Huntington's Beach sidewalks. It took only a few minutes to reach Bridgett's apartment on 14th Street.

When the appointment time for her dance lessons grew near, Robin realized they had lingered a little too long. If she walked to the studio, she would probably be late. She asked to borrow Bridgett's yellow Schwinn twenty–four-inch, ten-speed bicycle with the handlebars turned up. The girls wheeled it out of the apartment laundry room and Robin climbed on. Her route would take her near the spot where the "photographer" had been so friendly.

Robin flashed a radiant smile, waved to her friend, and pedaled away. The two friends would never meet again.

At five–fifteen, dance studio owner Beverly Fleming telephoned Marianne Frazier, Robin's mother, to ask why her daughter hadn't shown up that day. When Frazier had seen Robin in the apartment at about eleven that morning, she hadn't mentioned any plans that would keep her from completion of the dance lessons. Both women knew that Robin would never deliberately miss a class. Stunned, and trying to fight off a sick feeling, Frazier called Bridgett Wilvert's home and learned that Robin had borrowed the bike at three o'clock and left for the studio. The news gripped Frazier like the jaws of a wild animal tearing at her throat. This couldn't be. Robin was always so punctual and reliable. And she had never failed to call home to explain any absence. Robin's siblings, along with neighbors, started checking everywhere they could imagine to see if anyone had seen the little girl.

As a single mother, Frazier had built a strong sense of responsibility in her four children. She had brought them from Wisconsin two years earlier. Wishing to leave behind an unhappy life and marriage, she had rented a truck, packed it with everything she owned, and driven to California. Looking for a place to land, she chose Huntington Beach because of its reputation as a safe, clean community.

Robin had been attending dance classes from the age of four. Her mother, by working two jobs, managed to make ends meet, and even squeezed out enough to pay thirty–two dollars a month for the lessons. Recently, times had turned tougher. Frazier had been involved in a car wreck on May 2 and hadn't been able to work for a period of seven weeks. It had appeared the dance lessons would have to be discontinued. The studio owner, though, helped with a solution. She had agreed to let Robin answer telephones one hour before her classes in exchange for the lessons until Marianne could resume her job.

IT HAD NEARLY BROKEN FRAZIER'S HEART when, at about the same time of her exodus from Wisconsin, little Robin had needed serious surgery on her esophagus. The child had prayed to God, and promised that if He would let her survive, she would spend an amount of time in church equal to the time she used on her dancing. The prayer had been answered and Robin fastidiously complied with her half of the bargain.

As dusk rolled over Huntington Beach and the sun settled toward the Pacific horizon, fear engulfed Marianne Frazier like a dark storm rolling in from the sea. For her, Robin's last day of life was the first day of a never-ending nightmare.

Frazier's voice shook uncontrollably as she telephoned the Huntington Beach Police Department. It is not unusual for law enforcement agencies to delay investigating reports of young people who have been missing a few hours. But not this one. Officers launched an immediate search and investigation. By eleven o'clock that same night, they had spread an all-points bulletin with a full description and photograph of Robin Samsoe.

Investigators interviewed Bridgett Wilvert that evening. Her comments about a man who had taken photographs of the two girls on the clifftop that afternoon caught their undivided attention. But she had trouble trying to describe him. With the help of an officer who had studied hypnosis, Bridgett assisted police artist Marilyn Droz in developing a composite drawing of the photographer. The sketch would appear in local newspapers and on television news shows the next day.

City employee Richard Sillett passed by a store window and saw Droz's composite sketch. The familiar face sent Sillett rushing to telephone the police. On the afternoon of June 20, in the course of his job as a survey-party chief, Sillett had been examining the alignment of a bicycle trail below the cliffs. He had observed a man walking down the incline toward the ocean. Sillett, an amateur photographer himself, owned several cameras and habitually noticed photo equipment carried by other people. His attention had been caught by the fellow's 35–mil limeter Olympus camera equipped with a telephoto lens, suspended from his neck by a wide colorful strap. The two men had made brief eye contact but hadn't spoken. As soon as Sillett saw the composite sketch, he made the connection.

In the late afternoon, while Marianne Frazier suffered torment with each minute dragging into eternity, hoping and praying that her missing daughter would turn up safely, a part-time employee of the U.S. Forest Service spotted something unusual in mountains forty miles away. Anita Craven, 20, a slight woman with shoulder-length brown hair, wearing oversized glasses, worked as a seasonal firefighter. According to her subsequent statements, which tended to vary in some details, she experienced a series of unnerving events.

As shadows grew longer on Wednesday afternoon, she steered her Datsun B210 up the narrow, winding Santa Anita Canyon Road climbing into Angeles National Forest's rugged hills north of the famous horse-race track, Santa Anita Park, where Seabiscuit had raced into legend. As she slowed for a curve, Craven noticed a blue Datsun F10 hatchback parked on the uphill side of a sharp turnout at mile marker 11. Something else, though, caused her to remember the sight of an ordinary parked car. A few feet in front of the automobile, a medium-built man with dark brown hair was "forcefully steering" or "pushing" a young girl with long blond hair toward a dry stream bed. The man glanced toward Craven as she drove slowly around the bend, past a water tower.

Even though the incident seemed strange to her, she continued on her way to the forest service barracks at Chantry Flats. She didn't bother to tell anyone about it.

ON THE FOLLOWING DAY, Craven made the same round trip down to the city of Sierra Madre, and once again encountered an oddity on her early evening return up the mountains. At a place called

Rendezvous turnout, approximately 1.6 miles from mile marker 11, a white Volkswagen speeding downhill forced her to veer sharply to avoid a collision. As she swerved, she nearly struck the rear of a blue Datsun F10 parked on the shoulder and projecting almost into the traffic lane. Craven felt certain it was the same car she'd seen on the previous day.

Recovering control of her car, Craven, passed the parked Datsun, and caught a glimpse of a man leaning against a nearby rock wall. He wore pants that seemed dirty, and a white T-shirt that "appeared to be sort of dirty or have a stain on it." Craven felt a deep suspicion that something must be wrong. Why would this vehicle and this man be up here twice in two days, in roughly the same area? What had happened to the little blond girl?

Both incidents continued to weigh on Craven's mind. After sunset on Monday, June 25, she drove to the turnout at mile marker 11 and parked her car. She left her engine running, and headed up a narrow path. After she walked about forty paces, a foul stench almost made her turn back. Using her flashlight a little farther up the path, she spotted a small tennis shoe on the ground next to a pair of white shorts and a red T-shirt.

It's difficult for anyone to predict how they might react to discovering a dead human body, especially that of a child. The sight terrified Anita Craven.

The pitiful, naked corpse she saw was bloated. Pieces of flesh were missing from the head, perhaps due to carnivorous animals. Parts of the hands and feet were also gone. Wild creatures weren't responsible for all the damage though. It appeared that someone had used a knife on the victim, since it seemed to be "pretty cut up."

FEAR AND HORROR CONVULSED through Craven's mind and body. Reversing her course, she fled back to her car with as much speed as she could muster. In a daze, she drove to her parents' home near the Santa Anita racetrack. Inexplicably, Craven kept the whole experience internalized and told no one. It would later be theorized that she was "consumed by a sense of guilt" believing that if she had stopped to investigate on June 20 after observing the man pushing a little girl into the woods, perhaps the tragic death would not have occurred.

The mental strain of carrying such a traumatic burden is immeasurable. Under the circumstances, it is remarkable that Anita Craven would be able to work near the grisly discovery site just five days after seeing the car and the man a second time. On June 29, she joined forestry service crew to spray fire retardant near mile marker 11. Why she didn't inform the other members of what she had seen remains unanswered. She followed a colleague, William Poepke, up the same path where she'd found the human remains, behaving as if she had forgotten the whole thing. About one hundred feet from the road, Poepke bent over, picked up a bone he thought belonged to a dead deer, and playfully tossed it at Craven. It would later be reported that "Craven was not amused; she knew the bone was human."

That night, at approximately seven o'clock, Craven continued her bizarre behavior by returning to the area again. Perhaps she wanted to confirm that the bone thrown at her by the other firefighter was, indeed, part of the body she had seen. Once more with the aid of a flashlight, she gazed in horror at the small skeleton that had once been a living person. This time, the arm bones had vanished.

Craven poked around and made another discovery. Near the skeleton were six .22 caliber shells. She carefully picked them up and slipped them in her pocket. Eventually, she would comment that shotgun shells were commonly found in the area, along with broken clay pigeons, so she did not associate the shells with the child's death. To Craven, the ammunition had nothing to do with the human remains. Perhaps this is why she later threw them away, again without telling anyone.

Before she left, she again observed the sad little pile of clothing, including the tennis shoe, shorts, and T-shirt. She did not touch them.

On July 2, the Forestry Service crew, including Anita Craven, returned to mile marker 11 to continue spraying fire retardant. William Poepke, accompanied by two other fire crew members, at last discovered the skull and several bones, more widely scattered than when Craven had seen them. They summoned the police.

Crime scene technicians and detectives examined the skeletal remains and meticulously searched the area. Because the body parts were in an advanced state of decomposition, with several of the bones showing signs of having been gnawed by animals, the cause of the child's death could not be determined. Nor could the postmortem examination reveal whether she had been sexually assaulted.

Another strange aspect would also remain a mystery. Neither the forestry workers nor the investigators found any clothing. The only thing they turned up was the single tennis shoe, with the strings still tied as if the footwear had been removed in a hurry. Fortunately, it provided a vital link to Robin Samsoe who had been missing nearly two weeks.

The little girl had used a ballpoint pen to carefully print something on the blue and yellow shoe. A crime lab technician, would later report that he observed words on one side of the sole reading, "Robin plus Ralph" and "Robin plus Jason." On the other side, he saw the words, "Wendy plus Allen." Secret puppy-love notes Robin had recorded on her shoe provided a silent reminder that this vibrant child had special dreams, friends, and a heart full of love.

ANITA CRAVEN RELUCTANTLY ADMITTED to investigators that she had seen the remains days earlier, but took an uncooperative stance in which she failed to divulge any details about her forays to the discovery site. One of the officers interviewing her was Detective Art Droz, husband of Marilyn Droz, the artist who had drawn the composite sketch.

* * *

CONFIRMATION THAT THE SKELETAL REMAINS were those of Robin came when her dentist produced X-rays that matched teeth in the skull. The victim of a human predator had died more than forty miles from her home.

A few other potential clues also turned up in the search by Huntington Beach detectives. The searchers found blond human hair, a piece of rope, bloodstained leaves and what appeared to be a bathing-suit strap. More important, located about four feet from the bones, officers discovered a mud-caked, twelve-inch knife that bore tiny rust-colored stains, perhaps left by blood. They noted the knife's brand name, Kane Kut, and sent it to the crime lab for further examination.

About a mile from the body site, searchers found Robin's beach towel, also stained with blood. It appeared that someone had used it to wipe a "bloody, straight-edged instrument."

Although the autopsy results could not decipher the cause of death, they did reveal that the child's lower teeth had been fractured in a manner "consistent with a traumatic blow to the mouth." Stains found on the towel and on the soil at the crime scene were of a blood type "consistent with the type found in bone marrow extracted from Robin's remains."

Laboratory examination of the knife proved the spots on it were, indeed, human blood. In 1979, though, DNA had not yet made its debut as a forensic science. The stains were so small, they would never yield samples large enough for further tests.

In Huntington Beach, Marianne Frazier at last knew that her little angel, Robin, would never come home. Now, she could only hope that the child's killer would be found.

Detectives working the case held the same hope. They got an exciting break when a parole officer telephoned and said he knew of someone who strongly resembled the artist's sketch of the suspect that had appeared in newspapers and on television.

The Suspect

PAROLE AGENT DENNIS McNAUGHT'S HEART RACED
when he saw the sketch by police artist Marilyn Droz in both
The Orange County Register and on a television news report.
The drawing bore a strong resemblance to a man with whom
McNaught was well acquainted. He telephoned the Huntington Beach
Police Department to report that Rodney James Alcala might be the
man they sought in the Robin Samsoe case.

McNaught knew all about this guy, both the good and the bad. Born
on August 23, 1943, Alcala was 35 years old, although most people
would probably guess that he was younger. Standing five feet, eleven
inches, with a slim build, he might even be called handsome with his
brown eyes, high cheek bones, dark eyes and full mane of curly, chocolate brown hair. If women were attracted to him, he still hadn't taken
any of them as a wife. Blessed with a high level of intelligence, he had
earned a degree at UCLA.

But the man also had a dark side.

Alcala, said McNaught, had been on parole from state prison for a
child molestation conviction. There was another incident, he added. In
1974, Alcala had abducted a thirteen-year-old girl in Huntington Beach!
Furthermore, he was currently out on bail related to a charge of assaulting and raping a fifteen-year-old girl in Riverside County.

Detectives thanked the agent and instantly contacted the California Department of Motor Vehicles. That learned that Rodney Alcala's driver's licence showed an address in the city of Monterey Park, which was less than ten miles from the site where Robin's remains had been found. He also drove a 1978 Datsun, similar to the one reported by Anita Craven.

Probing deeper, investigators learned from parole agents Boyd Johnson and Alex Rubio that Alcala's home had been subjected to a routine search in 1978. (California law provides, as a condition of being released early, for paroled convicts to be searched at any time without a warrant, as long as the officers know in advance that the suspect is on parole or probation.) When the agents looked in a briefcase Alcala owned, they found numerous photographs of nude females, many of them of young girls.

When asked about the pictures, he had admitted taking one of them, featuring a pubescent nude girl, near the Sierra Madre Monastery area, which was a little over two miles from the Samsoe crime scene. Los Angeles police Detectives Charles Oakley and Troy Galloway, both part of a task force investigating the notorious "Hillside Strangler" serial murders, had participated in the search. When the detectives observed numerous photographs of young children at the beach, Alcala admitted that he used photography as a way to introduce himself to young women. It struck the officers as peculiar that Alcala's camera seemed to have focused primarily on the "crotch and buttocks of the children."

Alcala's prison records obtained by the Huntington Beach police included a number of psychiatric reports indicating the inmate was a "sexual deviate and a pedophiliac," or child molester. He could "show sexual aggression coupled with sadism."

Each new revelation seemed to build a powerful case against Rodney Alcala as the person who had photographed Robin Samsoe and

Bridgett Wilvert on June 20, and who might have abducted and murdered Robin. Another fact added even more weight. The female victim in the case for which Alcala was sent to prison was of "similar size and maturity . . . as Robin Samsoe," but younger.

It had taken place eleven years earlier. Alcala had been convicted of raping an eight-year-old girl!

The horrifying story was recorded in trial testimony of the victim and witnesses. On Wednesday, September 25, 1968, said Mary Adams, she was walking to school in Hollywood. A man in an automobile followed her and asked if she wanted a ride. Mary told the man her parents did not want her to talk to strangers. The man replied, "Oh, I know your parents." He promised the child he would take her to school, so she trustingly climbed into his car.

Someone else saw the incident. Donald Haines was driving on Sunset Boulevard when he spotted a man with long dark hair halt his car in an intersection crosswalk, block the path of a young girl, and start talking to her. Haines sensed something wrong. He drove another block, made a U-turn and hurried back to the scene. By this time, the child had entered the dark-haired man's car and sat on the left side of the back seat. When the car took off, Haines followed but maneuvered carefully so the other driver wouldn't notice. He observed as the other car stopped in front of a house and the driver escorted the child into the residence.

In an attempt to see the vehicle's license plate number, Haines drove slowly past. There were no plates on the front or rear of the car. Now alarmed, he drove to a pay phone and called the police.

A black and white unit arrived about ten or fifteen minutes later, driven by Los Angeles Police Department Officer Christopher Camacho. When he knocked on the front door, he glanced toward a window and saw a slim man with curly dark hair standing inside completely nude. The man yelled, "Wait a minute, I will be right back." When he failed to return promptly, Camacho kicked in the door, rushed inside and saw Mary Adams lying nude on the floor, apparently dead. She was "in a spread eagle position with an iron bar, about one foot in length and one inch in diameter, across her neck . . . . There was blood between her legs . . . blood all over the floor." The child's clothing lay about five feet away, along with a pair of men's shoes, jockey undershorts and a white T-shirt.

As he searched the house, Camacho heard a muffled cough, returned to the stricken child, and discovered that the bar had moved from her neck. He summoned an ambulance, then scoured the neighborhood in an attempt to find the defendant.

But Rodney Alcala had fled. He withdrew six hundred dollars from his checking account, then put a long distance between himself and the crime.

During a search of the residence, the police turned up stacks of photographs depicting nude boys and girls.

Mary emerged from a coma several weeks after the attack, unable to sit up, and was bedridden for months.

It took three years to find Rodney Alcala. In New Hampshire, he had changed his name to John Berger and found employment at a girls' school. Alcala was arrested on a warrant for unlawful flight to avoid prosecution, and extradited to California. He was convicted in March 1972, of raping Mary Adams and sent to prison. After serving a little more than two years, he was released on parole in August 1974.

If that case didn't convince police that Alcala was their man, two other events mentioned by parole agent Dennis McNaught provided even more reason to look for him.

TAMMIE BARNES WAS THIRTEEN YEARS OLD in 1974, but looked younger with no pubescent or breast development. On October 16, she sat on a bench in Huntington Beach waiting for a bus to take her to school when a man exited a yellow Fiat, approached her and introduced himself as "John Ronald." He spotted her name on school books and spoke to her as if they were old friends. In a brief conversation, she told him she was nearing her fourteenth birthday. He offered her a ride to school. At first she refused, rose, and edged closer to the bus stop. He followed, coaxing and teasing. She had already missed her first class. The stranger seemed charming and friendly, so Tammie laughed and finally accepted his offer.

On Beach Boulevard, Alcala drove toward Main Street with his passenger. When he zoomed past her school, he ignored her requests to be dropped off. Instead, he continued toward Pacific Coast Highway, telling her he was going to look for an apartment and would bring her back later. Tammie asked him again to take her back to the school, only to hear him bark orders for her to shut up. On that chilly autumn day, there weren't many people around where he pulled over into a parking lot near cliffs overlooking the beach. When Tammie tried to walk away, he jerked her back and led her to the cliffs. Fear caused her to put up very little resistance. As they descended, she made one more attempt to scramble back up the incline, but he gripped her ankle and pulled her back down.

They reached an area covered by boulders, where they sat down. Still exuding his oily charm, Alcala invited her to smoke marijuana. She had never tried it before, and didn't want to, but out of fear she acquiesced. According to the girl's subsequent testimony, the man "french-kissed" her and said he wanted to be "passionate." The incident might have ended tragically, but it was interrupted by a curious park ranger who thought he smelled marijuana and stopped to see what was going on. He arrested both of them for drug possession. Tammie later identified Rodney Alcala as the man who said he was "John Ronald."

Alcala insisted that Tammie had furnished the marijuana and suggested they smoke it. But he ultimately pleaded guilty to felony possession of the drug and was returned to state prison for three years. The steel doors opened to let him out once again in June 1977.

Nine months later, immediately following the 1978 parole search by agents Johnson and Rubio, in which Alcala was found in possession of marijuana and nude photos of young girls, he was locked up again. But this time it lasted just a few weeks, and he was released. Remarkably, he was also discharged from parole.

Alcala, though, just couldn't resist temptation. On February 12, 1979, just four months before Robin Samsoe was murdered, he was driving in Sierra Madre, near Pasadena. Fifteen-year-old Jennifer Carlson stuck out her thumb to hitch a ride. Two cars stopped for her; one loaded with kids about her age, and a blue Datsun F10. She saw the dark-haired driver place his hands in a praying gesture, as if begging her to ride with him. She spent the night with him at his house, during which he showed her pictures of nude children. According to an official report, "They engaged in sexual relations with her apparent consent."

The next day, he suggested that they take a ride up to the mountains. In an isolated area of Riverside County, he drove up a winding dirt road, pulled over, and parked. Alcala brought out his ever-present camera and asked her to pose in the nude. Jennifer complied not only with his wishes to pose, but his sexual needs. Yet, something lit the fuse to his explosive personality. He grabbed the frightened teenager by the neck with one hand, used the other to beat her with a stick, and began biting her breasts. When he jammed her yellow T-shirt down her throat, she lost consciousness. Upon waking, she found her ankles and wrists securely bound with ropes. Alcala raped and sodomized the helpless victim. Fearful that she might be killed, Jennifer pretended to be friendly with him as he drove back to a populated area. She asked to stop at an Arco gas station so she could use the restroom and clean up. As soon as an opportunity presented itself, she escaped and called the police.

Investigators later described her as "beaten, in a hysterical state." At a hospital, she was treated for chest injuries, rope burns, bite marks, and abrasion. She led them to Alcala and identified him as her assailant.

In a tape-recorded interview, to which he agreed, Alcala admitted taking Jennifer to a dirt road in the mountains. His version of the events differed slightly from hers. He confessed to photographing her in the nude, and said that she "simulated" sexual acts with him. He had tied her up, he claimed, as part of the photographic scenario. "We started to take photos and then I tied her up and she started to struggle." At some point, the allegedly consensual activities ceased, and Alcala acknowledged choking the girl until she lost consciousness. He tied her wrists and ankles. After she revived, he stuffed her shirt in her mouth to stop her from screaming. He didn't deny the sexual assault, and referred to himself as "a rapist."

Asked why he bit the victim, he stated, "You're in an unreasoning situation. Your brain and you just don't know what to do. It's not like do this, do that. You're not reasoning. You've lost your ability to reason. You're not thinking. . . . I raped her."

No one could argue with that.

Even though he faced serious criminal charges, Alcala was released on bail. And in June, he decided he needed more photographs of young girls at the beach.

ON JUNE 19, THE DAY BEFORE ROBIN VANISHED, two other girls spent most of the day on the sand at Huntington Beach, near the pier. As bikini clad Lynn Davis, 15, and Michelle Ellis, 14, walked to a parking lot, a slim man carrying a camera approached and asked if he could take pictures of them. He said he wanted to enter the photos in a "bikini of the month" photography contest. The two teenagers agreed to pose. After the shutterbug had snapped perhaps ten pictures, he said he had some "joints" and wondered if the girls would like to go for a ride and get "loaded" as payment for posing. They declined. He persisted, then asked them to at least give him their phone numbers so he could contact them in case he won the contest. The girls refused, turned their backs to the stranger, and walked away. Both of them later identified the photographer as Rodney Alcala.

On Wednesday, June 20, teenagers Wanda Ford and Tina Gardner went roller skating at Sunset Beach, a few miles north of the Huntington Beach Pier. A man they subsequently identified as Rodney Alcala waved and asked them to stop long enough to pose for some photographs for a class contest. Tina refused. Julie, clad in a new bikini, allowed him to snap a few pictures.

Later that day, according to witnesses, he encountered and photographed Bridgett Wilvert and Robin Samsoe.

Police investigators took statements from all of the surviving young females and added them to a growing case against Alcala. Because the suspect had once fled to New Hampshire, they expanded the investigation to Atlantic seaboard states as well. From New York came more information supporting suspicions against the suspect.

In 1977, the body of an adult female was found buried in a New York forest. Several other women told investigators that a man named John Berger had photographed them in that locale. A search produced the victim's personal calender which contained the name of a suspect. A handprinted entry on the date the woman disappeared read "John Berger." When detectives finally traced the pseudonym to Rodney Alcala, he admitted seeing the victim that day, but denied any involvement in her murder. The case remained open.

With the cooperation of Monterey Park police, Huntington Beach detectives maintained a surveillance of Alcala throughout the Robin Samsoe investigation. The Monterey Park residence where he lived with his mother was watched around the clock.

* * *

HUNTINGTON BEACH HOMICIDE DETECTIVES Craig Robison
and Bill Morris led the team of investigators. Long hours on the job had
been making their home lives almost nonexistent. Even though they
had identified a suspect, they continued to search for any evidence related to the death of Robin Samsoe.

Morris arrived at his residence on Tuesday night completely exhaust-
ed. He took off his shoes and flopped into his favorite chair. The television blared a repeat episode of a show called "The Dating Game." It had
been taped and aired the previous fall season. Three bachelors sat behind
a screen while an attractive woman asked them for responses to questions
loaded with sexual innuendo, racy stuff for 1979. Just as Morris closed his
eyes, he heard a familiar name spill out of the TV speaker. The master of
ceremonies joked, "Bachelor number one is a successful photographer
whose father found him in the darkroom at age thirteen fully developed.
He is into skydiving and motorcycle riding. Meet Rodney Alcala."

Morris nearly fell out of his chair as he leaned forward to see the
grinning face of the man they were investigating. Alcala wore a chocolate brown leisure suit, with fashionable bell bottoms and a white shirt
sporting an oversized collar, unbuttoned halfway to the waist. A gold
chain dangled from his neck. When he stood up, a little later in the
show, platform heels made him taller than his normal five–eleven. His
bush of full, curly, dark hair extended just below his shoulders. More
than a few female viewers may have thought him attractive.

WITH FULL ATTENTION FOCUSED on the screen, Morris saw host
Jim Lange introduce bachelor number two, an actor from New York,
and bachelor number three, a musician, then bring out the woman with
whom a date would be the prize. Cheryl, who appeared to be in her late
twenties, had red hair, and wore a full-skirted patterned dress that concealed her figure. But when she sat down, she daintily lifted the skirt to

cross well-shaped legs, and leaned forward exposing a considerable amount of cleavage with tan lines.

Each bachelor, at Jim Lange's prompting, greeted her with a sly comment. Alcala's wide grin revealed uneven teeth. He commented, "We're going to have a good time together, Cheryl."

She responded by directing her first question to him. Doing her best to sound sexy, Cheryl asked, "What's your best time?"

Without missing a beat, Alcala replied, "The best time is night time."

"Why?" Cheryl teased.

"Because that's the only time there is."

"What's wrong with morning or afternoon?"

His voice oozing suggestiveness, Alcala said, "They're okay. But night time is when it really gets good. Then, you are really ready."

Cheryl gave the other two men their turns, then emoted, "I'm a drama teacher and I'm going to interview each of your for my private class. Number one, take it."

In a throaty growl, still grinning, Alcala said, "Ohhh, come on over here."

Numbers two and three, doing their best to sound seductive, gave equally silly answers.

Heating up the banter, Cheryl said, "I am serving you for dinner." The camera zoomed in on Alcala as he grinned and groaned, evoking laughter from the audience. Cheryl added, "What are you called, and what do you look like?"

When Alcala's turn came, he said, "I am called the banana, and I look really good."

Cheryl began to show a hint of favoritism toward bachelor number one, Alcala. She asked him to be a little more descriptive. "Peel me," he invited, his mouth wide open. Again the audience chuckled.

Cheryl flirted, "Later, number one, later."

After a commercial break, the host invited Cheryl to make her selection. She said, "Well, I like bananas. I'll take number one."

After both losers exited the stage, Alcala trotted out and encircled her waist with his right arm. The emcee announced the "fabulous" prizes. They had won tennis lessons at a popular club, and an all-expense-paid date to Magic Mountain theme park north of Los Angeles. Neither Cheryl nor Alcala appeared very enthused about the booty. Other contestants on previous shows had been treated to weekends at resorts across the country or in Mexico.

It didn't matter. According to later reports, they never kept their date. Allegedly, Cheryl had recently broken up with her boyfriend. But when he watched the show, he contacted her and begged for a reconciliation, which she granted.

Detective Bill Morris slammed a fist into the other palm, feeling as if he had won the best prize. There was the murder suspect showing his face to the nation on television. Surely, such exposure would prompt calls from people who had seen his picture in newspapers and on television news. Maybe even someone had seen him with the victim, or at least on the beach during those crucial hours of June 20. Morris called Craig Robison with the astounding news.

Surveillance officers noted that Alcala's hair matched descriptions of being dark, long, thick and curly. Perhaps motivated by the artist's sketch, the suspect made some changes. On June 23, he straightened it with an over-the-counter product. Before the month ended, he cut it considerably shorter.

On July 8, Alcala informed his girlfriend that he had decided to leave Southern California and move to Dallas, Texas, to set up a photography business. She accompanied him to the Monterey Park residence he shared with his mother to help him pack for the trip.

Three days later he turned up in Seattle, Washington, where he rented a storage locker. When he returned to California he did not tell anyone where he had been. Instead, he reportedly mentioned to his girl-friend that he had been to Dallas. On July 23, Alcala announced he was leaving for Dallas the following day. To another acquaintance, he said he was going to Chicago.

For homicide investigators, it became obvious the time had come to arrest Rodney Alcala before he skipped out.

Alcala in Custody

ON TUESDAY, JULY 24, POLICE OFFICERS ARMED with arrest and search warrants arrived at the Monterey Park home and took Rodney James Alcala into custody. They also impounded his Datsun F10 hatchback and found inside it a briefcase containing camera equipment and keys. An extensive search of the premises turned up several items of extreme interest, including a receipt for a storage locker in Seattle. An officer copied down the information contained on the receipt but did not seize it. In the kitchen, they found and confiscated full sets of Kane Kut kitchen knives, the same brand of bloodied knife recovered at the site of Robin Samsoe's remains.

The next day, using a warrant amended to include seizure of the storage locker receipt, an officer returned to pick it up. But it had vanished.

Two detectives traveled to Seattle with additional warrants. When they located the storage locker, they found it secured by two padlocks. No problem. They had brought the keys taken from Alcala's briefcase, tried them, and easily opened both locks. Among the photographic material Alcala had stored were slide pictures of Wanda Ford, the roller skater who had posed for him at a Sunset Beach parking lot. Several items of jewelry also reposed in the locker. Of special interest were a pair of small, gold ball earrings. Robin Samsoe had been wearing gold ball earrings on the day she disappeared.

No photographs of the murder victim or her friend Bridgett Wilvert were found.

At the Huntington Beach Police Department complex, early Wednesday morning, Rodney Alcala faced Robison and Morris in interview room number three.

HOW DOES A MURDER SUSPECT, particularly one who is quite intelligent, behave when being interrogated by experienced detectives? What kinds of questions do they ask? Few people have the opportunity to observe such an interview. Too often, the public may form grossly inaccurate impressions about police interviews based on what they have seen on television or in movies. In real life, the sessions are sometimes long and tedious, sometimes like a chess game with gambits, disguised offense, and subtle strategy. Every question, every comment from the interrogators will be subjected to close scrutiny by defense attorneys, judges, and appeals courts.

The first step for police officers is to make certain the suspect understands the Supreme Court edicted Miranda advisory, which informs the suspect of a right not to speak and to be represented by an attorney. Once past that, the officers tread on thin ice every inch of the way. Their goal, of course is to gain information about the alleged crimes to either clear or convict the suspect.

The challenge for Robison and Morris was particularly difficult considering Alcala's high intelligence level.

After introducing himself and his partner, Robison said, "We know what happened. We know that you are responsible for this little girl's demise, and that's why we are here. . . . I think that you can see that's the situation. We're being truthful with you." The officer followed by reading Alcala the standard Miranda rights, verified that the suspect understood, then asked, "Okay, do you want to talk to us about it?"

Alcala mumbled, "I don't know what to say. I don't know what you are talking about."

Sliding a photograph of Robin Samsoe across the table, Robison said, "Well, you see this little girl here? She was last seen by one of her girlfriends in Huntington Beach. We found her about ten days later in Sierra Madre, in kind of a rugged area, isolated. We found her bones. There wasn't a whole lot left of her. We found some other things out there. . . . We've identified those remains as being her. . . . She didn't get there by herself, and that's what we want to talk about. Okay? Do you understand?"

Alcala faltered in his answer. "I don't—you know—uh, I think it would be foolish, uh, to talk about an incident, uh, of this magnitude. . . . You know what I mean? You, you're charging me apparently with a very serious crime."

"That's true," agreed Robison.

As Alcala continued to demur, Robison brought him back to focus. "We know that you've been in prison. We know that you've been convicted of child molestation."

"Right."

"We already know about your background, okay? These sexual problems that you had at the time you were arrested in relation to this Los Angeles case, some years ago. Sexual problems involving children, young females, a preference for them. . . . Just so that you are aware, Rod, we had five people follow you all night last night. . . ."

Alcala's eyebrows shot up. He asked what the people tailing him had seen. Had they been in a movie theater with him and his girlfriend? He added, "That's really funny, because I sensed last night . . . uh, like a vague idea that I was being followed. . . . You know, that's really weird. Did you see everything I did?"

Alcala had been under surveillance, but Robison simply replied, "I wasn't there. I wasn't involved so I don't know where they followed you to. We've been keeping an eye on you." He quickly changed the subject to photography. Alcala mentioned that he had attended UCLA and taken film classes. Robinson followed with a few general questions about the topic, then became more specific.

"Who do you like to photograph?"

"Friends, mostly."

"Do you ever take pictures at the beach?"

"Occasionally. You know, like I have some beach scenes."

"Okay, describe those for me."

"Laguna . . . stuff like that. Sunsets."

"Any photographs of people who just happen to be on the beach?"

"Not that I recall. Matter of fact, I'd say that my scenes—"

"Do you come to the beach often to do this photography?"

"No."

"How infrequent? Once a month? Twice a month? Once every other month?"

"Quite infrequent."

"Where do you go?"

"I've been to Zuma." He referred to a long stretch of sand in northern Los Angeles County.

"How about Huntington Beach? You ever been down Huntington Beach way?"

"I was in Huntington Beach in seventy–four for sure."

ROBISON NODDED SILENTLY, WELL AWARE of the 1974 arrest of Alcala on the local beach for smoking marijuana with a thirteen-year-old girl he had lured to a section below the cliffs. He commented, "The reason we ask is that you were seen in Huntington Beach taking some pictures." He handed Alcala a copy of the artist's sketch.

After studying the drawing, Alcala spent the next few minutes quibbling about it, claiming it didn't even resemble him.

Shifting gears, Robison asked, "What about Sierra Madre? That's pretty close to where you live. I think there's a monastery up there, too."

Alcala mumbled, "I really couldn't say anything about that."

"Why are you reluctant to say yes or no on that point?"

"Like homicide is like a really serious, I mean, I don't know where . . . " He trailed off, then doubled back to the artist's sketch. "I've seen that picture and to me, that doesn't look at all like me, and, I don't know. . . . I don't think I should say anything in relation to Sierra Madre . . . you know. Because I don't know what you are doing. . . . You know, I, I'm scared and I don't know how to react in this."

Robison offered counsel. "In my opinion, the best way to react is to be truthful. You can only help yourself by telling the truth. . . . We didn't bring you in here expecting you to just shrug your shoulders and start pouring out your soul to us. And we tried to avoid doing anything to scare you . . . . We'd like to know what happened. We'd like to be able to tell the mother of this young girl what happened to her daughter. . . . I know it's got to be bothering you. Something like that would bother the hell out of somebody. Very depressing. You realize it."

Alcala evaded the ploy. "I've seen this in the movies. Right? I don't mean to make light- but everything you are saying is . . . that you know I've done a homicide."

"Did you do the homicide? Did you kill Robin Samsoe?"

Instead of an indignant denial, Alcala turned to evasion again. "I can't answer any questions like that, either way. Because anything I would say in relation to that . . . you know it just doesn't make any sense to discuss something that I'm not aware of. . . ."

"Rodney, Rodney! You are aware of this. You are aware of why we are here. . . . You're aware of what's going on with this little girl."

"Yeah, you are charging me with something."

Detective Bill Morris, making an appeal to Alcala's superior intelligence, spoke in a calm voice disclosing that certain items of evidence had been seized at the suspect's residence. Alcala wanted to know just what kind of evidence the police had against him.

Morris shot back, "We're not going to tell you that. We can't. We've discussed this with the D.A., and he feels it is best not to discuss with you at this point what evidence we do have, but we both know and you know what happened out there. . . . It's got to be doing something to your mind . . . unless you are so cold that it doesn't even effect you; a homicide wouldn't bother you at all."

Alcala didn't falter or stutter in his answer. "I have not ever committed a homicide. And that I'll say, at any point, ever."

With a nod, Morris instantly opened another avenue for Alcala to admit his complicity in the crime. "Okay, now that we've got that out, let's go one point further. Perhaps she was not the victim of a homicide. . . . Perhaps she was the victim of an accident and she died because of that accident. And if that's what happened, then let us know . . . ."

Alcala reverted again to evasion. "I can't say anything. I'm not smart enough, you know . . . I don't think it's wise for me to say anything more than—I have never, now or in the past, ever committed a homicide. . . ."

ROBISON MADE ANOTHER APPEAL for Alcala to "get it off of his chest" and perhaps consider a defense in trial based on mental problems. "We know you did it. I think you know you are responsible. Why you did it, now that is something else. I can't get into your head like a psychiatrist . . . . I can't make that diagnosis. But you know what's going on and you can tell us . . . how you reacted and what she did to make you behave the way you did . . . . Heck, we can't ask her obviously. . . ." Without making any promises, Robison hinted that Alcala might be eligible for psychological counseling or mental health care.

The two detectives continued, in tandem, offering Alcala the chance to admit that he killed Robin but not intentionally. Alcala sat silently, listening, showing no reaction.

Robison even threw in a reference to the next world. "There's a higher authority than us that you'll have to answer to eventually. . . . While we're still here on this earth, and while you can still do it...you might as well make the best out of this life, and you can start right now. . . ."

The drawn-out appeal to Alcala's moral conscience, to his logic, to his chance in the afterlife, to his possible desire for help, had taken a long time. Robison and Morris had made a powerful pitch. Now, it reached the critical point.

Robison asked, "Did she get in your car?"

Alcala took a breath. He said, "I'm not . . . " and his muffled voice faded away.

The interview continued for another hour with the same results. The nearest Alcala came to hinting of his culpability in the homicide occurred when Robison said, "You are the only one that we know of who last saw her alive, and that's why we are asking for your help to find out what happened."

Alcala's response was not a denial. "I'd like to help you, you know, but I just can't do it. I can't make a decision."

When the two detectives offered Alcala a chance to take a polygraph exam, he unequivocally refused. Asked why, he replied, "I was advised at one time several years ago never, ever, under any circumstances to do a polygraph."

THROUGHOUT THE INTERVIEW, Alcala asked again and again what evidence the investigators had uncovered. Robison and Morris refused to give any specifics. They simply said at least three witnesses had identified him as the man who photographed Robin and her friend near the cliffs. The sleuths had shown a tape of "The Dating Game" to several people and asked them if he was the man they had seen taking pictures of young girls on beaches, but had not yet told Alcala about it. Now, they decided to go ahead and play that card.

"People on 'The Dating Game' called," said Robison, "and I'm not counting those in the three I told you about. . . . This little girl who gave us . . . the identification, and who viewed your photos in a lineup, and who viewed you on 'The Dating Game'—it was like electricity in the air when they introduced you as bachelor number one. I was in the same room with her, and her mother was sitting right next to us. 'And now we meet our bachelors, and here's bachelor number one. . . .' I have no doubts that she would stand up right now in open court and point to you and say, 'That's the man who took my photograph, and that's the man who photographed Robin.' I believe it."

Alcala seemed unimpressed. "Who do I know that said it's me?"

"I'm not telling you, Rod," replied Robison.

Alcala continued to plead that he was confused by the detectives' confident assertions of his guilt. He wouldn't give up in his queries about the evidence.

By the end of the session, he had admitted nothing.

That same evening, Alcala was permitted to spend time alone with a female relative in the same interview room. If either of them realized the tape recording machine was still running, they never mentioned it. Most of the time they spoke in Spanish and used veiled terms. When the police later played the tape, they had it translated by a multilingual officer. Some segments of the conversation were inaudible, but most of it could be clearly heard.

During the first few minutes, Alcala and his visitor spoke of Alcala's visit to Knott's Berry Farm, a theme park about fifteen miles from Huntington Beach. They indicated it might have taken place on Wednesday, June 20, the same day Robin Samsoe vanished.

He revealed to her that he'd recently removed a number of his possessions from a garage. She asked where he had put them.

"In Seattle," he replied. "In the storage. I'm sure that's one thing that they don't probably have. The police can't look through it, which means I don't have to tell, and they'll have to guess. . . ."

Alcala asked her to look for the receipt

"The receipt for what?"

"The storage place. . . ."

"Who has it?"

"They have it or it's over at the house."

"What does it look like?"

"Yellow slip of paper, orangish-yellow. With a map . . . Triple A map. . . . They don't have anything. They say that a girl said I took photographs of her and her friend at the beach, and that's all. And, that because they found her body in Sierra Madre about fifteen miles from the house, you know, it's close, and then they said we have a lot other very good [evidence]. . . . He said people had called after the TV had telecast the picture, and people that knew me had called and said, 'That's Rod Alcala . . . Yeah, and they [obtained] the name from 'The Dating Game.' They said they showed it to the little girl and said, 'Oh, that's him.' "

The exchange wound down with Alcala complaining about the high bail a judge had set. "Two hundred and fifty thousand dollars bail. Can you believe it?"

A few minutes later, Alcala's visitor departed.

WHILE INCARCERATED AT THE ORANGE COUNTY JAIL in Santa Ana, Rodney Alcala met other inmates and established a certain rapport with a few of them. He spoke several times with Carlos Cardenas, who had been arrested for child molestation, and David Jackson, and later regretted the conversations.

On September 17, 1979, a preliminary hearing was held in Orange County Superior Court to determine if there was enough evidence to try Rodney James Alcala for first degree murder. Deputy District Attorney Richard Farnell presented the facts for the people before Judge John H Wyatt Jr. John Drummond Barnett and Jeffrey H. Freidman represented the defendant.

Orange County jail inmate Carlos Cardenas settled his stocky frame into the witness chair. Farnell asked, "When did you first talk to Mr. Alcala about his case?"

Cardenas replied, "Well, I think he went to chow and on the way back I said, 'Hey, what are you in for?' You know, like that. And he just looks and goes, 'Didn't you hear?' I go, 'No.'

He told me, 'It was in the newspapers and on TV.' I said, 'I don't read the newspaper.' He says, 'I'm in here for murder, you know, and rape, a twelve-year-old girl.' "

Farnell wanted to know more. "You asked him if he did it?"

"Yeah, I asked him if he did it. . . . He just got upset and goes, 'Yeah, I did. . . . I've been busted for it. . . .' That was it. . . . He told me that he was taking pictures at the beach and he saw these two little girls and he . . . taking pictures of them, and he said [someone] came up so he got scared and took off . . . he went running around or whatever. Later on, he seen the girl by herself and he drew up by her and said, 'Hey, you want to take some pictures? I can make you a movie star, or something like that.' And he told me he just stopped her bike. . . . He didn't drag her in the car, she just . . . got in the car on her own."

Answering Farnell's questions, the informant claimed that Alcala had lured the girl with promises. "Like, 'I can make you a movie star, real famous like a model. . . .' He told me he took her up in the hills, and after he had her up there, he took her for a walk, and just threw her down and started molesting her, you know. I [asked] him, 'Did you have sex with that little girl?' He told me he was doing kinky sex. . . . I was sick of hearing it, but I just tried to get him to tell me all of it. I was laughing with him. He got all excited. He started telling me all kinds of things, what he was doing with her."

"He was laughing?"

"Yeah. He told me that the little girl was like, you know, fading away. Like she knew." Cardenas said the victim mentioned something about identifying Alcala.

"The girl said she would identify him?"

"Yeah, so the next thing, you know, he killed her. He said if she would have lived—he would have gone in jail for so long. So he did what he had to do."

"Did he say how he killed her?"

"He, you know, like the little girl was—he was molesting her, you know, and he said she was moving around—she started sweating, crying . . . like she was dazed and tired trying to get this dude off of her and he just started beating her up until he killed her, man, sliced her, whatever."

"He was beating her?"

"Yeah, that was it. He looked at her—he said she was lying there—he said he freaked out and just, you know, like that. So he got in his car and took a drive and went home later on."

The witness spoke of Alcala's reaction to news reports shown on television that included an interview with a girl who said she could identify the artist's sketch. Prosecutor Farnell brought Cardenas back to the murder. "Did the defendant say anything more about how he killed the little girl he picked up?"

"He said he took her up in the hills and was going to take pictures of her there. He just threw her down and started pulling down her pants and molesting her . . . sick stuff, man, sick stuff." As he described the sexual acts, Cardenas seemed reluctant to use certain anatomical street terms. "It's embarrassing to say," he muttered.

Farnell tried to make it easier. "The girl's private parts, is that what you're trying—"

"Objection," said Barnett, the defender. "Leading and suggestive. This witness is a convicted child molester . . . and Mr. Farnell has to help him with private parts?"

Farnell wanted to know if Alcala had mentioned using any kind of a weapon. Cardenas answered, "The only thing he told me was that he had a knife and he was slashing."

"Did he say he dropped the knife?"

"Yeah."

The exchange shifted to another conversation Cardenas described having with Alcala, in which the defendant had expressed confidence that he would win his case and be exonerated. "He goes, 'Yeah, I will. They ain't got nothin' on me.' " Cardenas had asked, "They ain't got no pictures or anything?" He quoted Alcala's alleged reply, "No, man. All they got is me and my camera."

Defense attorneys know full well that jailhouse informants frequently barter testimony for shorter sentences or other favors. Sometimes, they tend to exaggerate the facts. Cardenas may or may not have told the entire truth about his alleged conversations with Rodney Alcala. Skeptics would point to the claim that Alcala had immediately admitted to this complete stranger that he'd been arrested for molesting and killing a young girl. In jails and prison, men who sexually assault and murder children are at the bottom of the pecking order and are often subjected to brutal treatment by other inmates. Alcala had been in prison several years, and would be painfully aware of this. In addition, he was intellectually superior to the men around him. Would he really have been so candid about such sensitive information?

On the other hand, experts on human behavior recognize that criminals sometimes have a deep need to talk to someone, and cellmates can seem sympathetic and trustworthy.

Farnell excused Cardenas and called Anita Craven to the stand.

Asked about her job, she replied, "I'm now a firefighter at Lake Arrowhead, U.S. Forest Service." On June 20, 1979, she had been assigned to the Chantry Flat Station near Sierra Madre.

"On June 21, did you proceed down a highway from your location of assignment?"

"Yes. I left about eight–thirty at night. The road is called Big Santa Anita but is known as Chantry Flat Road . . .." Craven, explaining that she had made the trip to buy groceries, described the near-collision with a Volkswagen heading in the opposite direction and how she had swerved to avoid it. At about ten or ten–thirty, on the return trip, she had seen a vehicle. Officers had shown her photos of various cars, asking if any of them resembled the car she had seen. Craven picked out a blue Datsun F10.

The preliminary hearing ended with a finding by Judge Wyatt that the evidence supported a charge of first degree murder. He ordered Rodney James Alcala to be tried by a jury.

Key evidence
The victim's earrings

The 1980 Trial

THE MURDER TRIAL OF RODNEY ALCALA opened in February 1980 while television audiences across the nation were glued to their screens watching the Winter Olympics at Lake Placid, New York. A young American named Eric Heiden zipped gracefully around ice skating courses and brought home five gold medals. An unheralded U.S. ice hockey team caused commentator Al Michaels to shout his immortal question, "Do you believe in miracles?" as the U.S. men stunned the favored Soviet Union and Finland teams to win the gold.

In stark contrast, the somber courtroom of Superior Court Phillip Schwab was the stage for the airing of human nature's dark side.

Prosecutor Richard Farnell delivered his carefully worded opening statements. Using friendly eye contact with each of the twelve jurors, he presented an outline of what he expected the evidence would show. Witnesses and exhibits, he said would prove that Rodney Alcala had kidnapped and murdered Robin Samsoe.

Defense Attorney John Barnett reminded the jury that anything either attorney said was not evidence. "We are trying to give you an overview so when the evidence comes in you'll have some sense as to the importance of it." He promised to break his case into three categories:

conduct prior to the incident, conduct subsequent to the incident, and then the incident itself.

"The conduct prior to the incident is the business of the three girls mentioned by the prosecution, Mary Adams, Tammie Barnes, and Jennifer Carlson.

"The conduct after the incident is basically inmate confessions, purported statements by Mr. Alcala to inmates at the Orange County Jail.

"And the third category of evidence is the incident itself and that is Mr. Alcala's relationship, and times and places, to Robin Samsoe.

"The prosecutor will seek to introduce evidence which shows that Rodney took Robin's picture in Huntington Beach on June the twentieth at one o'clock p.m. . . . By four p.m., Robin is missing from Huntington Beach and at ten o'clock. . . . Rod's car is seen by Anita Craven in Sierra Madre. . . . That is generally what their case is about."

"The evidence will show that every key prosecution witness in this case, every one of them, is or has remarkable changes of memory after they are contacted either by district attorney's investigators or by police officers from Huntington Beach.

"The Tammie Barnes incident: I think the evidence will show that she was merely playing hooky. She was smoking marijuana with Mr. Alcala and she got caught . . . She originally said that she was forced to smoke the marijuana, and that is what Mr. Farnell told you, that Mr. Alcala forced her to smoke marijuana.

"That isn't true, and she'll recant that statement and say, 'Well, no, he didn't force me to smoke marijuana.' She is just out there playing hooky. She . . . had at that time a reputation for chronic truancy; she had a reputation for fantasizing a great deal and as being a liar, a rather proficient liar, and she had lied on many occasions before.

"The Jennifer Carlson incident is a purported rape in Riverside County. Now Jennifer Carlson has a couple of days of consensual sex with Mr. Alcala. She posed in several exotic pictures for Mr. Alcala and then she freaks out. She freaks out and she starts a fight with Mr. Alcala and they wrestle. She later freaks out again and says that she was raped.

"Four of the last seven years Jennifer Carlson has spent in mental institutions. She has a history of drug abuse. She has a history of taking mind-altering drugs included but not limited to PCP or what is commonly called angel dust. And she has made accusations like this before.

"That is what I believe the evidence will show on the pre-incident conduct.

"The next thing is the purported confessions by Mr. Alcala . . . to jail inmates. I think the evidence is going to show that originally Mr. Alcala refused to talk, and then the inmates began . . . to extract statements from him and they threw urine on him and tried to set his bunk on fire. They threatened to beat the story out of him and . . . kill him.

"Mr. Alcala didn't confess to killing Robin Samsoe, number one, because he didn't do it, and number two, because he was told prior to going in there that the inmates in that particular tank . . . were snitches . . . would inform and he would get the death penalty. So Mr. Alcala did not confess although there will be several inmates who will come in here and say that he did.

"Now all of these people in that tank, while they are not geniuses by any means, they know the system. Okay? They know they can profit by informing. And they know it doesn't have to be the truth. They know that in a big case, if they have information they are going to be able to trade on that. These are all people who have a history of informing. . . . They are narcotics addicts. They are child molesters. They know they are not going to make it out on the streets. They know that they are going to need help from the authorities. And so, whenever they can, they establish a little credit.

"And the inmates had extensive knowledge about this case from news coverage. They'll tell you that they read a lot about this case in the papers.

"Mr. Galindo, I believe, will be a witness. He goes by Cisco. He told other inmates he's not going to testify unless he hits the streets. Okay? He's a long time narcotics addict and informant. And he knew by snitching off Alcala that he could establish credit. . . . Mr. Galindo says that the information about the bike came from the newspapers. The information about photography came from an investigation in the D.A.'s office. He says that Mr. Alcala told him he didn't stab the girl and that there was no talk about molestation.

"All right. Another inmate who may testify is Al Davis. He's a narcotics addict. He read at least two articles in this case, and at least in a portion of his explanation about what happened, he said, 'I'm not sure if it was him saying it or it came from the newspapers.'

"Every time Al Davis is arrested, he turns and seeks to give information to a friend and associate, somebody he's ingratiating himself to.

"Next, we come to Carlos Cardenas. He's another inmate in the PC tank. Now he says the reason he's informing on Mr. Alcala is because it made him sick what Mr. Alcala did. And it made him so sick and so embarrassed he couldn't even bring himself to say the words 'penis' and 'vagina.' He's just a good citizen revolted by the nature of the case and that's why he is coming forward; not for any gain but because that incident so revolted him.

"Well, Carlos during this time was convicted of sodomizing a four-year-old boy. He believes that if he goes to prison with that on his record he will be killed. He was told by other inmates, 'Carlos, this is your ticket out. Say something about Alcala. Maybe you'll get protection.' Well, he didn't get protection, he got sent to prison. But his motivation in saying anything about Mr. Alcala was the chance that somehow, somewhere, he is going to get a [reward] for his testimony.

"Now these are the people we are talking about here. We've got Carlos Cardenas, Mr. Galindo and Mr. Davis. And you'll have to determine the credibility to give to these people.

"Okay, that takes us to the evidence in the case. The people seek to put Mr. Alcala at the beach, at three o'clock on June twentieth, taking Robin's picture. They'll bring in Bridgett Wilvert . . . and she'll say, 'Yes, that's him.' But the evidence will show that when first shown a photographic lineup, with Rodney in it, she couldn't make any identification at all. And then later on she says, 'I'm pretty sure it's this one.' And then she says, 'He's the closest one.' And finally, through a series of events, she becomes positive.

"Jackye Young fails to make an identification of the photo lineup of Mr. Alcala.

"Then, we have the business about Mr. Alcala's car being seen on June 21st at 10 p.m. [the day after Robin vanished]. Now, that's the testimony of Miss Craven . . . . It could not be that day.

"We have her view about the car, forgetting about what the date is. You'll have to decide what you believe the evidence is as to what date it was. But her view of the car is, well, the evidence will be she's going to round the corner . . . it's kind of a sharp curve, it's dark and there's no lighting up there."

Barnett summarized Craven's account of the near-collision with a Volkswagen. It had all happened in the blink of an eye, the defender said, with Craven swerving around to avoid a wreck. How could she possibly recall details about a parked car allegedly belonging to the defendant?

"Additionally, we'll prove it wasn't Mr. Alcala up there because he was elsewhere. We'll prove he wasn't there at that time. She couldn't have seen him.

"So, you may notice there is nothing on my chart about the knife or the jewelry, the bike or the haircut. The knife adds nothing to the case. There is no tie to Mr. Alcala. There are no prints that link that knife. There is nothing that links Mr. Alcala to that knife.

"There is nothing about the jewelry because the jewelry is not identified. It is similar, but nobody will testify that she was wearing any jewelry on the twentieth at all. It is described as similar, and we will show that Rod had that jewelry prior to June twentieth . . . .

"The bicycle . . . there is no showing that the bike . . . was in any way connected with this case. The tape on the bike in El Monte was black and white. It was in good condition and the owner didn't know whether it was a twenty–four or a twenty–six-inch bike. Bridgett's bike was in poor condition and had yellow tape on it.

"With respect to Rodney getting his hair cut, yes, he did get it cut around the twenty–fourth or twenty–fifth. However, it was discussed with other people . . . he had been talking about changing his hairstyle weeks before that—at the end of May.

"The prosecutor says you are going to have to grapple with this testimony; in his opening statement he said that Miss Craven is a victim. Well, we are going to show you that she could not possibly have seen Mr. Alcala's car on the twenty–first because he was elsewhere.

"We are going to show you that in August, a Detective Hooper from the Huntington Beach Police Department went up and talked to Anita Craven, showed her a picture of Robin; showed her a picture of Mr. Alcala and said, 'Did you see these people before?' "

Craven, said Barnett, denied having seen the victim or the suspect.

AFTER A PAUSE FOR MAXIMUM EFFECT, the defender continued. "The prosecutor yesterday spoke about evidence as to why she didn't come forward sooner. Remember that he said the God-awful things she saw prevented her? She felt responsible. That is the reason she hasn't come forward? Well, the evidence is going to show that Miss Craven was a firefighter. She worked horrible fires; that she was not upset at people being carted away in body bags, corpses. She had seen people burned horribly and that just didn't bother her, had no effect on her. In fact, when she saw the remains of Robin Samsoe, she said that didn't bother her. It was only when the police came . . . that she started becoming upset.

"Now I believe that she will testify that the police came up. And she is asked a question, 'Who were these people?' she'll say, 'I couldn't tell you. They didn't identify themselves or anything. And then I told them I wasn't going to talk with them because I had nothing to say and they started giving me this big line about people murdering other people and it's all my fault and trying to make me feel guilty and everybody show ing me pictures. . . . All they said was I was just not giving them the information they wanted to hear.'

"That's what the police did. They are up there blaming her in some way for the murder, harassing her and telling her, 'We are not getting the information we want to hear.'

"We'll show you at the preliminary examination Miss Craven swore to tell the truth, the whole truth, and nothing but the truth. She mentioned nothing about seeing Mr. Alcala with Robin. As for being a victim, we'll show you that she was intimidated by the police from the beginning, from the outset, that she was threatened by district attorney's investigators, that she had a nervous breakdown. She was unable to sleep. She was unable to study. And she was suicidal.

"In this weakened state, in this state caused by the police, the harassment, the threats, she sought refuge. . . . She wanted help. She'll say that. And who does she get? Who is the unbiased fair person to help her sort this out? To help her deal with the fact that the police are harassing her and telling her, 'You are not telling us what we want to hear.'

"Well, it's a policeman from Huntington Beach. Of course, he doesn't identify himself as such. He is introduced as some sort of a counselor. He knows the facts of this case. Surreptitiously he poses as a counselor . . . and tapes her conversations. He embarks on a charade, and some of the conversation is this: Miss Craven is struggling to separate fact from fantasy. Officer Droz says, 'It is best to go with the feelings. . . .'

Barnett's next statement rocked the courtroom. "Robin wasn't kidnapped on June 20. Robin was in Huntington Beach on June 21. Robin couldn't have been in Sierra Madre on June 20 as Miss Craven is now going to apparently testify, because the next day she is in Huntington Beach.

"We are going to prove that through two witnesses. One is Officer Hattabaugh. After Robin is reported missing, the police go around Huntington Beach with pictures of Robin to see if anyone has seen her. They go up to an individual named Tim Nellis, show him the picture of Robin Samsoe, and ask, 'Have you seen this girl?'

"'Yes, as a matter of fact I just saw her ten minutes ago.' He positively identifies her picture. His recollection is as fresh as it could be. He just saw her. And then he adds something kind of interesting. 'You know what? She was on a yellow bike.' A yellow bike!

"Well, as you recall, Robin had borrowed Bridgett's yellow bike on the twentieth. Mr. Nellis doesn't know Robin Samsoe. Mr. Nellis doesn't know Rodney Alcala. Mr. Nellis just happened to see Robin Samsoe. There is no way, no way, he could have known that girl was on a yellow bike. Officer Hattabaugh will testify he specifically did not tell Mr. Nellis the girl they were looking for might be on a yellow bike. Mr. Nellis comes up with that fact, so Robin was in Huntington Beach on the twenty–first. This is important for three reasons.

"Number one, it renders Miss Craven's testimony useless to the people.

"Two is that it breaks the connection. You see, if Robin is still in Huntington Beach on the twenty–first, the fact that Mr. Alcala took her picture—and I'm not admitting that by any means, but assuming that for the purpose of argument—she's alive on the twenty–first.

"And that is pretty important, because that brings us to Mr. Duarte, Juan Duarte. Now on the twenty–second, eleven–thirty at night, at road marker number eleven, he's seen by police officer Crawford. . . ."

Barnett pointed to a graphic map of the mountain area. "Now this is where Mr. Duarte's car was. There are no lights there. No one else was there. Eleven–thirty at night. And officer Crawford pulls in and sees the car with no one in it. He's a little suspicious, so he gets out of his car.

"Remember, down here about one–hundred feet or so from the road, from this area, is where the remains of Robin Samsoe are found. All right. The car is parked up here. Mr. Duarte, eleven–thirty at night, is walking down this path towards this street. And Officer Crawford sees him. Officer Crawford pulls his service revolver and engages Mr. Duarte in a conversation. And the conversation went like this." Barnett unfolded a police report and read aloud to the jury.

"What are you doing up here?"

"I'm waiting for my girlfriend."

"What's her name?"

"I don't know." Barnett added that Duarte may not have said any thing at that point

"Where's she coming from?"

"I don't know."

"What were you doing up there in the brush?"

"Just taking a piss, man."

"What are you doing with those channel locks in your pocket?" Barnett explained that channel locks are a type of pliers with longer handles.

"You never know what could happen up here in these mountains."

"This conversation takes place right here. . . ." Barnett again indicated a site on the map. ". . . a hundred feet from where Robin Samsoe's remains are found. Now, Mr. Duarte has an alibi for the twentieth. He's working. But we know Robin was alive on the twenty–first. We don't know when she left Huntington Beach. We don't know that. We know that she was seen in Huntington Beach on the twenty–first of June. We don't know when she left.

"So Mr. Duarte doesn't have any alibi at all. Additionally, Mr. Duarte said he was at the beach that day. He said he was at a different beach; certainly wasn't at Huntington Beach, but he did go to the beach that day and he had a towel in his car. Also had a broken window in his car. . . .

"That is what I believe the evidence will show."

Judge Schwab asked, "Does that conclude your opening statement?"

"Yes, sir."

PROSECUTOR FARNELL LAUNCHED THE FIRST PHASE of his presentation by putting a series of young girls on the witness stand to inform jurors how Rodney Alcala had asked to photograph them, then offered them rides or even marijuana. Lynn David and Michelle Ellis testified about being approached by the defendant at Huntington Beach on June 19, the day before Robin vanished. They recalled that he had spoken of a "bikini contest" and tried to get their phone numbers. Both had contacted the police when they saw Alcala's picture on television.

Next came Wanda Ford, 15, who told of posing for photos while roller skating at Seal Beach on June 20. Investigators had found her picture in the Seattle storage locker. Her companion Tina Gardner corroborated the testimony.

Bridgett Wilvert positively identified Alcala as the photographer she and Robin had met on the cliffs. Jackelyn Young, too, said it was the defendant she'd seen with the two girls. Richard Sillett pointed to Alcala as the man he'd seen carrying a camera not far from the Huntington Beach Pier.

The next step on Farnell's agenda was to introduce a piece of evidence that could be crucial to the entire case. Everything else hinged on witnesses, timing, and other circumstantial evidence. This represented the only physical link between Alcala and Robin Samsoe.

Robin's mother was sworn in. She seemed fragile, with moist eyes, as the subject of a pair of small, gold-colored ball-type earrings were brought up by Farnell. They, too, had been seized from the Seattle storage locker, so they had clearly been in the defendant's possession.

Farnell spoke gently. "Mrs. Frazier, did you ever have a set of earrings that were just round, gold balls?"

"Yes, I had."

"Do you remember where you bought those earrings?"

"Probably a variety store. They were very inexpensive."

"Do you have a recollection of how much you might have paid?"

"Maybe three dollars."

"When you bought those earrings, were they just simple, round gold balls?"

"No. They had a bottom attached to them."

"Would you describe that for us?"

"Like a little chain with another loop on the bottom. Another little—not loop—a little ball like on the bottom of them."

"There was a chain and then a smaller ball?"

"Uh-huh."

"Dangling from the round earring?"

"Yes."

"Did something happen to one of those earrings?"

"It broke."

"How did that happen?"

"Well, they were very inexpensive and I don't know how it broke. They were just — cheap."

"They were not pure gold?"

"No."

"Were they gold plated?"

"No."

"When a part broke off one of the earrings, did you do something?"

"I clipped the bottom of the other one off, and tried to clip both sides even, so that they could still be worn as little posts."

"Did Robin ever borrow any of your jewelry?"

"Many times."

"Did Robin ever borrow those particular earrings from you?"

"Yes."

"Did you see that particular jewelry at the police department?"

"Yes."

Marianne Frazier believed the altered earrings in evidence were indeed the ones she had owned. Her testimony turned to the day Robin disappeared and the traumatic contact with Beverly Fleming, the dance studio owner, in which both women realized that Robin was truly missing.

It would be the jury's responsibility to decide if the round, gold-colored earrings found in Alcala's locker were the ones Robin had worn to the beach that terrible day.

ANITA CRAVEN, THE U.S. FOREST SERVICE employee who had stumbled upon Robin's remains, came next. Her accounts of seeing Alcala's car and a man who resembled him had undergone several modifications. To courtroom observers, she appeared nervous and frightened.

Her answers to the prosecutor's questions created a tableau in juror's minds of Craven seeing someone she thought was Alcala "sort of forcefully steering" the girl up the gully and of discovering the child's decomposed and partially missing remains.

Asked by Farnell if it was the same man she saw on both occasions, Craven said she was almost certain, but not "one hundred percent positive." With each new question, the witness seemed more nervous and agitated. She interrupted her narrative with long pauses and rocked back and forth in her chair.

She testified about returning to the body site on the evening of June 25, late enough to require the use of a flashlight. Part of the face was gone, and the naked corpse was "pretty cut up." The hands and feet were missing, but Craven could not say whether they had been severed and could not "remember" whether the legs were hacked up. The head was "next to" the body, and she could not tell if it was severed. Nearby, she saw a blue and yellow tennis shoe and what looked like shorts and a T-shirt. She found no knife.

WITH INCREASING INCIDENTS OF SILENCE and staring into space, Craven's behavior was so erratic that the judge held a hearing in his chambers to decide if she could continue. Farnell said, "Whether she saw knife cuts on the body, she hasn't told us yet. And when asked about what she saw, she sits there and won't respond. The inference is that what she saw was so horrible, that she's not able to relate to it. And that has caused her a great deal of anguish."

Defense attorney Barnett commented, "Well, I don't know what she's going to testify to. But I know what she has said in the past, and that is that she's worked fires and she's seen horribly burned bodies and corpses and put them in body bags and it didn't bother her. And seeing the body didn't bother her."

Farnell disagreed. "She never said that. She never said seeing the body didn't bother her, did she? She said just the opposite. In fact, that was the tenor of what she said when she had seen bodies before. She said they didn't bother her but this one did."

Since Craven had nearly reached the end of her testimony, the judge decided to let her finish.

AFTER THE WITNESS FINALLY STEPPED DOWN, Farnell brought in two inmates from the Orange County Jail. Four jailhouse informants had provided statements to investigators, Carlos Cardenas, David Jackson, Al Davis, and Francisco "Cisco" Galindo. The District Attorney decided to rely on Davis and Galindo to convince jurors that Alcala had confessed the murder to fellow inmates.

Al Davis testified that he overheard a conversation between the defendant and Cisco Galindo. According to Davis, Alcala denied stabbing

Robin, saying instead that he had "slapped her unconscious." Later, said Davis, the defendant had told him that "nobody seen me take her." They would never convict him, Alcala allegedly said, without the "film" and the "bike," and they would not find the bicycle. In a conversation about photography, the defendant reportedly said that he liked to go to a place in the mountains near water towers where there was a view of city lights. A water tower stood not far away from the death scene. Alcala, according to Davis, had said that the victim's little girlfriend had been unable to identify him, even under hypnosis.

Cisco Galindo replaced Davis in the witness chair and said the defendant had mentioned getting Robin into his car by offering to pay her for magazine photos, which wouldn't take very long, and by promising to drop her off at the dance studio. Once underway, he locked Robin's door. Galindo said he asked the defendant what route he took to the mountains, but Alcala had been evasive about it. He had mentioned driving along Pacific Coast Highway. Galindo added that he "thinks" some conversation took place about Robin being "worried or scared" and that she "wanted to get out of the car."

At some point, said Galindo, Alcala asked Robin if she had ever posed nude and had she ever been naked in front of a man. She started crying, and the defendant began "slapping the shit out of her." According to Galdindo, Alcala had described it as "a weird sensation" and a "trip." The bike, he said, had been abandoned behind a "Thrifty Drug Store or a Thriftimart or some kind of thrift store," and Alcala believed the police would never find it.

The missing bicycle was never found. However, the manager of a charity thrift shop in El Monte testified that he had found a yellow Schwinn bicycle with turned-up handlebars behind the store during early July 1979, and had sold it. The bike, he said, had black and white tape on the handlebars and was in unusually good condition for a charity donation.

After Galindo was excused, a question arose about the reason for Alcala being placed in protective custody with the informants. In a hearing outside the jury's presence, Alcala testified that it had been at his request. "If I didn't get put in PC, I was going to be in a lot of trouble, 'cause I had a jacket as a child molester." In prison parlance, a "jacket" is a negative reputation. "I would have problems in jails because I was considered to be a punk first." Punks in prison are usually weaker men used by more powerful inmates to satisfy sexual desires. "And second, if someone.. finds out that I've been in prison for child molesting, that is a hazard. I'm really frightened about not being in a protective custody situation. . . ."

Defender Barnett asked, "Did you tell them that you had been assaulted before?"

"Yeah. I told them that I had been sexually assaulted at the L.A. County jail and that I had been beaten up when I was in prison."

"And what was their response when you asked to be put in protective custody?"

"They said they didn't know if they could put me in PC or not . . . . They said it depended on what I had done . . . that I had to have done something sexual, like rape."

"What did you say to that?"

Referring to the incident in which he had picked up Jennifer Carlson in February 1979, Alcala said he understood the officers to mean that protective custody assignment would be made according to statements he might make about his crime. "I said, 'So if I say I raped her, they would put me in PC?' They indicated that was true. So I didn't say anything for a few minutes. And then [one of them] asked me if I wanted to make a statement. I just nodded."

Farnell, his voice betraying skepticism, asked, "Mr. Alcala, are you telling us the only reason you admitted this crime was that you would not be able to get into PC unless you did?"

"I'd say yes."

"In other words, that is the only thing that caused you to admit to this crime and to make this tape that is nearly forty minutes long? Is that right?"

"I'd say it's the major thing. In other words, what I'm saying is that for me to say — for me to have made that tape, I needed something awfully strong to push me to say what I said on that tape."

Farnell's face telegraphed his disbelief. "How would anybody in prison or in the jail know that you were a child molester?"

"Okay. I had been in prison for approximately six years. I am very well known in prison both because I'm a child molester and because . . . of my legal activities. And I was on the men's advisory councils in various prisons. I know a lot of people in prison. A lot of people know me, or my name, and who I am. Okay? They know I'm a child molester. . . . Anytime you go to jail you are always going to run into somebody who knows you. You know, also from my experience in Los Angeles County, a lot of people know this. I had been in Orange County Jail before that. So it is not—I thought it was highly probable that there was going to be somebody in Riverside Jail that would know me or know I was a child molester."

THE NEXT SEGMENT of the prosecution's case virtually lit a fire under the defense team. Barnett strenuously objected when Richard Farnell decided to introduce information about Alcala's previous criminal behavior into the guilt phase of the trial. The issue would turn out to be profoundly important.

Under California law, this is seldom allowed, except in the penalty phase. Disclosure of prior crimes is usually considered far too "prejudicial" to be used in the guilt phase. Certain exceptions do exist, though.

Before the trial started, prosecutor Farnell sought Judge Schwab's approval to use Alcala's previous convictions and arrests related to luring young girls, by the use of photography, into situations that resulted in sexually abusive behavior. Farnell developed a chart to demonstrate all the similarities in the incidents related to Mary Adams, Tammie Barnes, and Jennifer Carlson. The prosecutor contended that evidence of Alcala's prior crimes, even uncharged ones, should be admissible since they were almost identical to earlier offenses. Similarities suggested the same person committed all of them.

Judge Schwab studied the district attorney's motion and written rationale, which cited several legal precedents. It noted, "All that need be shown is a 'discernible pattern' rather than uniqueness. The chart of similarities . . . clearly shows all three incidents have several unique points of similarity, including approaching of young girls, coaxing these girls into a car, abducting of the girls to locations safe from public view, his house, mountains, remote beach, use of photography, etc. These distinctive acts easily suffice to tie the offenses together sufficiently for admissibility. Even if this were not so . . . the number of similar but not distinctive acts is many more than cited by the courts approving admissibility of prior acts. . . . These similarities make this a classic case where evidence of uncharged offenses should be admissible."

After careful consideration, Schwab decided the district attorney's argument had merit, and granted the motion. Farnell put a series of police officers on the stand, cops who had investigated the complaints from the three young female victims. Barnett continued to object. He cross-examined vigorously, while jurors listened and scribbled notes as rapidly as they could. The testimony strongly suggested that Rodney Alcala had a distinct predilection and strange appetite for pre-pubescent females.

Another issue needed clarification. If Alcala had lured Robin into his car, could he have stashed the bicycle in it too? To settle this matter, the judge agreed to have the Datsun F10 hatchback parked close to the court, and allowed the trial to convene in the parking lot. Jurors observed a demonstration answering the question. The bike easily fit into the luggage space behind the seats.

WHEN FARNELL RESTED the prosecution's case, defender John Barnett launched his parade of witnesses. Jurors had heard, in his opening statements, about someone named Tim Nellis seeing Robin in Huntington Beach on the day after Alcala allegedly photographed her near the pier.

Nellis took the stand and said he had been in Huntington Beach, near 17th Street, to visit a relative. At about four o'clock on the afternoon of June 21, he had seen a little girl "riding a yellow, ten-speed bike down the alley." Barnett showed him a photograph and asked if he recognized the person pictured. He said it was the child he had seen. Approximately fifteen minutes after spotting the rider, Nellis said, he had spoken with a police officer who had shown him a photo of a missing girl, and he had "no doubt" it was the same child

"Do you remember what she was wearing?"

"Yes, she was wearing a white top. And I'm not sure what she was wearing beneath it."

The answers seemed to satisfy Barnett, so he turned the witness over to the prosecutor for cross-examination.

Farnell asked, "Had you ever seen that girl before that day?" No, he hadn't.

Handing the witness a photo, not the same one Barnett had used, he asked, "Are you sure that's the picture of the girl?"

"Yes, it sure looks like her."

"Okay, this is the girl you saw on that day?"

"Yes."

Without a pause, Farnell asked that the photo be numbered as one of the prosecution's exhibits, and continued his questioning. "Mr. Nellis, the little girl you saw was riding a yellow bike—is that right?"

"Yes."

"And you told the police the bike was a little big for her?"

"Yes, it looked a little big."

"And did you notice the handlebars on the bike that you saw?"

"No." He couldn't say whether the handlebars were turned up or turned down.

Nellis reaffirmed that she wore a white top. The prosecutor asked, "Did you see any red top with letters on it that said, 'Here comes trouble'?"

"No, I didn't. I didn't notice that at all."

"And did you think the girl you saw might have had a dress on?"

"I'm not sure. I couldn't say for positive."

After a few more questions about her clothing and whether she carried anything with her, Farnell asked, "Okay. How sure are you, sir, that the girl you saw is the girl in the picture?"

"I'm positive."

It would later be revealed that the photograph Farnell had shown the witness was not Robin Samsoe!

On redirect examination, Barnett made it clear that Nellis had made the identification to a police officer within just a few minutes after the actual sighting.

The issue now lay in the hands of twelve jurors. Would they believe that Robin Samsoe had changed her clothing, and was riding the yellow bike within a few blocks of her home twenty–four hours after she had been reported as missing by her distraught mother, and while police searched the city for her? The witness seemed certain, and had no apparent reason to fabricate such a story. Could he have been one of those strange people who craves attention? Could he have been well-meaning but simply mistaken? The jury would have to decide.

JOHN BARNETT NEEDED TO COUNTER another prosecution thrust; the testimony of two jailhouse informants who told jurors that

Alcala had made statements to them about abducting, beating, and killing Robin Samsoe. He brought in his own informant, Jimmy Small, who had been incarcerated with these men.

Small admitted that he was currently serving a term in Chino State Prison on a forgery charge and had about forty–seven days to go. He had been in Orange County Jail the previous July and August, in protective custody along with Alcala, Davis, and Galindo. Before the defendant had arrived, Small, said, he had discussed the case with Davis and Galindo. "It was a pretty heavy case and that if we could get information out of Alcala that we might be able to work something out with the District Attorney's Office or somebody to get a modification of our sentences. Maybe keep—like for myself, for instance—maybe from going to state prison. Galindo wanted immediate release. And I really don't know what Davis wanted because he only had a couple of weeks left."

It had been Small's idea, he said, to have Galindo "write things down so we could keep our stories straight. . . . I supplied about ninety percent of it. . . ."

"Where did you get it?"

"Out of the newspapers and made up the rest. . . . Mr. Galindo and I asked the deputy if we could go out and sweep on the tier, and we went up and talked to Mr. Alcala. Didn't mention anything at all about his case."

"Were you able to get any information from him?"

"None, whatsoever." He later modified the statement; the only thing they got from Alcala was his interest in photography and that he had "a small station wagon."

"Who thought up the idea about Mr. Alcala having a tough time getting the bicycle in his car?"

"I believe I did."

"How did you come up with that particular part of the story?"

"Well, that particular incident—we just wanted to make things up that would sound believable and not too far-fetched." He had thought the bike bigger than it actually was. They had learned from news reports that Robin was riding a bike. " . . . We just sort of put our heads together and came up with that."

The inmates had also considered fabricating a story about what finally happened to the bike, stated Small. They planned to say that Alcala had dumped the bike somewhere in the mountains near the body discovery site. "We had an arrangement with an inmate who was getting out pretty soon." The accomplice would be paid $150 to purchase a bike and "plant" it. "He was going to go out . . . and get a yellow ten-speed bike, and beat it with a hammer, and take the serial number off, and spray paint the bike, and just generally abuse it so it wouldn't be too recognizable, and go out and bury it near where the little girl's body was found." Then, they planned to tell the district attorney that Alcala had revealed to them the missing bike's location.

"What happened to that plan?"

"Nobody could come up with the money."

On cross-examination, Farnell needed to undermine Small's credibility. He elicited admissions about "numerous" arrests and previous use of heroin. Small couldn't explain why he had never contacted the District Attorney's Office to barter the information regarding Alcala, nor why he never learned what make of car the "small station wagon" was.

"Were you present in the cell when Mr. Alcala talked to Mr. Galindo?"

"Yes."

"Did you ever hear him say anything about 'The Dating Game'?"

"No."

"Did you ever hear Mr. Alcala say anything about the girl he kidnapped not getting a good enough look at him?"

"No. I thought Galindo made that up."

"Did you ever hear Mr. Alcala say that he wanted to take pictures of the girls?"

"No."

"Did you ever hear him say nobody could put him at the beach?"

"No"

"So if Mr. Galindo or Mr. Davis knew the type of car that Mr. Alcala had, they didn't get it from you, did they?"

"They got it out of the newspaper."

"Well, do you know whether it was in the newspaper, sir?"

"I'm pretty sure it was."

Farnell switched to questions about Small's "three hundred-dollar-a-day" drug habit, the crimes he committed to support it, and his intentions to get out of jail by snitching on other drug pushers or "fences" who bought stolen property. He admitted there was "some truth" in the allegations.

"You wanted to be an informant in this case, didn't you?"

"I had thoughts about it, yes."

"And Mr. Davis and Mr. Galindo beat you to it, didn't they?"

"No, sir."

"When you talked to Mr. Alcala, you advised him to stop talking to Davis and Galindo, didn't you?"

"Right."

A barrage of similar questions had Jimmy Small reeling before he was dismissed.

TO CONTINUE THE DISMANTLING of a snitch who ratted on snitches, Farnell summoned a probation officer who knew Small quite well. The prosecutor asked, "From your knowledge of Mr. Small, from your experience with him, from your contacts with him over the period of time you supervised him, is it your opinion that Mr. Small is not a believable person?" Yes, he said, and other law enforcement people also distrusted Small. The jury heard that Small was reviled and mistrusted by both his inmate peers and law officers who dealt with him. In that light, it would be difficult to give his testimony much credence.

Defense attorneys often employ a strategy of shifting suspicion to someone else for the crime. John Barnett had found a possible suspect in Juan Duarte, who had been questioned by an officer near the crime scene. Farnell argued against the admissibility of such evidence. In a heated hearing, Barnett repeated the events he had described in his opening statement, and embellished them. "It's eleven–thirty at night. There are no lights in the area. He's coming out of the bushes less than a hundred feet from where Robin's remains are ultimately found. The police officer asked him, 'Have you ever been busted before?' 'Yes, sir. I've done time for murder. I was a juvenile at the time.' 'Why did they let you out?' 'I was paroled in seventy–eight.'

"Additionally," Barnett continued, "at the preliminary hearing, he admitted to being at the beach that day, but a different beach. And he identified a woman named Crystal with no last name as being with him. He also made other incriminating statements."

Farnell also had more to say about Mr. Duarte. "Work records, time cards, indicate that he was working on the twentieth. Witnesses remember him being at work. That he went to a beach on the twenty–second has absolutely no bearing on this case." Even if he had, said the prosecutor, Duarte worked in Los Angeles. If he had finished work at five in the afternoon, it would have taken him at least an hour to drive to Huntington Beach. Robin was already missing by that time.

Barnett had an answer. "It's true that he has a time card for the twentieth. However, it's our position that Robin was seen alive on the twenty–first by a guy named Tim Nellis. Therefore, the exact date of her abduction is unknown. Duarte's alibi for the twentieth is illusory. . . . Our purpose is to show that Duarte, not Alcala, probably did this killing."

The argument also included the issue of revealing to the jury that Duarte had admitted serving time for murder.

"What is the relevance of the fact he was convicted of murder?"

"It shows his state of mind and his nervous reaction to the police officer. He is up there late at night. He gives ridiculous answers to the officer's questions."

"Of course he was nervous," replied Farnell. "He's on parole. One of the conditions of parole is no drinking, but he had beer in his hand when the officer stopped him. He thought he would go back to prison for the violation." Besides, Farnell added, "There's no relation whatsoever between a robbery-murder and a sex kidnapping and molestation of a young girl. There's absolutely no nexus."

Barnett disagreed, and threw in another fact. "The murder weapon in Duarte's case was a .22 caliber pistol. Six shots were fired. Anita Craven, when going back to the scene, found several .22 caliber shells and threw them away."

Judge Schwab allowed testimony by Officer Crawford and Juan Duarte. They told of the night encounter on June 22 in the Sierra Madre mountains. It appeared that Duarte might be a logical suspect. But Farnell had done some additional homework.

He summoned a management employee of the company for which Duarte worked, and introduced evidence that Juan had worked until five o'clock, not only on June 20, but on the following two days as well. Duarte's role as a suspect crashed and burned.

In another tack, the defense worked hard to show that Anita Craven's testimony was "confabulated," a product of improper police interrogation methods which played upon her confusion and emotional turmoil. Barnett introduced tapes of extensive interviews conducted by police officers to suggest that she had been brainwashed and that her testimony was riddled with false memories. It would be another challenge for the jury to sort out during deliberations.

ON MONDAY, APRIL 28, 1980, Richard Farnell stood before the jury to deliver his final summation of the case. Like the lawyers' opening statements, these summations were not evidence, but simply their versions of what had been presented in court. These closing arguments may be compared to old detective movies in which Sam Spade or Charlie Chan gathers everyone in the drawing room and methodically explains how he has solved the crime.

"Good morning, ladies and gentleman," he greeted. "First of all I would like to discuss with you just what the charges are and what the evidence must show for each one. The first charge against the defendant, in count one, is kidnapping. . . . Three basic things [are required] to prove a kidnapping. The evidence must show that the person was unlawfully moved by physical force or compelled to move because of a reasonable apprehension of harm.

"When Robin Samsoe got into the car and the defendant began driving her, he reached over and he locked the door. At one point, Robin said she wanted to get out at the next corner, but the defendant continued. When that happened, the kidnapping began. When she wanted to get out and he would not let her out, but continued to transport her, he embarked on a kidnapping. And that took place over a period of an hour and a half as Robin Samsoe was transported by the defendant up to the mountains in the Sierra Madre foothills.

"He was moving her by the unlawful use of physical force. She knew that if she resisted, she would come to harm. When they got up to the foothills and the defendant removes her from the car and he begins forcefully steering her up the ravine, the kidnapping continues; the force, the pushing of her.

"Of course, when Robin wants out of the car she is no longer consenting to being with the defendant.

"And finally, the third element; the movement was for a substantial distance. That is more than a slight or trivial distance. . . . What we have here, of course, is the movement of Robin from Huntington Beach, a substantial distance, for an hour and a half up to the mountains, from the turnout up into the hills away from the roadway, back where it's secluded, where the risk of harm to Robin is greater.

"The second count, count two, is murder. Murder is the unlawful killing of a human being with malice aforethought.

"No question Robin is a human being.

"Unlawfully. This is to distinguish between, for example, when a police officer shoots a fleeing robber. That is lawful. There is no lawful killing in this case; absolutely no question about that.

"With malice aforethought. What is malice? Malice may be expressed or implied. In our particular case, I believe we have malice expressed by the acts of the defendant who has manifested an intent to unlawfully kill. He did this when he took Robin up there and he stabbed her and cut her.

"Aforethought simply means that the mental state must occur before the act, not after the act. No question that this has occurred.

"Now, the defendant has the right to have you instructed in two degrees of murder; first degree and second degree. There is no question that under our facts, the facts presented in this trial, that the murder is of the first degree.

"Second degree murder is unpremeditated or may occur during the course of other felonies such as kidnapping.

"First degree murder involves three separate elements:

"Deliberate and premeditated murder. Intentional as opposed to an accidental or unpremeditated killing. Intentional killing. There is no question that when the defendant took the knife up there with him and he stabbed Robin, when he hit her, when he broke her teeth out, there is no question that his killing was intentional. He intended to do what he did.

"As the defendant drove . . . up to the Sierra Madre foothills, what is going through his mind? He is thinking, he is contemplating. He knows that after he attacks Robin that he is going to have to kill her. Because if he doesn't, she'll report him, exactly the same way Jennifer Carlson reported him. He has to kill her. He is deliberating. He is thinking about it.

"He takes a knife out of the car, and goes up the ravine with that knife. Each step of the way he is thinking about what he is doing. He is planning. He is deliberating.

"Premeditated. Simply means to consider beforehand. In other words, deliberation must occur before the killing . . . and there is no specific time required. The cold, calculated killing can be formed in a person's mind in a very short period of time.

"So the murder of Robin Samsoe in this case was deliberated and it was premeditated. The defendant had planned it. He had been looking for a little girl to take with him for his sexual desires for at least two days; trying to get a little girl to go with him from the beach. And finally he succeeded by finding Robin Samsoe.

"You also have a verdict [to consider] in special circumstances.

"Special circumstances, as you will consider them now, involve two separate findings. First, there must be murder found in the first degree. And secondly, the special circumstance that you must find that a kidnapping occurred.

"Beyond that, you do not consider at this stage, the penalty. That is not to be discussed by you at this time. When you find the defendant guilty of first degree murder, and then you determine if the murder occurred during the course of a kidnapping, you have determined that the special circumstance exists.

After a few comments of courtesy, Farnell thanked the jury and sat down.

John Barnett's final summation lasted considerably longer than the prosecutor's. He dwelled heavily on the proposition that Robin may not have been abducted on the day in question. There was no physical evidence, he asserted, such as hairs, fibers, fingerprints, blood, or anything else that linked his client to the murder. The entire case was circumstantial, he said, and full of holes. Testimony from jailhouse informants was unreliable because each of them had ulterior motives. He asked the jury to find Rodney Alcala not guilty.

THE DEFENSE PLEAS WERE IN VAIN. Twelve jurors struggled nearly a week before voting unanimously that Alcala was guilty of murdering Robin Samsoe. In the ensuing penalty phase, they recommended that he be put to death for the crime. Judge Schwab, who had the option to hand down a sentence of life without parole, or death, chose the latter.

Alcala was transported to San Quentin.

Rose Bird's Supreme Court

California law demands that every murder conviction resulting in a penalty of death must be automatically reviewed by the State Supreme Court. Most condemned inmates wait for years, even decades, before their appeals begin.

Rodney Alcala's 1980 conviction and sentence came before the California Supreme Court in 1984. The deck was stacked in his favor.

Chief Justice Rose Bird, an attractive, brilliant woman, age 47, had made her view of capital punishment patently obvious. She eventually voted to overturn all sixty-one of the capital punishment cases she reviewed. Bird's colleagues, especially Associate Justices Cruz Reynoso and Joseph Grodin, aligned themselves with her on most of them, leading to a furious public outcry that the court was ruling not by law, but by their personal biases against capital punishment. Rose Bird had been appointed by Gov. Jerry Brown, who made no secret of his abhorrence of the death penalty.

In examining records of the 1980 Alcala trial, the court focused primarily on three crucial issues appealed by the defense.

First, said the appeals lawyers, no credible evidence was ever introduced to show that Robin Samsoe had been forcibly kidnapped. The implication was that she had willingly gone with Alcala.

Second, according to the defenders, nothing supported the finding that Alcala had premeditated the victim's death. Since premeditation is an essential part of first degree murder, affirmation by the court would necessitate overturning the guilty verdict and the death penalty.

And third, the trial court had allowed jurors to hear about Alcala's prior crimes including a few for which he had never been charged with criminal conduct.

After studying trial transcripts, the justices said about the forcible kidnapping issue: "All parties concede that, at the time of Robin's disappearance, force or fear was a necessary element of the kidnapping. . . . We think a rational trier of fact could find beyond a reasonable doubt that force or fear was used to transport Robin. Even if the victim's initial cooperation is obtained without force, or the threat of force, kidnapping occurs if the accused subsequently restrains his victim's liberty . . . and compels the victim to accompany him further. The force . . . need not be physical. The movement is forcible where it is accomplished through the giving of orders which the victim feels compelled to obey out of fear for harm or injury. . . .

"Here, there is both direct and circumstantial support. . . . The people introduced evidence that Robin was a responsible child, highly motivated to meet her late-afternoon ballet appointment. Yet she never arrived for that appointment . . . ." They noted Anita Craven's claim to have seen Robin in the defendant's company after the scheduled appointment time. Jackye Young, they observed, testified that Robin had found the defendant "strange." "The jury could reasonably infer that she had not accompanied him voluntarily."

The justices also commented that inmate Galindo had testified about the defendant's statement that he had lured Robin into his automobile with a ruse about magazine photos, then locked the car's only passenger side door. She "wanted out of the car" and asked to be let out at the next corner. "The death scene was far from Pacific Coast

Highway, suggesting that Robin was kept in the car for a substantial period after she asked for her freedom." The defense contentions, said the court, "lacked merit." Strike one against the defense.

Regarding the premeditation issue, the justices said, "The evidence . . . suggests the defendant met and photographed Robin, devised and executed a scheme to abduct her, kept her in his car by force or fear, drove her a considerable distance from urban surroundings to a rural area, then took her on foot away from the road to an even more secluded spot where others were unlikely to intrude. The jury could conclude he carried a knife with him to the death scene and used it to kill Robin. Anita Craven testified that Robin's body was 'all cut up.' A Kane Kut knife containing human blood , and a towel with 'wipe' stains of type A blood, were found nearby. There was a set of similar knives at defendant's home. . . . The evidence suggests that defendant had committed a serious felony, kidnapping, of the victim and believed she was the only person who could implicate him." Killing her would, they noted, eliminate the only witness to his crime. "Under all the circumstances, we find ample evidence of premeditation and deliberation."

Strike two against the defense.

Now, they examined the introduction to the jury of prior crimes.

The defense, said the justices ". . . argues that the crimes should have been excluded in any event as more prejudicial than probative. . . . The People invoke the statutory exception which allows admission of prior conduct to show 'motive . . . intent . . . plan . . . or identity.' The jury was instructed that it could consider evidence on each of those issues."

The justices took issue with the prosecution claim that all of Alcala's incidents with young women fit the same pattern. Jennifer Carlson, they noted, "was never restrained in defendant's car by trick, force, or fear. Neither outdoor settings nor the use of photography figured in the Mary Adams incident. . . . There was no element of photography at all in the Tammie Barnes incident." Several other "inconsistencies" bothered the court members. "We conclude that the prior acts were inadmissible on all of these [prosecution] theories, and that the error was prejudicial on all charges."

Associate Justice Joseph Grodin wrote the crucial finale. "We will conclude that the convictions and special circumstances findings must be reversed, since the admission of prior offenses constituted prejudicial error on those issues. . . ."

The defense, with two strikes against them, swung and hit an out-of-the-park home run. But the game wasn't over. The Orange County district attorney soon announced that Rodney Alcala would face a new trial, still charged with murdering Robin Samsoe. The death penalty would be sought again.

A colorful, cantankerous, controversial judge in Orange County would inherit the second trial. Donald A. McCartin's remarkable background prepared him well for the assignment.

PART II

MEMOIRS OF A JUDGE

Judge Donald A. McCartin

The McCartin Story
(In his own words)

"If you don't keep your sense of humor in this business,
you'll lose your mind."
—*Judge Donald A. McCartin*

My life has been full of fortunate encounters with remarkable people, some famous, some notorious, all unique. And I've had some incredible adventures.

I was a "child of the Depression," born April 21, 1925, to Aaron and Ruth McCartin in Minneapolis, Minnesota. In my infancy and early childhood, we lived at 4306 Sunnyside Road, near the country club, in Edina, Minnesota, which was the ritziest place in the region. Still is. We had a maid and a live-in nanny. While the majority of people in this country endured great hardship after the 1929 stock market crash, I was one of the lucky ones shielded from those difficulties.

My early education consisted of eleven years in local schools. I did okay in the classroom, and despite mediocre athletic skills played basketball in high school. Sometimes I'd get frustrated and trip the guys who'd go against me, so I didn't last long on the team.

We moved several times to different homes around Minneapolis. One of the first relocations I recall was to a Cape Cod-style home on St.

Albans Road in Belgrove. Years later, after I had left, my parents moved
again from a gracious residence in Holdridge, another suburb, and sold
it to Bob Short. People knew him as the owner of the Minneapolis
Lakers, the professional basketball team that moved to California and
became the Los Angeles Lakers.

I don't have many memories of my younger life, but one recollection stands out in my mind. It took place in November 1930, when I was
five. My folks held a big party for a number of people in our basement
amusement room. I asked my dad, "Who is that gentleman who
appears to be sleeping on the couch?" Actually he was drunk.

My father answered, "That man is the new governor of Minnesota
who just got elected." It was Floyd B. Olson, age 39 at the time. He took
office on January 6, 1931, and died of cancer on August 22, 1936, while
still occupying the Capitol in St. Paul.

We descended from a long line of flour millers, but due to a bad
decision by an ancestor, my inheritance did not include shares in a
mega-firm similar to General Mills. Flour had put Minneapolis on the
map during the late nineteenth century, and my family owned a big mill
powered by St. Anthony Falls on the Mississippi River. But some great-
great uncle didn't believe in buying insurance for the firm. The whole
thing burned down and we were no longer in the milling business.
When I attended a fifty-year reunion of college classmates, a bunch of
us went on a tour. We saw the old ruins and someone asked, "Is that
where the flour mill was?" I just nodded.

Another relative, this one from my mother's family tree, might have
changed the course of history had he been a little more vigilant.
Benedict O'Driscoll, a Union Army major in the Civil War, was at Ford's
theater in Washington, D.C., on the night President Lincoln attended to
see a play called "Our American Cousin." John Wilkes Booth shot
Lincoln, leaped down to the stage, and made his getaway. I'd always
heard that Major O'Driscoll was there to watch out for Mr. Lincoln, but

can find no historical reference to it. If that was the case, he didn't do a very good job.

Our family roots are in Ireland and I grew up in the Catholic faith. My ancestors were originally from County Down, and were among the true ancient families in Ireland, going back to around 400 B.C. All McCartins, whether spelled McCartan or McCarten, are ninety—nine percent Catholic. In Downpatrick, Northern Ireland, where St. Patrick is buried in a cathedral named for him, St. McCartin lies in the adjacent tomb. The St. Anthony church in Minneapolis has a stained-glass window inscribed with the names David and Mary McCartin, two important donors. They were my father's grandparents.

My grandmother came from the Murphy clan, and my dad was one of her four children. Marion McCartin, his sister, reclaimed her mom's maiden name by marrying Ignatius Murphy. They were pioneers in the use of radium in medicine, and radiology, preceded by Marie and Pierre Curie. Marion and Ignatius both died in their early fifties—of cancer.

My father, Aaron, almost became Moses McCartin. When he was born, his parents opened the Bible to pick a name, but came to a page telling the story of Moses. They had the wisdom to make a second stab at it, turned to another page, and found Aaron. I'm glad. I don't think I'd like being Donald Moses McCartin.

In addition to being a practicing Catholic, my father was a rock-solid Democrat. But he married a rebellious woman who became a staunch Republican and a bridge player. She supported Alf Landon for president when he ran against Franklin D. Roosevelt.

EDUCATION WAS IMPORTANT to both of my parents. My mother was valedictorian at her high school, but in those days not many women went on to college. She compensated for the academic shortage by voracious reading, sometimes devouring four books a day. Dad had college degrees in accounting and law. A reserve colonel in the National Guard, he was called up at the outbreak of WWII, but failed the physical. Somewhere along the way, he developed military ambitions for me that would eventually have a major impact on my life.

Life in Minneapolis, like anywhere else, had certain school-kid customs that probably didn't make much sense. For example, if you lived in Minneapolis, you tried to stay away from St. Paul. You didn't shop there. We looked down on St. Paul. They were "bad" people. You didn't socialize with them. It was like the Hatfields and the McCoys. The only time I ever went there was after high school graduation, to attend Macalester College.

When I was in high school, my father said I had to work to help support the family, which of course was a big joke. So I took a job under him at Juster Brothers clothing store in Minneapolis. This was about 1941. I bought a used 1938 Packard with a rumble seat which made me really popular; everyone wanted to double date with me. As the driver, I was focused on the girl up front with me, and ignored whatever was going on back there in the rumble seat. One night after dropping off my date, I came home in pouring rain. I went up to my bedroom which was over the garage. While I was getting ready for bed, I heard this strange noise coming from underneath in the garage. I went down to investigate, and found the other couple I'd forgotten about. When it had started raining, they had crouched down and closed the rumble seat over them. It had locked and they couldn't get out. I had to get dressed again and take them home.

I attended high school through the eleventh grade, and entered college in December 1942, a year early. Even though most Catholic boys went to the University of St. Thomas in St. Paul, I decided on Macalester College in the same city. I would have been forced to wait until spring to enter St. Thomas, but Macalester's schedule allowed immediate entry. The school, founded in 1874, also had a good reputation for academic excellence and has a history of illustrious graduates.

Kofi Annan, secretary-general of the United Nations, from Ghana, would also choose Macalester and graduate in 1962.

It was a Presbyterian institution, and I had to suffer through chapel every day. My economics instructor was Hubert H. Humphrey who later became Minnesota's senator, then U.S. vice president under Lyndon Johnson. In 1968, Humphrey's presidential aspirations were defeated by Richard M. Nixon. My father had helped Humphrey get started in politics by running his 1942 campaign for mayor of Minneapolis.

At Macalester, my roommate was another Minnesota native, Pete Mondale. His younger brother, Walter "Fritz" Mondale, also graduated from our school. Fritz eventually replaced Humphrey as the state's senator, then served as Jimmy Carter's vice president, and eventually ran for, and lost, the top office in 1984. Pete had an IQ about three times greater than mine, so he didn't have to work very hard at school. He would roller skate up and down the hall in the evenings when we were all trying to study. Sometimes I joined him in mischief. We would steal hams from the kitchen and take girls down to the river for a picnic. At our fiftieth reunion, I spoke to Pete Mondale, but he didn't remember us doing those things, or rolling marijuana cigarettes either.

My father had visions of me as a career officer in the U.S. Navy. Influenced by his wishes, which probably grew stronger with the eruption of WWII, I changed schools. After a year at Macalester, I went south to Dubuque College in Iowa, enrolled in a V-12 program arranged by my dad. Similar to NROTC (Naval Reserve Officer Training Corps), it consisted of a sixteen-month program of classes, then transfer to a sixteen-week midshipman school at a major university.

At Dubuque, my unit was commanded by Lt. Dunsmore, who ran the program like we were Nazis. I had so many demerits I was nearly always restricted to the barracks. Cadet trainees were in one big dorm — the other dormitory was for women. But eight of us guys were assigned to a room in the women's dorm. Dunsmore was known as "The Fox" and would creep down the halls trying to catch us in any kind of misbehavior.

During the first four months, I was on restriction most of the time and I couldn't go home when the one-week break came. I wasn't even allowed to go to church. Dubuque is a Catholic town, so I wrote a letter to the local parish priest, using my left hand. I am ambidextrous; can write with either hand. In the letter, I said I was a V-12 student who wanted to attend church but was prevented from going by my commander.

Two or three weeks later, all hands were called to a meeting in the gymnasium. I stood in the front row, close to The Fox, and could see my letter in his hand.

Dunsmore said, "I don't know who wrote this, but we don't take Navy problems to the outside world." He read it aloud to everyone. All I could do is stand there with a red face. Fortunately, nothing more ever came of it, and I finished my sixteen months successfully.

When the time came for transfer to a university midshipman program, I lucked out. I had heard the ones at Notre Dame and other places were really tough. But I landed in the most cushy program of all, at Northwestern University, Chicago campus. It was pretty much a joke, really. The only thing you had to do was run up twelve stories to the top of Abbott Hall. We couldn't use the elevator; they wouldn't let us. The four months sailed by, and I was commissioned as a nineteen-year-old U.S. Navy ensign in March 1945.

World War II ended in Europe two months later, but combat in the Pacific theater continued until September. I fully expected to see some fighting.

Most cadets, after being commissioned, were sent for more training or directly off to the war. Not me, though. Somehow, I was sent down to Miami Beach and lived at the Everglades Hotel on the seventh floor.

I spent most of my time playing bridge. When they finally started me on sea duty training aboard a minesweeper, I suffered horrible seasickness. I was going with a girl whose father was a doctor, and every Monday she would send me out to sea with plenty of medicine, but it didn't help. I almost died. After ten weeks of torture on small vessels, I asked for the biggest ship in the Navy. They assigned me to the USS Tennessee, a famous old battleship that had nearly been sunk on December 7, 1941, at Pearl Harbor.

From Miami, I was sent to Philadelphia, then to San Francisco as a jumping-off point to catch up to the Tennessee. In San Francisco, they didn't have room at the BOQ (Bachelor Officer's Quarters), so I stayed at one of the big hotels. I really thought I was going to be shipped out at any time, but they assigned me a job for a couple of months. My duty was sending everyone else out to war. Here I was a little ensign dispatching other guys to Pacific combat, into the heat of battle. After that, they finally said it was time for me to go.

My destination was Okinawa, where the USS Tennessee caught a kamikaze attack before my arrival. The circuitous route they chose took me to the Admiralty Islands, close to Australia. That's a long way from Okinawa. You can see how screwed up they were. If you don't know where a battleship is! I crossed paths with any number of guys who were looking for LSTs (landing craft) and such, which might be anywhere. But I don't know how they could lose a battleship. Somehow, we still won that war.

On the final leg of the journey, they put me aboard a cargo ship loaded with food headed for Okinawa. I arrived on the Tennessee just a few days before the war was officially ended. The big battle wagon was extremely crowded, with officers sleeping anywhere they could, including the halls. So there I was at the end of the war on a battleship, looking like I had helped win the war. But I knew I hadn't.

The USS Tennessee was the flagship for the Seventh Fleet. The same

day I boarded, we transferred the flag to the USS Pennsylvania. That
made room for some of the excess number of men. That very night, a
lone Japanese plane flew over and dropped a bomb on the Tennessee,
resulting in quite a bit of damage, but nothing disabling. It was the last
ship hit by an enemy bomb. The next day, the flag was transferred back to
the Tennessee, and we sailed off to patrol around Okinawa and prepare
for the invasion of Japan. Fortunately, that event never happened. A pair
of atomic bombs convinced the Japanese that more fighting was useless.

In Yokohama Bay, I was temporarily on another vessel tied up near
the USS Missouri. So, on that historic day, I sat with a grandstand view
of Gen. Douglas MacArthur and watched the whole Japanese surrender
ceremony.

In October, word came that someone had decided to send us home
to the States. I had been on active duty only about a month and a half.
The interesting thing is, the Tennessee and the Pennsylvania, our sister
ship, were the only two U.S. warships that could not get through the
Panama Canal. When they were hit in Pearl Harbor, they had to be refit-
ted, which included adding big blisters on the sides for protection. So we
had to take the long way around the world to get to the East Coast.

I had left the States from Philadelphia, and arrived back at
Philadelphia on the fourth anniversary of Pearl Harbor day, December
7,1945. So I had a free trip around the world; got to see Ceylon (now Sri
Lanka), Singapore, Rio de Janeiro, and several other exotic ports.

I WAS LOOKING FORWARD to discharge the following April. While I
waited, I inherited the duty of decommissioning the Tennessee. I, a
lowly ensign, along with one other Lieutenant-junior grade, put the
grand old battleship in the mothball fleet, to eventually be dismantled
and sold for scrap metal.

When we finished, we had nothing to do, so they sent us to a Navy
facility near Fenway Park, Boston. I spent a lot of time watching the

Boston Red Sox. I had been a big Yankee fan from birth, so I didn't really enjoy that very much. With a lot of time on our hands, we played badminton in the Quonset huts. It was all a big joke and a terrible waste of time. I finally got out in August 1946 and went back to Macalester College.

My dad had other plans for me. He hated lawyers, even though he was a lawyer himself. He was also an accountant and went into business with a large clothing store, called Juster Brothers, in Minneapolis where he headed the Retailers Association. In addition, he wrote articles for Esquire magazine. Deep inside him, though, I believe there was a frustrated military leader. He had been a colonel in the National Guard. He met my mother and proposed, but she wouldn't marry him unless he promised not to pursue a military career. I think he must have regretted leaving the service because he really wanted me to stay in the Navy. I didn't care much for the Navy because I was a little too hot-tempered and didn't like to take orders. So I got out and went to college.

I graduated from Macalester in June1947. During the first semester I had taken nine credits and planned to attend through the next summer on the G.I. Bill. But I decided to accelerate my work in order to graduate in June, and took nineteen credits the second semester. When I got out in June, my dad started his campaign. "Go back in the Navy, go back in the Navy." By that time I had decided I wanted to go to law school, but felt that I had nothing to say about it because, of course, in those days you did what your parents wanted you to do. That next fall, I went back in the regular Navy, as an ensign in the supply corps.

FOR A PERIOD OF TIME, I was stationed in Annapolis at the Naval Academy, living in the BOQ with rooms as big as some houses. There were very few other single officers there. I was on the second floor, in one of only eight rooms. If I showered too long, water would overflow, seep through the floor, and rain on officers eating down below in the mess hall.

Someone one would run up and shout, "Ensign McCartin, please, turn the shower off, it's starting to leak through in the dining room!"

During that time I found a good way to commute home to Minneapolis to visit on weekends. Two of the men in the BOQ were U.S. Navy pilots. My future wife, Ruth, living in Minneapolis, would get them dates with pretty Minnesota girls, so they would gladly fly me there. We'd all go out for the weekend, then fly back to Annapolis.

Being one of the only eligible bachelors, I went to all the Academy dances. Once, I had to be the escort for Margaret Truman, the president's daughter. And once it was Secretary of State Jimmy Byrne's daughter. You'd get stuck with some real "winners." This is one reason I finally got married while I was there, in May 1948. A buddy of mine, who had agreed to be my best man, couldn't believe I was actually going to tie the knot. He was so certain that I wouldn't go through with it that he didn't even bother to show up. My dad stood in as best man.

My goal, at that time, was to become a pilot. But it looked like I would have to spend two years at sea before I could enter flight training.

The United States Marine Corps entered the picture. At that time, the Marine Corps had a program that sent you to Quantico, Virginia, for one year after which you could go down to Pensacola for flight training. I thought, "This is great. Why waste my time here in the Navy?" So I resigned my commission. Two days later, I was sworn into the USMC as a second lieutenant.

IT DIDN'T TAKE LONG TO REALIZE that Marines are Marines, and that I had no "gung ho" spirit. I found myself at the base with a hard-bitten major named "Moose" who had played football for Macalester College while I was there. He was the roughest, toughest gyrene in existence. We would take forced walks at night, and if somebody dropped off a cliff or disappeared, he wouldn't let anyone go back until the next day to see if they were alive or not.

My new wife was a schoolteacher. We lived off base in a Quantico apartment above a café. Every night, I heard the same song on the juke-box down below. It was called "Slow Boat to China." They played it night after night. I thought it was going to drive me nuts. My wife laundered and pressed my shirts at home. We had these tough inspections and my shirts never passed. I was required to keep a bunk in the barracks, too, with the sheets and blankets drum tight so that a quarter would bounce from it. I was having a "wonderful" time. I thought to myself, "This is absolute bull." We'd play war games, run through the woods, then come back and clean our M-1 rifles. I got smart. When we'd be out there in the boonies, I would never fire my weapon, to keep from cleaning it that night. They got on to me pretty soon, and were able to tell the rifle had-n't been fired. Good old "Moose" would stop me out there, grab my weapon, and fire it to make sure I would have to clean it.

This routine didn't appeal to me very much. I was fighting "WWIII" but my real enemy was the Marine Corps. After about five or six months, the solution came from the U.S. Navy.

I found out they had instituted a new policy allowing ensigns to go directly to Pensacola for flight training without the two prior years of sea duty!

So I promptly resigned from the Marine Corps and a few days later accepted a commission as an ensign in the U.S. Navy once again. I remember saying to someone at Quantico, "I'm going to Pensacola, and when I get my wings I'm going to come back here and bomb you with horse manure."

AT PENSACOLA, MY GROUP included two ensigns I had known on the Tennessee. One of their fathers had designed the F4UCorsair fight-er plane used extensively on aircraft carriers. We used SN-J trainers which were considered pretty hot at that time. You got eighteen hours in the air, instead of the 100 hours previously required in those "yellow peril" aircraft. During training, we had some strange experiences. In night flying, you'd get very disoriented. One guy went down too low and ran into a Greyhound bus. Another fellow walked into a spinning propeller. But it was a great class and a lot of good men in it.

In the fall of 1949, I was scheduled for my solo flight. My instructor, a fellow named Prewitt, great guy, said, "McCartin, you're a lousy flyer, but you can make crosswind landings better than I can." We had to bring the plane in at an angle, and I could do pretty darn good landings. On your solo, you dumped your instructor off, then you go off and fly, then come back and pick him up. I dumped him, took off, and was in the middle of my solo. I could see him down there waving frantically to come down. I landed, picked up my instructor, and found out a hurricane was blowing in fast. We were ordered to head immediately for Memphis, Tennessee, and not to land until we got there.

So I had to wait until we got back from Memphis several days later, and start all over with my preparation for a solo flying test.

DURING THE TIME IN PENSACOLA, the actual training took place at Whiting Field, forty miles from our living quarters. I commuted with three other married ensigns, driving back and forth, an eighty-mile round trip. One of the group was an African-American, who happened to be among the first black ensigns out of the Naval Academy. For some reason, he just couldn't get the hang of flying at all. And night flying was a real disaster for him. He almost landed on top of me one time. They gave him two or three chances to make a satisfactory night landing, but he failed and they washed him out. He said to me, "Don, I don't want to say anything about it, but the reason I flunked out, I'm sure, is because I'm black." It's too bad he believed that, because it simply was not true. He just couldn't fly very well.

My wife and I, with our little son Mike, lived in quarters at Navy Point. We sometimes had family members visit. One of them, my very attractive cousin, Jan Huxtable, from Chicago, stayed on for a while. There was a shortage of women around the military base, so Jan sometimes made two or three dates for a single night, and spent all day trying to get out of them. One of the cadets she dated was Jack Whisler. When he came around, she would whistle the theme from a popular radio mystery show, "The Whistler," just to watch him blush. Jan's cousin, Vicky Huxtable, was another beauty. She appeared in small television roles with Abe Vigoda, who played the character Detective Fish on the "Barney Miller" television series, and eventually had his own show, titled "Fish." Years later, Vicky attended some function where she met Bill Cosby. He liked her surname and asked if he could use it in his upcoming television series. That's how Cosby's character, Dr. Huxtable, got his name. Vicky wound up developing a line of sauces and dressings called "Huxtable's Delectables."

WE HAD A BASEBALL TEAM representing Pensacola Naval Air Station, and I played first baseman. I broke my left hand in a game, and they put a cast on it. We had completed instrument training and were about to go into the next stage, formation flying at Safley Field, I believe. If you got your wings, you were obligated to spend three years as a naval officer. But the injury took me out of training. I sat around forever, mostly playing bridge. All of my fellow class members and my friends went to Corpus Christi, Texas, for advanced training and I was left behind in Pensacola. I wondered, "What am I doing here? Do I really want to invest all this time in the military? Maybe I should go back to law school."

A few months later, at the beginning of spring, 1950, my hand was still screwed up. So I went to the commander and told him I had decided to offer my letter of resignation. He asked what I planned to do, and I mentioned that I would probably go to law school in the fall. We agreed that I would make my departure effective the following September, and sent in my letter.

I departed from Pensacola with several months yet to serve. They assigned me to duty aboard a heavy cruiser, the USS St. Paul, which seemed appropriate since I was from Minneapolis, Minnesota (although I had avoided actually going into the city of St. Paul until I was in college). I reported aboard and met the executive officer, Commander John S. "Jack" McCain, Jr., who would eventually become an admiral. His father had been a four-star admiral in WWII. McCain was the most dynamic person I have ever met. He was short, only about five–six, and had silver-gray hair. He would rub his hands together and say, "Okay, Mac, here's what you are going to do. You're going to be my personnel officer, which means you are going to do absolutely nothing. We have a slight problem on the St. Paul. It's known as the 'French cruiser.' You're going to get rid of these fags."

Of course, that language is politically incorrect and insulting today. But it was the way many people thought and expressed their feelings about homosexuality in the forties and fifties.

McCain wanted to rid the ship of homosexuals, and I was assigned the task of finding out who they were. He told me that the men so identified would be offered an undesirable discharge and if any of them refused, they would be subject to court-martial. With those steely blue eyes and unquestionable authority, he said, "You're going to do this for me, Mac."

To be honest, I didn't know at that time what a "fag" was. I think I was approached once in Philadelphia, but I was too naive to know what it was all about. So I asked, "Well, sir, what's the problem here?" He said, "We've got the wrestling team, which is the core of all these fags." There was a rumor that word had been spread in various ports indicating the St. Paul was tolerant of homosexuality, which may have inspired more than a few requests for transfer to the ship.

After I learned exactly what Commander McCain meant, I was wondering just how to go about such a job. There were about eleven–hundred men on the ship for me to screen.

I learned that we were going to take a large number of midshipmen on a cruise within forty–five days, and that the captain wanted all of the homosexuals off of his ship before then.

Fortunately, I got some help. An officer from ONI, Office of Naval Investigation, soon arrived and teamed up with me. Fred Reeves and I worked arduously. We ended up identifying approximately seventy or seventy–five officers and enlisted personnel on the St. Paul who fit the category, including a chaplain and a medical officer. We even rooted out a few marijuana smokers, and busted them, too. Within a few weeks, I had close to twenty men scheduled for courts-martial. A number of others agreed to consider undesirable discharges.

It was a strange tour of duty for me. Here I was some bonehead lieutenant jg, sleeping in the executive officer's cabin. But it wasn't too bad, being McCain's "fair-haired boy."

McCain told me, "Mac, you and Fred Reeves are going to write up this report for me." He had inherited a sticky problem, and worried that his naval career was in serious jeopardy. I like to think Reeves and I came to his rescue at the right time.

After completion of that task, we were cruising the Pacific, on our way to Hawaii, and I had very little to do as "personnel officer," so spent most of my time playing a deck game with McCain he called "Quarts." We tossed rope hoops over a net to each other, something like deck tennis, or what was once called on the Queen Mary "tennequoits."

I always wanted to please the commander, and I think I disappointed him only one time. It happened because I didn't know what "ambulatory" meant. We had brought a group of wounded soldiers and sailors aboard for transport to a hospital. McCain said to me, "We've got twenty four men. Of those, eighteen are ambulatory." It was very clear to me. So I sent a telegram to the hospital port saying we have six guys who could walk but the other eighteen need ambulances. When we got there, I thought McCain was going to kill me.

By mid-June, I began counting the days until September, when my resignation would become effective and I could return to law school. But June 25 changed my life, and the course of history. North Korean troops launched an attack that day on South Korea, and lit the fire of a war that was to known as a "police action." I was in for the duration. I had been the luckiest guy in the U.S. Navy, having my way, easy duty, didn't even know what a gun was, and suddenly it all changed. We actually ended up going to Formosa at first, instead of Korea, with the idea of heading off a Chinese invasion of that island. Pretty soon, though, we got right in the thick of it along the Korean peninsula.

We saw our share, and more, of naval combat for the next year at sea. In January 1951 we kept those big guns hot, lobbing shells ashore north of Inchon. Up and down that coast, we supported plenty of strike missions. It was a hectic period for me and everyone aboard.

In June, we returned to San Francisco for some refitting and stayed through September. That's when I got to know Jack McCain's family, at least briefly. We'd go to Vallejo, where I met his son, John, who was about fifteen at the time. I knew that Jack McCain played tennis and exercised regularly with calisthenics and rope-jumping. So I showed young John how do some of those fitness routines.

MY WIFE HAD BEEN WORKING for the Costa Mesa Daily Pilot newspaper in Southern California. She would drive up to San Francisco so we could be together on weekends, and bring our son, Mike. One time, when she was on her way up, our old car broke down in Tulare, about halfway between Los Angeles and the Bay area. Commander McCain let me use his car to go get her. He was one of the greatest men I ever met. His wife was awfully nice too, sometimes babysitting little Mike during my wife's visits.

Of course, the commander's son, John McCain, would eventually be known to the world as a heroic prisoner of the Viet Cong during the Vietnam war, and later as a U.S. senator representing Arizona.

Back at sea in the fall of 1951, we participated in numerous gun strikes along the Korea coastline. It was at this time that I made up my mind to start doing something about my future. My first choice was to leave the Navy and return to law school. But if I had to remain in uniform, at least I wanted to resume flight training and become a pilot. I was a stubborn guy ready to fight for what I wanted.

"Mr. Roberts" was a pushover next to me. I started a letter-writing campaign that put his to shame, and bombarded the Navy with mail. I was firing off letters at least weekly to demand my rights. McCain agreed with me. Unfortunately, he was reassigned and sent to Washington, D.C. Before he left, I made an appeal to him. I said, "Commander, I did my best to help you with a big problem. Now I need help. If I have to stay in the Navy, can you do anything to get me back to Pensacola where I can complete flight school?"

He said, "Don't worry, Mac. I'll get you back into flight school." Well, McCain got back to the States and with that glowing official report Reeves and I had written, he looked like a hero for ridding the Navy of those "undesirables." But he must have forgotten about getting me to flight school, because nothing happened.

So I continued my barrage of letters.

MCCAIN'S REPLACEMENT was Commander Amos T. Hathaway. He stood about six–six, which forced him to duck when he came through the hatch into our wardroom. He had been the fencing coach at the Naval Academy and was a tough taskmaster. My job suddenly changed. The "personnel officer" now had to go to general quarters. During GQ under McCain, I would go down, lock myself in the personnel office, and eat frozen strawberries and listen to the radio.

It changed drastically under Hathaway, who I nicknamed "Anus T." As much as McCain loved me, this guy hated me. Just like James Cagney in "Mister Roberts," he said to me, "McCartin, write one more of those letters about getting relieved, and I'll kill you." So that was the end of my letter-writing escapades. And I served longer, I think, than any other officer on the St. Paul.

We were the flagship for the fleet, meaning we had the admiral aboard. Three or four carriers would be in the center of the formation, surrounded by other protective ships. The flag, St Paul, and Helena, its sister ship, would also be in the center, along with perhaps ten destroyers. Sometimes, it would become necessary to shift the flag to another vessel.

On one memorable occasion, when I was in CIC (combat information center), my watch on the St. Paul, I had the responsibility for joining up with the flag. I got in a little over my head. We were in the middle of a howling storm in Korean waters, among thirty or forty other ships. This particular time, they had the flag on one of the destroyers. That was a problem. I didn't know how to give the course and speed necessary to join up with the destroyers. I came sailing in, bellowing different orders for course and speed, and changing my mind every few minutes. I gave the captain about six or seven changes in course and heading. I didn't know what to do. Finally the captain asked, "McCartin, do you know what in the hell you are doing?"

I said, "Not really." We finally had to get the regular CIC officer out of bed to get us straightened out. To make a long story short, I almost sank the Seventh Fleet out there.

That time, I was more like Ensign Pulver than Mister Roberts.

A TRAGIC INCIDENT TOOK PLACE during the Korea battles. It occurred not far from Inchon, where huge tides and forty-foot swells constantly threatened to capsize the ship. The captain and "Anus T." decided they were going to put an officer's club on the beach there. We sent a rowboat out with ten sailors and three officers to begin preparations. They disembarked, and we never saw them alive again.

A court of investigation was assembled, and good old "Anus T." made sure I got assigned to it. That's partly why I continued to pursue my goal of becoming a lawyer. My roommate in the Navy during this period, Stu Hancock, was an attorney who had attended the Naval Academy. His father was the chief justice of the New York Supreme Court. I was assigned to work on this investigation and Hancock said, "You're a natural at this. You should be a lawyer."

Eventually, pieces of the missing boat were found along with a couple of bodies. They sent us back to Taipei, Formosa (now Taiwan), to conduct the board of investigation. I learned that one of the three missing officers was the son of a congressman. Naturally, he had a lot of questions, but we had very few answers. There was never a satisfactory resolution.

Later, I had to do another board of investigation when one of the ships batteries misfired and killed nine or ten sailors.

I finally left the St. Paul in April of 1952. They took me off with a helicopter. The flight was nothing new to me because I had often spotted for the gunners from aboard the chopper.

Two days after I departed, a powder fire broke out in the forward eight-inch turret that blew up and killed thirty men. My quarters, which had been right under the turret that exploded, were demolished.

In September, I ended my active U.S. Navy career but stayed in the reserves.

I APPLIED FOR ADMITTANCE to several law schools and was admitted to Stanford, USC, Loyola, and UCLA, but wound up attending the University of Minnesota. I figured that my dad had a lot of connections in Minneapolis. He was head of the Retailers Association, head of the annual Aquatennial parade, held several other important posts, and was a powerful member of the "good old boys" network. I hoped he could help me out through the financially tight times.

My wife had taken a leave from her California job to stay with me in Minnesota. We now had two sons. She was originally from Redwood Falls, about forty miles from Minneapolis, so had lived through the icy weather before. But our living conditions in a Quonset hut near the university campus were miserable. There were actually icicles hanging from the ceiling four feet long! After one winter, she decided that was enough. We moved to California, and I was going to commute back and forth by air travel.

That didn't work out very well, so I moved into a dorm on campus. Being in the U.S. Naval Reserve, I was committed to serving two weeks of active duty in the summer. Luckily, they sent me to California where I could be with her and the boys temporarily.

To make ends meet, I worked two jobs; one in a clothing store for my dad and the other as a librarian in the law school. I did my studying in the library. If anyone came up to me and asked for something, I'd say, "Get it yourself." I almost got canned for that.

IN SCHOOL I HAD A PROFESSOR for a code pleading class named Charles Alan Wright. He graduated from Yale before he turned twenty–one, and was the most egotistical guy I'd ever met. He'd walk into class and ask a question that no one could answer. Then he'd get angry and say, "No one knows anything," and send us all home. We had full class periods only about one-third of the time. My folks owned a house at Lake Minnetonka (which was later purchased by a governor of Minnesota). Professor Wright said, "What we're going to do—instead of a test, we're going to go to McCartin's house at the lake and have a party. Anybody who doesn't show up at the party will flunk." I attended and got a "C."

In the ensuing years, I lost track of Charles Alan Wright, although I did hear that he was a professor somewhere in Texas. In 1973, I was reading about President Nixon's impeachment problems and noticed a reference to "Mr. Nixon's attorney," Charles Alan Wright.

When he passed away in July 2000, obituaries noted that he had been a professor at the University of Texas, Austin, and proclaimed him one of the most influential lawyers in America. As leading authority on the U.S. Constitution, he authored the fifty–four-volume Federal Practice and Procedures, the top academic reference used not only by lawyers in federal practice but high court justices as well.

After I graduated in June 1955, I traveled to California again for two weeks of Naval Reserve training. Feeling at loose ends, I returned to Minnesota, not sure just what to do next. I was making a meager living by working for State Farm Insurance, but wanted to start practicing law. I talked to Joe Hoffman, a classmate and fellow University of Minnesota graduate. We teamed up as informal partners and started looking for something that would produce money for us. Hoffman had one case we were living on; his barber had been rear-ended in an auto accident and had a stiff neck. We had nothing else.

At the Naval Reserve meetings, I had befriended a guy name Joe Robbie who was also a lawyer. He said, "Come work with me. Both of you guys can come in. We aren't partners, but we can still work togeth-er. You can keep what you make." Robbie had a little dark, one-room office, with one secretary, across the street from my dad's workplace on South Sixth Street in Minneapolis. I said okay, but I didn't give up my day job with State Farm.

Hoffman was about ready to take his barber client case to trial and ask for ten thousand dollars damages plus medical and other costs. Robbie said, "I'll show you how to try a case." So he presented it to the jury. They were out less than 10 minutes and came back to ask the judge if they could award more than the ten thousand dollars.

Robbie was a mesmerizer and a heavy drinker. A big Democrat. He was also a close buddy of national hero Joe Foss. A Marine Corps Medal of Honor recipient in WWII, Foss was later a brigadier general in the Air National Guard, governor of South Dakota, and the first commis-sioner of the AFL (American Football League.) In the commissioner job, Foss was in a position to help his pal, Robbie.

Even though I had made a small start in the legal profession, my wife wanted to move us permanently to California. I finally agreed, and glumly told my colleagues, Hoffman and Robbie. I hated to say goodbye. State Farm Insurance offered to transfer me to California, where I could remain employed by the company. I accepted and moved to Costa Mesa in Southern California's Orange County. In those days, there were still vast orange groves covering most of the area. In the spring, the perfume of citrus blossoms sweetened the air. Walt Disney had recently built his new theme park in Anaheim, just a few miles from Costa Mesa, and it was surrounded by orange trees.

COSTA MESA BROUGHT BACK MEMORIES from 1952 when I had worked temporarily for a firm called Eldon Manufacturing Company. Their products included tear gas hand grenades. They had a testing facility near Costa Mesa, in the wide open agricultural fields, where "braceros" (Hispanic farm workers) labored, and where dairy cattle grazed peacefully We got complaints about the cows crying and that our tear gas was polluting their milk. At 17th Street and Newport Avenue, there was a roller-skating rink. A bunch of kids broke into the Eldon storehouse, stole grenades, and tossed them into the skating rink. That was all long ago. Today, Orange County's most popular shopping mall, South Coast Plaza, covers the whole area of the dairy, the crops harvested by braceros, and the old Eldon site.

By early 1956, we were settling into the lifestyle of Costa Mesa. The region had a terrific climate, with breezes sweeping in from the ocean. I thought the future in this clean atmosphere, with balmy weather, looked bright.

Robbie and Hoffman, in Minnesota, stayed together for awhile, then went on to bigger things individually. Hoffman became known as "the mall maker." He was the driving force behind Minnesota's gigantic, famed Mall of America. He is owner of

Hoffman Development Inc., and a partner in a law firm Larkin, Hoffman, Daly, & Lindgren Ltd.

Joe Robbie, on the advice of Joe Foss, applied for an AFL expansion franchise in 1965, and was accepted. He launched the Miami Dolphins team. I always wondered where he got the necessary money. With the minor league lawsuits we handled, such as representing claims filed by low-income American Indians, I knew he hadn't saved anything near the fifty–thousand dollar initial investment he would have needed. I found out in 1997 when I attended the fiftieth anniversary Macalester reunion. Bob Hoffman picked me up at the airport and I said to him, "One thing that has always puzzled me —where did Robbie get the big bucks together to buy the Dolphins?"

He said, "Didn't you know? He went to high school with Danny Thomas. Danny did most of the financing." As a popular television and movie star, Thomas could afford it. It was kind of funny in a way. If you ever saw Robbie and Thomas together, you would have thought they were twins. Robbie later purchased Thomas' interest in the team. By 1967, Joe had amassed a fortune large enough to build a new football stadium and name it after himself. He died in 1990.

In Costa Mesa, I still yearned to use my legal education. I had passed the Minnesota bar in 1955, and decided to take the California bar exam. But in law school, I had taken only about nine of the twenty–five subjects that would prepare you for the California exam. I went to a cram course in the mornings and worked in the afternoons, for about six weeks.

On the morning of the test, I drove to Los Angeles with another applicant, Bob Huckenphaler, who would later become my law firm partner. The downtown smog was so thick you could hardly see the upper floors of tall buildings.

I had never taken classes on estate tax or income tax laws, but a counselor had said, "Don't worry. Out of the five questions, you can option one out. Just option out the tax law question." When I opened the exam, I was jolted. One of the five questions was about estate tax and the second was about income tax! Two out of the five were tax law questions. I hadn't taken cram courses on either one. So I decided to write on income tax. I knew almost nothing about it, and I'm sure I got a zero on that question. I hoped that I could score well enough on the others to raise the average to a passing level.

WHILE WAITING FOR THE RESULTS, I continued working for State Farm. I took the test in June, and had to wait until September or October for the scores. This was 1957. My wife worked for a newspaper represented by a Newport Beach law firm, Hurwitz and Hurwitz. She arranged for me to meet the lawyers, Max and Bob. They said, "While you're waiting for the bar exam results, why don't you work for us? We can give you some things to do." Max was real nice guy and said, "We need an Irishman in the firm. We're both Jewish, so that will make a nice balance." I said okay.

I was there just a few days when one of them said, "Here, take this motion and file it in court." I realized that it was something a licensed lawyer should do and said, "Look, I haven't passed the bar. We'll all go to jail!"

"Don't worry about it," they said. "We do things informally here." So I appeared in court with the motions. I remember talking to a Charlie Corolla who was an interpreter on the third floor. He said, "McCartin, I think one of these days I should go in and tell them that you haven't passed the bar."

I said, "Don't worry, I'll pass it." But I wasn't as confident as I sounded. When the results finally came, I breathed a sigh of relief. I had passed.

I went up to the federal court in L.A. to be sworn in. Max said, "Incidentally, once you are sworn in, I have a case for you in federal court at one–thirty this afternoon. You can handle this for us." I couldn't believe it! I was going to be sworn in that morning, and handling a court case the same afternoon. And to top it off, Judge Yankwich, who was swearing me in, was the one hearing the case. It was a disaster. But I managed to scrape through.

The following Monday, Max gave me another case to handle in court: a lawsuit over a car wreck. "You take it, show up in court, and I'll be there." He never showed up. I'm trying the case. I wondered what my client, an accountant, thought of the whole deal. The opposing attorney, Charlie Fox, was an "in-your-face" harsh type of guy. I'm doing the voir dire. I got one question out of my mouth, like "What's your name?" or something, and he yelled, "I object." "Jesus," I thought, "What have I done now?" He was just all over me. He objected to everything. It was the worst day of my life.

I HAD ALWAYS BEEN DISAPPOINTED that Jack McCain had never followed up with the help he had promised me. In all that time, I hadn't heard from him. I followed his career and learned that he had ended up as CINCPAC, commander in chief of all the Pacific forces. He had the Marine Corps, Army, Navy, everything. He of course retired as a full admiral.

Years later, I read an article that said Admiral John S. McCain, retired, was going to be the guest speaker at a Newporter Inn dinner, just a few miles from Costa Mesa. I decided to attend, and watched as he gave a speech. Afterward, with a lot of people gathered around, I muscled my way to the front and said, "Admiral McCain, do you remember me?"

He said, "My God! McCartin. You're back!" I thought he was going to faint.

I had visions of him in the old Navy days when he did his share of drinking and cussing. He had often used the term "hogwash," and I had found myself adopting it in recent years.

He said, "You saved my naval career, and I never even answered your letters." I laughed. We sat down and relived the war completely. It was a great evening, and my respect for him never faded.

The last time I ever saw McCain was that evening at the Newporter Inn. (Vice Admiral John Sidney McCain Jr., who preferred to be called Jack, died in 1981.)

IN MY FIRST YEAR with Hurwitz & Hurwitz, Max went to England on a vacation in December. He was married to a gentile. And she hated Jews. Bob Hurwitz drove his wife and son to Mexico for the Christmas holidays. On the return trip, before they reached the U.S. border, he rear-ended a truck that had no tail lights. His wife and son were killed. It just destroyed poor Bob.

Meanwhile, with Max in England, I had to run the law firm all by myself. We had some big clients including the Newport Beach City Council. We also represented some Newport Beach police officers who were accused of burglaries. My friend Bob Huckenphaler was also with the firm. They offered to make me a partner, but after being with them for two years, I decided to strike out on my own. Huckenphaler and I set up shop on Harbor Boulevard in Costa Mesa.

We were on the second story. Below us was an Orange Julius store. We'd go down for an Orange Julius drink nearly every day. Next door to it was the Martin Real Estate office. The owner had a little bratty kid who used to drive me nuts. He would come over to the Orange Julius shop and bug us while we had our drink. When the kid grew up though, he did okay as a television comedian and movie star. His name is Steve Martin.

My partner and I often used a small private partnership called Madison and Farrell for service of our legal papers. One of the partners, Mike, served most of my papers in the early sixties. He was a native of St. Paul, Minnesota, and an ex-Marine. I guess he got tired of the legal business, because he also became an actor and skyrocketed to fame in the television "M*A*S*H" series. Today, he's an activist with the Death Penalty Focus organization, working to abolish capital punishment. In February 2004, Mike Farrell helped prevent the execution of a prison-escapee named Kevin Cooper who was convicted in San Bernardino County of slaughtering a married couple, their ten-year old daughter, and a houseguest, age eleven. The 9th Circuit Court of Appeals granted a stay just a few hours before Cooper was scheduled to die.

WHILE WE WERE HAVING A HOME BUILT we rented a water-front house on Balboa Island, an attractive community in Newport Beach. Our next-door neighbor was Ben Alexander. Old-time television fans will recognize that name as the actor who played sidekick to Jack Webb in the "Dragnet" series. Webb was Sgt. Joe Friday, and Alexander was officer Frank Smith. My sons loved going over to his house and playing "cops and robbers" with the affable actor.

I could kick myself now for turning down an offer to buy the Balboa house. It had four bedrooms, five baths, and was twenty feet from the ocean. But the owner wanted too much, $80,000. Now, it would sell in the seven-figure range.

The kids were aware of another movie star in our neighborhood after we moved into our new home in San Juan Capistrano. Creighton Chaney, better known as Lon Chaney Jr., lived just a short distance away. His reputation for playing in horror films, such as "The Wolfman" and several Dracula and Frankenstein movies, had my boys intimidated. On a Halloween night, I accompanied them on a trick-or-treat expedition, and tried to get them to knock on Chaney's door, but they were too terrified of him.

Our law firm began to pick up steam in the early 1960s. I handled some remarkable cases.

Among them was the extraordinary story of Dr. Samuel Frazier.

In August 1963, I got an emergency telephone call on a Sunday night from Dr. Frazier, a prominent Costa Mesa physician. He said, "Don, we got a problem. There are robbers out here trying to break in."

It turned out the "robbers" were Costa Mesa police trying to catch him in the act of having sex with female patients. He was suspected of taking advantage of them as they lay unconscious on an examination table. The police also had information that Dr. Frazier was performing abortions, which were illegal at the time.

It came as quite a surprise because Dr. Frazier, at age 35, was one of the most respected men in the community. He stood about five–eight, had a trim build, kept his dark hair cut short, and wore black-rimmed glasses. He had once appeared on the cover of Time or Newsweek magazine with Dr. Paul Dudley White, President Dwight Eisenhower's personal physician and founder of the American Heart Association.

Dr. Frazier was the father of four children and a member of St. Andrew's Presbyterian Church of Newport Beach. His religious wife would read the Bible and make him read it in the evenings and on weekends. But Sam had a few secrets.

Before the U.S. Supreme Court made its historic Roe v. Wade decision in January 1973, which changed laws against abortion, Dr. Frazier covertly performed the procedure for selected women. One of his abortion patients, whose operation was a top secret, was married to a high-ranking Huntington Beach city official.

When Sam agreed to do an abortion, he would bring the woman into his office at night and put her to sleep with Trilene, a brand name for trichloroethylene. The substance, which worked like chloroform, is no longer used today as a medical anesthetic gas. But it worked well for his needs.

He followed this routine with numerous women. While they were semi-conscious, he would have sex with them! If any of them felt anything, Sam explained that he was doing "manual manipulation of the uterus," his term for doing a regular instrument abortion.

Unfortunately for Dr. Frazier, two of his patients complained, and the police started closing in. It caught him off guard because, as the city physician for the Costa Mesa Police Department, he considered himself almost immune from investigation. He regarded many of the officers as personal friends. When the arrest came in August, Sam was confident he could simply talk his way out of it. But they charged him with performing unnatural sex acts on a twenty–seven-year-old mother, and doing an abortion on an unmarried twenty–year-old Newport Beach nursing aide.

I AGREED TO HELP HIM and took on the case. It turned into an extremely complex web of legal maneuvers with law suits and counter suits. The public was fascinated by it. Tom Keevil, editor of the Costa Mesa Daily Pilot, knew if he put an article about Sam in the paper on Friday, he would sell every copy over the weekend. Housewives would be out in their yards waiting for delivery of the paper.

The district attorney was Kenny Williams. Dr. Frazier called me for legal advice, but kept talking to Williams, offering to take a lie detector test. The D.A. told him, "You have to get your lawyer. I can't talk to you." Eventually, Sam did take a polygraph test and passed it clean as a whistle. I don't know what he used, but he evidently drugged himself with something to get through it.

By November, a grand jury issued an indictment against Dr. Frazier charging him with seventeen counts of rape, sex perversion, and one count of abortion. Before the case went to trial, I made a request of Judge Bob Kneeland, the former district attorney. He signed an order to the prosecution witnesses saying, "You may speak to defense attorney Donald A. McCartin if you so desire." I arranged for court reporter Les Slayback, who took longhand notes, to accompany me at meetings with all of these witnesses. To each one, I said, "I have a court order here that says I may speak to you." I didn't mention that they didn't have to say a word to me if they didn't want to. From all of the complainants, I got detailed statements. Every one of them gave me just what I needed. Judge Kneeland later said, "I'll never sign another order like that."

The case went to trial in February 1964. My old mentor, Judge Howard Cameron, presided in Department 12 of Superior Court, which was in a converted church, downtown Santa Ana. The walls were so thin in there, you could sit in the judge's chambers and hear the jury deliberating in the adjacent room.

JUDGE CAMERON WAS MY IDOL; the roughest, gruffest, meanest judge of all time. The D.A. was George Jeffries, who still practices in Newport Beach. He was like a bulldog when he got hold of you. In contrast, I was Mr. Nice Guy.

During jury selection, I told each candidate, "The evidence will show that my client had consensual sexual relations with the four prosecution witnesses." I made it clear that Dr. Frazier was not on trial for having intercourse and that they shouldn't judge him on his moral conduct, but on the specific crime of which he was accused.

Using the statements I had obtained, I put these women on the stand and tied them in square knots. Of course, they couldn't remember half the stuff that took place while they were semi-conscious during the incidents. I just destroyed them.

Jeffries made the mistake of antagonizing Judge Cameron by asking repetitive questions. The judge said, right in front of the jury, "If you ask that question one more time, you are going to jail instead of Dr. Frazier." I liked that, and stored it in my memory for future use.

NEAR THE END OF THE TRIAL, just before lunch, Jeffries delivered his rebuttal statement to the jury, four men and eight women. He said

Dr. Frazier had been a busy fellow with his female patients. In addition to performing abortions, and having sexual intercourse with six of them, said Jeffries, the doctor also performed oral sex on the women. During my closing argument, I stated that my client couldn't possibly perform all those sex acts unless he had four arms. When Jeffries argued his case to the jury, he said something I will never forget. He blurted out, "McCartin said it's impossible to do all these things at once. Well, you just go into the jury room and try it, and you'll see you can do it."

I'll tell you, the courtroom blew up. Here's George waving his hand around making these gestures, saying these sex acts can be done. Judge Cameron had to call the lunch break to settle things down.

WHEN THE JURY CAME IN with a verdict, they convicted Dr. Frazier on one rape count plus the single abortion count, and acquitted him on all other charges. Frazier had been confident of complete exoneration. All during the trial, he'd been sitting there showing no interest in the whole thing. He would slide handwritten notes over to me saying, "Hey, let's go fishing." He was acting like it was a tea party or something. I said, "Look, on the cross-examination, will you please pay attention and help Chris." But he kept acting as if the whole thing was nonsense.

After the verdicts, I immediately made a motion for a new trial on the rape conviction. Judge Cameron listened, then turned to the D.A. and said, "Mr. Jeffries, did you read her testimony? She went back for seconds!" Everything the woman said was riddled with contradictions. Cameron threw out the rape conviction, leaving Dr. Frazier with only the single abortion rap.

We appealed all the way to the U.S. Supreme Court, but lost by a six-to-three decision. Dr. Frazier had to serve a sentence which turned out to be less than two years. Later, after Roe v. Wade, he even got his license back to practice medicine.

*   *   *

ANOTHER TRIAL IN WHICH MY CLIENT was accused of sexual antics took place near the end of 1966. He was charged with "gambling, possessing obscene material, and living in a bawdy house." Today, something like that would just draw a laugh, but in the sixties it was a crime.

My client, I'll just call him Jerry, had done nothing more than throw a stag party for a buddy of his who was getting married. One of the local police officers even attended. Jerry figured that the police department probably wouldn't openly approve of his party, but certainly wouldn't regard it as something worth raiding. The guests included an impressive list of well-known young businessmen in their late twenties and early thirties; executives, stock brokers, real estate dealers, and even a few representatives from the legal profession. No, I wasn't there.

They all gathered at Jerry's Corona Del Mar home and paid fifteen dollars each to cover the cost of food, liquor and entertainment. The "bawdy" behavior was limited to watching a stag film and a dallying with few female "guests." Jerry was an equal opportunity employer—the three women represented the African-American, Asian, and Anglo communities. The film was probably tamer than a lot of stuff shown on television today. In the midst of their celebration, the police raided the house and arrested several of the guests who didn't escape via rear windows. Among those who got away were a couple of judges!

I thought the charges were ridiculous, and made the district attorney a plea offer. If they would drop the obscenity counts, my client would plea guilty to gambling. That could save the expense of a full-blown court trial. At first, he tentatively agreed, but then backed out and insisted on taking the case to a jury.

Presentation of the evidence ended on Wednesday, November 30, and the jury began deliberations. The six men and six women worked all day Thursday then kept at it late that night. Finally, they came out after eleven o'clock to announce their verdict. They were hung five to seven for acquittal on all the sex-related charges. They convicted Jerry on a single count of gambling. That's exactly what I had offered the D.A. two months earlier. It had all been a waste of taxpayer's money. Judge Donald Dungan criticized the D.A. for his handling of the case.

ONE ESPECIALLY BIZARRE DEFENSE CASE I handled came to me before sunrise on a warm, summer Sunday morning. Groggy from being awakened by the jangling telephone at 4 a.m., I heard an astonishing plea.

The desperate voice of a man I had represented in a divorce case yelled, "You gotta come help me. I've been arrested for murder and so has my girlfriend. I don't have any idea what they are talking about! The police busted into her apartment and hauled us to the Huntington Beach jail. My God, we're stunned. Please help!"

I dressed quickly and broke speed laws en route to the jail. After calming down my client, I listened to the beginning of one of the strangest problems I had ever encountered.

My client, Jack Benson, worked as a rocket engineer for a major Southern California aerospace firm. He was a member of the team charged with assembling a vehicle that would take Scott Carpenter and Buzz Aldrin to the moon in July 1969. Benson had spent the weekend with his girlfriend, Lisa Lake, at her apartment. At about midnight, after going to bed and falling asleep, the couple heard someone battering on the entry door. Disoriented, they were too alarmed to answer. A few moments later, officers splintered the door and charged into the bedroom. They took both Benson and Lake into custody on suspicion of murder.

Detectives separated them, and interviewed both suspects. But the police gave them no details about the murder or how the couple was allegedly involved in it.

After a brief session with Benson, I spoke with Lisa Lake. I wouldn't be able to represent her, but could at least hear what she had to say.

It turned out to be precious little; no more than what Benson had told me. She had no idea, she claimed, what the whole thing was all about.

By obtaining a copy of the arrest warrant, I finally learned what led to the police action.

The dead body of an adult female murder victim had been found at an intersection just off Pacific Coast Highway, close to the ocean. Her corpse was lying near her wrecked vehicle. But she clearly had not expired from injuries sustained in the collision. Someone had savagely slashed her throat from ear to ear. The other vehicle, Lisa Lake's blue Toyota, sat abandoned a few yards down the street. It appeared that the killer, perhaps under the influence of drugs or alcohol, had perhaps slammed into the victim's car. Maybe a heated argument had ensued, and the enraged Toyota driver had killed the woman.

When police arrived and checked the license plate and registration, they traced it to the car's owner. Homicide detectives had immediately obtained a warrant for Lake's arrest. Jack Benson was with her, so they took him in too. Since her apartment address was on the registration, she had not been difficult to find.

During the subsequent police interrogation, detectives had asked Lake if the Toyota belonged to her. She said it did.

"When was the last time you drove it?"

"Saturday. Jack took it to have it washed." That explained Benson's fresh fingerprints, along with several others, found by a forensic specialist on the exterior and on the clean vehicle's interior.

"Where are the keys to your car?"

"In my purse." Officers had already searched her handbag and found the keys inside.

"Are there any spare keys?

"I don't think there are any spares.

"How did your Toyota get to an intersection on Pacific Coast Highway last night?"

"I don't have any idea," said Lake, in tears.

Interrogation of Jack Benson shed even less light on the killing. He had met Lisa a couple of months earlier where she worked as a waitress, and they had started dating. He had taken her car to be washed. But neither of them had been in it since then. He had parked the Toyota in its assigned carport stall and they hadn't left her apartment.

"Do you have a car?"

"Yes."

"Where is it?"

"I pulled it in right behind hers on Sunday evening and left it there."

Both Benson and Lake insisted that her Toyota had been in the carport all night.

The police had already checked the carport, and found her space empty. Another vehicle, registered to Jack Benson, was parked directly behind Lake's vacant slot. One of the officers had placed his hand on the engine, and found it to be cold.

Another resident of the apartment happened to be a Huntington Beach police officer whose assigned parking place in the carport was next to Lake's. He told investigators he had arrived home at about ten that night, and Lake's Toyota was there.

The officers arrested Lake and Benson. He used his one telephone call to contact me

The next morning, I spoke to one of the detectives, Dale Mason. I had know Mason from previous cases and established a friendly working relationship with the impeccably dressed officer. "How about hooking them up to a lie box?" I suggested. I knew that polygraph, or lie detector, results would not be admissible in court, but if Benson and Lake could convince the machine of their innocence, it might help persuade the prosecutor to reexamine the charges.

"Okay," said Mason. "Let's do it and see what happens."

* * *

I WAS ASTONISHED when the polygraph results indicated that both Benson and Lake were not telling the truth! My client couldn't believe it either. Lake wept uncontrollably when she heard the news. With this turn of events, I even began entertaining doubts and wondered if they actually were in cahoots. Could they have been in a wreck after which one of them flew into a rage when the other driver reacted in anger? Did either Benson or Lake lose control and slice the woman's throat? Perhaps Benson had done it by himself, or maybe Lake had gone out for more liquor, food, or something, crashed the car, and killed the woman. I regarded myself as a pragmatic, logical person, but I have to admit, I was totally mystified.

I didn't particularly want to, but I went to Benson's former wife, who was a very good-looking woman. I asked if her ex-husband had ever displayed a violent temper. She would say only that Benson had been "acting weird lately," since the divorce. She could offer no help. I rationalized to myself that a lot of engineers act weird.

Sometimes, when all else fails, the power of the press can work wonders. I contacted my good friend, Tom Keevil, editor of the Costa Mesa Daily Pilot newspaper and asked him to write a little exposé on the case. Keevil agreed to help me by running the story.

The article described what had happened, then added that the killer would probably be covered with blood. In the last paragraph, the editor asked the public for help in identifying anyone seen in the area that night with bloodstains on their clothing. My telephone number was included along with a request to call me with any information that might be related to the incident.

It worked!

One day after the news story ran, I received the call I needed.

The owner of a Huntington Beach motel told me that two Hispanic men had stayed in one of his units on the night in question, and one of them had blood all over him. I immediately contacted the only police department and passed the information on to them. Detectives rushed over to interview the motel owner. They were pleasantly surprised when they inspected the motel registration record. The two "guests" had foolishly signed it with their real names. It took only a short time to round them up.

When the two suspects were arrested, they were easily linked to the murder case. One of them caved in to interrogation and confessed. The other denied his involvement, but his partner implicated him. They had burglarized Lisa Lake's apartment several weeks earlier, but had found nothing of any value. All they took was a set of car keys. When they tried the keys on Lake's Toyota down in the carport, they fit. She had completely forgotten about her set of spares, and was unaware they had been stolen. She didn't even know anyone had entered her residence.

From that night on, when the thieves needed a car, they would push the Toyota from the carport and start it at a distance where the owner couldn't hear them. They would drive it around town, then return it before Lake woke the next morning. On the night of the murder, when they encountered Benson's car parked behind the Toyota, they had simply pushed it out of the way, taken the Toyota, then shoved his vehicle back where it had been.

The police had been correct about the accident leading to murder. The thieves had collided with the victim's car and then argued with her when she wanted to call the police. Since the men were in a stolen car, they certainly didn't want any cops at the scene. When the conflict had flared, they silenced the woman by slashing her throat. Unable to drive the damaged Toyota away, they had walked to the motel and checked in to clean themselves up and stay for the night.

A jury convicted both men of murder.

WHY HAD BENSON AND LAKE FLUNKED the polygraph test? My subsequent interviews with both of them revealed the strange twist.

Each one had suspected the other of perhaps being guilty! They wondered if the other person might have awakened during the night, and taken a short trip to a convenience or liquor store, collided with the other car, and killed the driver in a rage. So during the lie detector test, neither of them was telling the complete truth. Lake felt responsible for the mess they were in and came close to compounding the tragedy. At one point, she said, she had considered a guilty plea in order to free Benson so he could continue his important work.

For my part, I breathed a big sigh of relief. If that case had gone to trial, I think they probably would have been convicted.

OVER THE NEXT DOZEN YEARS, I handled a huge assortment of cases with clients running the whole spectrum of behavior. I didn't lose many. To be a good defense attorney, I realized the two elements are essential. First, you must believe your client. Second, you have to pick cases that have a sound defense. I carefully screened all of my cases for these two things. If I could see no solid defense, then I didn't take it. As a result, I never lost a criminal case.

My law practice took me through more than twenty years of various litigations and trials. Also, through a divorce and remarriage. Karen, my present wife, and I were married in 1973, but please don't ask me the date. I know it's very close to her birthday, October 25, but I can't pin it down exactly. A fellow I used to play tennis with had his anniversary on the same day as ours, and he would always remind me. But he passed away and now I can't recall the right date.

I have four sons. The oldest, Mike, is a judge. Mark is an emergency room physician. The two younger ones, Casey and Duffy, are educators. And Karen brought a pair of daughters, Tracy and Cheri into our family.

By the time my son Mike graduated from law school, I was getting a little weary of the private law practice. He came into my firm to help out. I've kidded about it and said I hired him because he couldn't get a job anywhere else, and that I accepted a judgeship because he was driving me crazy. In reality, he was a fine lawyer and is now a respected judge himself.

I stayed in the law partnership right up until I was appointed to the bench. That happened on August 2, 1978. Gov. Edmund G. "Jerry" Brown Jr. appointed me, and I'm still puzzled about how that happened. He was a well known anti-death penalty liberal. Somehow, I slipped through his people's screening process. I welcomed the opportunity, though, to emulate my role models, Judge Howard Cameron and Judge Robert Gardner.

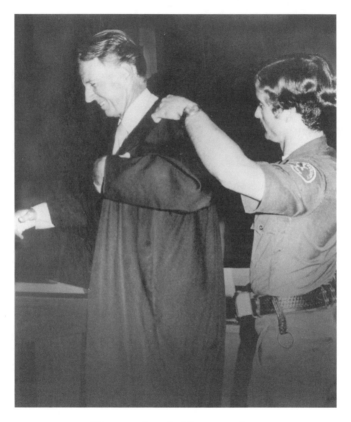

Donning the robe
for the first time

7

Here Comes the Judge

Before you first put on those black robes and pick up a gavel, you ordinarily get a mentor judge for a period of time to show you the ropes. I came in on a Monday, and Judge McMillan, who got me appointed, smiled and said, "I'm your mentor. Go to Department 4 and take the OSC (Order to Show Cause) divorce calender and don't bother me again."

I did exactly as he told me. After I'd been on the bench a few months, I wondered why I hadn't been given one other customary session. Newly appointed judges always get to go to Berkeley, in the San Francisco Bay area, for a two-week orientation school. I told McMillan I'd never had my turn yet up at Berkeley He said, "You ain't going. It would ruin your style."

I GUESS MANY PEOPLE ASSOCIATE ME, as a judge, with the trials in which I sentenced nine men to death row. But there were many, many others that featured a wide spectrum of oddball behavior and bizarre events. One of them involved a Huntington Harbour doctor who was famous for reconstructive hip surgery. He killed his wife and said he did it in his sleep! His excuse was remarkable. He claimed to be afflicted with narcolepsy.

At the doctor's first trial, he told of going to his estranged wife's residence for the purpose of exercising his court-approved visitation rights to pick up his children for the weekend. She refused, and said her attorney was there to assist her. She even refused to let him see the kids. The doctor pushed his way in and grabbed a knife from a kitchen drawer. He slashed and stabbed his wife and her attorney to death, in full view of both children. In his defense, he blamed it on narcolepsy. He said it caused him to fall into a deep sleep and rendered him unable to remember his actions. Several jurors bought his story and wouldn't vote for a murder conviction. The hung jury resulted in a mistrial. When the D.A. decided to try the doctor again, it landed in my court.

Deputy D.A. Richard Farnell prosecuted while Ed George and Al Ramsey represented the defendant. Ramsey and George wanted to negotiate a plea for voluntary manslaughter. The district attorney wanted a murder conviction and wouldn't give an inch.

During the trial, in which the doctor once again used the narcolepsy excuse for the double homicide, he would frequently drop his head down, apparently asleep. You could see it on television news clips.

After two weeks of testimony, the district attorney got worried and came into my chambers. He said, "Judge, there's something I want to do. But this is a politically sensitive case and I would take a lot of criticism." He asked me for a favor. "If I agree to accept a plea of manslaughter, will the court take the heat?"

I was surprised because I knew Ramsey and George would give anything for that kind of a bargain. The D.A. wanted me to be the heavy, though, call them in, and make the offer so it wouldn't appear that he had caved in.

I brought the two defense attorneys in and said, "Okay, guys, I've got a deal for you. We'll accept a plea of voluntary manslaughter." They were ready to kiss me after the plea was entered.

We brought the jurors out. I asked the attorneys, "Do you gentlemen want me to poll the jury?" They did. So I polled them. It was twelve to zero for first degree murder! Only one of the three alternates would have held out for a lesser conviction. Al and Ed thought I was God! The D.A. felt like killing himself.

Years later, I conducted the ceremony when the defendant's son was married.

OCCASIONALLY, I TOOK DIVORCE CASES to fill in gaps between murder trials. In one of those instances, the wife was suing for divorce and her husband had cross-filed for alimony plus other relief. This husband happened to be an employee of his wife's father, who had cut off his salary, taken away a Mercedes he used as a company car, and then fired him. In my final judgement, I awarded alimony to the husband, restored his use of the Mercedes, and ordered the additional relief he requested. In those days, it was virtually unheard of for a divorced husband to receive alimony. When the courtroom cleared, I heard all this yelling and screaming outside. My bailiff went running out to see what was going on. He saw the wife trying to throw her husband off the eighth floor balcony, and had to forcibly break up the struggle.

A MAJOR THEME IN MY COURTROOMS was my reluctance to waste time and expense on irrelevant and unnecessary proceedings. I refused to allow prolonged bickering among lawyers, redundant delays, or testimony that had no bearing on the issues. To me, that is one of a judge's major duties. The primary responsibility is to conduct a fair trial for both the prosecution and the defense. I think this can be done without so much waste.

Early on, I dispensed with stuffy procedural customs, such as formal court openings. Instead of having everyone stand up when I walked in, I would just say, "Let's go," or give my bailiff a thumbs up signal.

There is an evidence code in the law, number 352, that permits a judge to limit things in order to keep a trial moving along. I am one judge who used it to full advantage. I hate to see trials prolonged due to frivolous motions, wasted time, and inefficiency, unnecessarily spending taxpayers' money.

One thing that drove me crazy was attorneys to whom "NO" didn't mean no. I sometimes told them, as my old role models Judges Gardner and Cameron had, 'If you ask that question again, you're going to jail instead of your client." True to my mentors' values, I was also impatient with long, drawn-out motions. When I was an attorney, I filed a motion in a drug possession case in Gardner's court. He had made a tentative ruling, and I got up to present my side of the issue, he said, "McCartin, I don't want to hear a word from you. If you say anything, or argue this particular point, I will change my ruling. So I remained silent while Gardner said, "The D.A. should be locked up for bringing the case, and you should be embarrassed to collect a fee from your client." That was Gardner, and I learned from him. He was later chief justice of an appellate court.

When I had a non-jury trial, and heard enough to make up my mind about the outcome, I'd say to the attorneys, "I don't want to offend you gentlemen, but I have my mind made up and you are not going to sway me with your rhetoric, period. If you want to make a remark or two (this was usually directed at the D.A.) you may do so, but you are going to lose."

One of my frequently used phrases, often directed at an attorney presenting irrelevant or useless material, was, "Why do I care?" It is simply a signal that the lawyer needs to move on to something important, not an indication of apathy at all, or that I really don't care.

I ONCE SENT MY BAILIFF, "Mitch" Miller to Norwalk to arrest attorney Rob Harley. Before the lunch break, Harley had mentioned to me that he had to appear in Norwalk that afternoon on a different matter. I said, "This case takes priority." When he didn't show up as scheduled in my court at one–thirty, I issued an arrest warrant and ordered my bailiff to bring Mr. Harley back. Not quite two hours later, he stood before me. Defense attorneys get many of their clients by assignment from judges, and the county pays them. Pro bono means handling a case without pay. As punishment for Mr. Harley, I sentenced him to handle five pro bono cases.

Mitch was an integral part of my courtroom team, along with my patient and always cheerful clerk, Gail Carpenter, and reporter Sandra Wingerd. They weren't immune to my teasing either. Once during a trial, Mitch had stepped out into the hallway for a moment. I told the jury, "I want to be reincarnated as a bailiff. They do nothing." Gail kept my wall calender updated with trial and hearing schedules. Once in mid-March, when a couple of attorneys picked a particular date for some court business, I took a closer look at the calender and announced, "Gentlemen, we can't hold our hearing on that date. The only case I have that day is a Mr. Saint Patrick. Let the record show we won't require him to appear either."

I KNOW THAT I HAVE A REPUTATION for making offbeat or "colorful" remarks during trials. An article in The Orange County Register, by reporter Jeanne Wright, said, "McCartin is something of a legend around the Santa Ana courthouse. He is considered a master of the witty and acerbic aside. Defendants, prosecutors, and defense attorneys have felt his verbal sting . . . McCartin has done everything from amusing and rankling attorneys to ordering one arrested in his courtroom. There are jurors who find him adorable and highly entertaining. Many of his fellow judges say he has earned their undying respect . . . [but] there are attorneys who assiduously avoid his courtroom. Others say they welcome the chance to do battle before McCartin because he calls it as he sees it."

I do call them as I see them. About the "witty and acerbic" comments I make, I told the reporter, "I don't mean them; I just say them." If I used humor while speaking to juries or attorneys, I certainly never intended to compromise the seriousness of a trial. I firmly believe in the law and the importance of fairness in administering it.

On the other hand, I think humor can be used effectively in many situations. My intent was simply to lighten up the tension and encourage people to relax. A trial can be extremely stressful to all parties, especially the jurors. These are generally people who would rather be anywhere else than sitting there and listening to repulsive, gory, sickening facts about criminal behavior, rape, murder, and so forth. I've seen jurors who seemed to be on the verge of a nervous breakdown. I always felt that if I could neutralize the tension a little with some off-the-cuff remark, and get a chuckle out of them, it was worth it.

During the trial of serial killer Randy Kraft, I couldn't resist when one of his lawyers, Jim Merwin, was telling the jury a story about Abraham Lincoln. I interrupted him and said, "You don't have to believe Mr. Merwin. I went to law school with Lincoln, and none of that story Merwin told you is true."

I didn't spare media representatives either. Jerry Hicks of the Los Angeles Times wrote an article recalling how I had treated him. He said, "I was once threatened with contempt of court. I had been bouncing from courtroom to courtroom, trying to stay on top of my beat. Superior Court Judge Donald A. McCartin saw me take a seat, then interrupted testimony to announce me in contempt for being late. My face turned beet red before the judge revealed that he was only joking. And this in the middle of a murder trial. But that was McCartin, whose laid-back manner sometimes marked his remarkable skills on the bench."

It wasn't unusual for me to use a bit of humor early in the proceedings, during jury voir dire. My usual procedure in that phase was to allow each lawyer, the prosecutor and the defense attorney, to ask prospective jurors a few questions. Then I would take over and do most of the questioning. Quite often, my comments were aimed at teasing attorneys. For example, in the trial of James Gregory Marlow (see Chapter thirteen), I asked a group of jury candidates if they had any friends who were attorneys, then added, "I know—attorneys don't have any friends, they have acquaintances." I can remember quite a few people smiling at that, even the lawyers. I couldn't resist carrying it a little further by asking, "Have any of you ever studied law, then decided to go into an honest profession after you regained your sanity?" That got an outright laugh, and I'm certain it did nothing to damage the fairness of Marlow's trial. He even laughed.

I felt the same way when I got a little critical of a rapist who acted as his own attorney, and was convicted in my court. His name was Ty Clayton. At the sentence hearing, he was ranting and raving about being denied a fair trial because his clothes didn't fit him and his shoes were too big. He claimed the jury convicted him because of his rumpled clothing and shaggy appearance. I had even loaned him one of my own neckties and suit coat to help him look better. So his outburst didn't exactly please me. I listened several minutes, then told him, "One day you look like a bum. The next day you want to dress up. You go from being Beau Brummel to looking like a bum, even in my tie. You might have at least tucked your shirt in. You wanted to go casual. The next day you wanted to go even more casual. I thought you were going to go without your pants." Of course, there was no jury to hear me.

Clayton had been a thorn under my saddle for the whole trial. They'd bring him over from the jail with his boxes of papers and some clothing. He'd flop down on the floor of his holding cell, wearing only his underwear, and lie there until the proceedings were ready to start. I'd have to go in and request his presence in my own inimitable style. He was never ready to go on time.

Before sentencing him to thirteen years in prison, I chewed him out not only for that conduct but because he had clearly lied under oath. I said, "You are a delusional liar . . . you are the biggest liar I ever had in my court in ten years."

In another case, Tom Goethals, who is now a judge, once tried to assure me that his opponent wasn't trying to mislead the court. I interrupted him to say, "I've never been misled in my life because I don't believe anybody." Of course, that's an exaggeration, but I may be a bit more skeptical then most people.

Now and then, I make a comment that is perfectly acceptable in one context, but politically incorrect in another. I remember a case in which my words were completely unintentional, but caused an uproar. Defense attorney Gary Proctor had represented a young black woman. She was convicted of a felony. While sentencing her, I was really giving her a lecture to try and convince her to straighten out. I finally said, "Young lady, it's time to call a spade a spade." Proctor nearly passed out and the courtroom was in a frenzy.

Later, Proctor acknowledged his realization there was no racial slur intended. He said, "My client and I took it as a humorous remark. When you appear before Judge McCartin, you soon learn to recognize when he's joking and when he's serious." I appreciated his understanding.

A DEPUTY DISTRICT ATTORNEY WROTE a letter to the Commission on Judicial Performance to clear up a similar misunderstanding. He had prosecuted an African-American, a former U.S. Marine, who had painted his face white, dressed up like a character from the Warren Beatty "Dick Tracy" movie, stolen a taxi, raced it in a high-speed pursuit from the police, and fired on them with a 9mm. handgun. At trial, the defendant requested the jury be dismissed because only one black person was on it, and she was an alternate. In a hearing, outside the jury's presence, I pointed out that the population of Orange County was only about two percent black. I said there wasn't much the court could do to change the racial composition of the jury except to perhaps pass out some black paint.

I hadn't paid attention to the fact that two newspaper reporters were in the courtroom. The next day, two articles made a big issue of "racially insensitive comments." The D.D.A who wrote to the commission in my defense said, "I am convinced that Judge McCartin's remark was in no way evidence of a racial bias; in fact, considering the context in which the remark was made, one has to strain to conceive of such an interpretation. Had the case not concerned a black person who had painted his face white, the play on words would never have occurred to Judge McCartin. The comment was made in passing, perhaps as a jest to a frivolous motion, and no one took notice of it at the time. In fact, even [the defendant's] attorney smiled at the obvious irony. . . . Donald McCartin is a colorful judge, but he has never, in my experience, demonstrated any racial bias or bigotry. Rather, he has followed the law in an indubitably fair and evenhanded manner."

THE RACIAL CARD CAME UP again during the murder trail of a seventeen-year-old Hispanic man. The defendant's family members wanted to testify in his behalf, but spoke limited English. Defense attorney Edison Miller asked for a court-paid, Spanish-speaking interpreter. I doubted that the witnesses statements were of any probative value in the case, and didn't see the need to waste time on something unnecessary. But I didn't state my opinion very diplomatically. I said, "If they come across the border, I'm not going to use the taxpayers' money on interpreters." Yet, I still granted Miller's request. At first, he was angry about my comment and accused me of being prejudiced against Hispanics. Later, he calmed down and said he hadn't understood that Judge McCartin often makes unusual, off-the-cuff remarks. Statements from that defendant's family had been unnecessary for a very good reason. I decided that circumstantial evidence presented by the D.A. was too weak to prove the defendant's guilt, and found him innocent without ever hearing the defense case. As I said, I call them as I see them. I think that decision also quieted a few of my critics who sometimes claimed I showed bias in favor of prosecutors.

In another murder trial, the defendant was accused of murdering a girl. He was quoted as previously yelling to the victim that he was so mad he could kill her. To me, that was inadmissible evidence, and I voiced it by saying, "So what? Sometimes I tell my wife that I'm so mad I could kill her."

Screening out prospective jurors can sometimes be fun. One panel included a little Japanese girl who I recognized immediately. She played tennis with my wife and periodically joined us for bridge games. I had difficulty keeping a straight face when I questioned her. No one else in the courtroom knew of our acquaintance. She was well educated and her grasp of the English language was better than mine. I asked, "How are you with the English language? Do you think you can understand it well enough to sit on this case?"

She primly said, "Yes, sir."

I explained, "We do get some Asians in here who don't understand the language well enough but say they do just to get on the jury." Then I asked her if she knew how to play bridge. She said she knew how to play the game. I asked, "Would you like to serve on this jury?"

She nodded and, "Yes, I would."

I said, "You are excused."

There were some confused expressions among the other jury panelists, so I thought it was only fair to tell them that the woman was my wife's tennis and bridge partner.

ONE JEST I MADE STILL EMBARRASSES ME. In jury selection again, I was explaining the trial process and the various roles of people in the courtroom. Trying to lighten things up a bit, I said, "The bailiff usually sleeps over in the corner but if I'm shot he'll come over and pick me up. The clerk keeps the judge awake. She also has another duty. I wear very expensive Thorlo sweat socks and I have long toenails that punch holes in them. I bring them in by the basketful. When the clerk isn't too busy, she darns my socks as one of her primary duties."

It was a murder trial in which the defendant was accused of killing a young woman, putting her in a bathtub, and stuffing a sock down her throat. I later realized that the D.A. must have been sitting there just dying as I went through my little comedy routine about socks. But you must understand, I don't read the cases before the trial starts. I take them as they come, so I had no idea that socks would be an important element.

WHILE I SINCERELY CARE ABOUT JURORS and try to look after their welfare, there was one case in which I was furious with them. A Vietnamese gang had raided a Garden Grove shop and killed the owner. The police department had not conducted a very thorough investigation, and failed to tape witness statements. Pretty sloppy job. The defendants' friends killed one of the witnesses and scared the rest of them off, several of whom left town. The remaining ones developed bad cases of amnesia. In testifying they would say "I don't remember" or "I'm not sure now."

Even though the witnesses tried to avoid answering, I thought the evidence supported conviction. But the jury ended up acquitting the defendants. I was sitting there steaming during the whole trial. I was ready to hand out some death sentences. When the "not guilty" verdict was read out loud, I told the jurors they were excused, but to go back into the jury deliberation room. I was so furious, I locked them in there. A couple of hours later the D.A. found out I still had them locked up. He said, "Judge, you've got to let them out." Of course I let them out, but I didn't say a word. Usually I compliment juries, give them a "well done." But not this bunch.

A LOT OF PEOPLE ARE SURPRISED to hear that I tried nearly three hundred murder cases. That sounds like I was doing two or three a week over the years. But what they don't realize is that defense lawyers often prefer to try homicides in front of a judge without a jury, especially if the charges are second degree murder or manslaughter, and prosecutors prefer it if there is a fairly sound defense case. I was often tabbed to hear these cases because I have a reputation for being fair. Probably half the murder cases I tried were without juries. Many of these were juvenile cases, in which the defendant is not entitled to a jury.

In my hundreds of trials, I heard just about every type of injury people can inflict on one another. Sometimes, the strangest cases come from marriage disputes. When Trisha Norris, still glamorous at 61, and her husband Gordon, 65, decided to split up, she not only refused to sell her half of their large ocean-view home, but insisted that he sign it all over to her. Mr. Norris refused, so Trisha decided to put a little extra pressure on him. She hired two men who posed as potential buyers of a nightclub Mr. Norris was selling. When the pair had him cornered, they first threatened to break his arms and legs. When he continued to resist, they jammed a lighted railroad flare close to his groin.

Trisha Norris and both men were arrested. The two accomplices pleaded guilty and I sentenced them to the 2½ months they had already served. Trisha preferred to fight the charges, and came to trial. One of the top Orange County private attorneys, Gary Pohlson, represented her. The husband testified about the threats. One of the men, he said, "asked me if I had ever smelled burned skin. I immediately signed the property over to her. I was terrified."

The couple had been living in the disputed house. She claimed the upstairs while he occupied the downstairs. I thought the whole thing was blown out of proportion. As a lawyer, I had handled countless divorce cases, and saw this one as not much different. What set it apart was the threat to the husband's sex organs. I guess that makes good, controversial news copy. The papers correctly quoted me as saying, "The best sentence might be to keep them married to each other for the rest of their lives. They deserve each other."

Pohlson's client claimed that she never knew about the railroad-flare threats and that she had hired the men just to "talk" to her husband. I found her guilty and sentenced her to a ten thousand–dollar fine plus unsupervised probation until the divorce was final. I ordered her and her husband to steer clear of each other. Everyone wanted her to go to jail, but I thought she had led a good life other than this messy divorce. Even the probation report submitted to me recommended a prison sentence. I told the probation officer who wrote it, "I was surprised you didn't recommend the death penalty." The defendant's husband groused about the outcome, furious over the very personal threats, and so did the prosecutor. You can never please everyone.

ANOTHER CASE PROVIDED a good illustration of this. I sentenced a career burglar named Daniel Principato to twenty–four years in prison. His attorney screamed to the press that the punishment was much too harsh to fit the crime. But Justice Sheila Prell Soneneshine, of the 4th District Court of Appeal in Santa Ana, reversed my decision, saying the I "erred" when I dismissed three felonies from the defendant's record. Sonenshine's decision resulted in the sentence being hiked up to forty–four years. In dissent, Justice Thomas Crosby, who passed away in early 2004, said that the twenty–four-year sentence I imposed "would surely be sufficient to accomplish Principato's retirement from his chosen field." He also stated that McCartin is not noted for his lenient sentences.

These are just a few of the memories about trials that are lodged permanently in my memory.

Being a judge, you get to know a lot of diverse people, and make some lasting friendships. It was a pleasant surprise to learn from one of my fellow Orange County Superior Court colleagues, Judge Dave McEachan, that he, too, had served on the USS St. Paul. His tour of duty came several years after mine. In 1965 he was aboard when segments of a motion picture titled "In Harm's Way" were filmed on the ship. Dave recalled that the star, John Wayne, was invited to dine with the captain and staff of officers but chose instead to eat with crew members. I had met Wayne in the early fifties when I pumped gas for a few weeks at the Newport Beach Arches Union 76 service station. He and quite a few other stars were regular customers. The station was adjacent to the famed Arches restaurant, one of Wayne's favorite eateries and watering holes. Today, the Arches is owned by a gregarious former U.S. Marine, Dan Marcheano, who is romantically linked with Cheri, one of my wife's two daughters. They travel all over the country on his motorcycle. Cheri is a teacher, and had as one of her special students the son of Sylvester Stallone.

IT'S FUNNY HOW NAMES can form links in the chain of memory. Like that well known "six degrees of separation" theory. John Wayne was sometimes a patient of the so-called "society doctor" of Newport Beach, Dr. Alan Cottle. A pretty young woman, Karen, who worked for Dr. Cottle had been my client when I represented her in divorce proceedings. After my own divorce, I married Karen. Before that, her two young daughters, Cheri and Tracy, were getting free rides at Disneyland because Karen's father, after leaving military service, took a position as head of security at the theme park as a lawyer.

I once represented Disneyland in a lawsuit involving a plaintiff who claimed a slip-and-fall accident on Tom Sawyer Island. Before I met Karen, her father took a different job, working as a clerk of the court in Newport Beach, and I met him when I defended my client "Jerry" of running a bawdy house. Life can make for some incredible circles of coincidence.

SITTING ALL DAY LONG DURING A TRIAL can be tedious and not very healthy. To keep in shape, I started running during the lunch break. Sometimes, I would get back at the last minute and slip my jurist robe over the running shorts and go right into the trial. But usually I was the cleanest judge in the county because I took three showers a day, one before going to work, one after running, and another when I got home. I also exercised by commuting to the Orange County Central Court on a bicycle, riding ten miles each way from my Costa Mesa home. It was just an ordinary bike with no gears to shift, like an old propeller-driven plane compared to fancy ten-speeds which are like jets. A year or so after I was appointed, a parked motorist opened his car door and it hooked the little wire basket on my back fender. The bike just stopped dead and I went over the handlebars. I was in pain for a month or more with a broken collar bone.

I also played tennis at the Jamaican Inn Tennis club with a doctor named Frank DiFiore. If you didn't know Frank, and tried to guess his profession, you might think he resembled a Mafia hit man instead of a skilled surgeon. His tennis style was awkward; just brute strength and a wild temper. But Frank was a terrific guy. I called him one Saturday morning and said I had a doubles game lined up. He asked, "Who we were going to play?" I said, "Rod Laver and Mal Anderson." He said, "You gotta be kidding!" "No," I said, "I really do." If you don't recall, Laver and Anderson were world-famous Australian tennis champions. In the late sixties, Laver won at Wimbledon four times, and was the first player to earn one million dollars prize money.

The match came about because Mary Laver, Rod's wife, had been one of my clients while I was in practice. So she set the game up for us. Unfortunately, the next morning was so foggy we couldn't keep the appointment. We didn't get to test our skills against the very best. But my path did cross Laver's again some time later. A robbery took place in his Corona Del Mar home. A domestic employee was arrested and charged with taking numerous valuables. The criminal case came up before Judge McCartin. Fortunately, Laver got most of his property back including prized tennis memorabilia.

Dr. DiFiore once had to sew up a bad wound on my wife's lip. We had a golden retriever named Nugget. He was one of those unfortunate dogs who needed surgery for a hip replacement. It cost me $6,000. I spent more on medical bills for that dog than I did on my four sons. Nugget had lots of other medical problems. One time when I arrived home from work, Nugget was on the floor, frothing and rolling, having an epileptic fit. My wife tried to pick him up and he bit Karen in the mouth, a serious wound. Just ripped it open. I said "I'll have Mike come from court and take you to the emergency ward and I'll take the dog to the vet." Those were our priorities, and she said, "Okay."

In the emergency room, Karen was sitting there waiting for the doctor, holding a bloody towel over her mouth. Dr. DiFiore walks in – you can hear his voice all over– and bellowed, "Don said I was supposed to come down here and sew your lower lip to your upper lip." I really had said that to him when I called him. Everybody in the emergency room thought this Don guy must be crazy.

EVEN THOUGH DOGS are an important part of my life, I denied a motion made by a defendant in one of my trials. He requested that he be allowed to bring his dog, named Spud, into the courtroom because it would help the defendant relax. Serial murderer Randy Kraft made several references to his dog, too.

I've sentenced savage killers to be executed, but I can't stand to let a healthy dog be euthanized. One of my Costa Mesa neighbors owned a golden retriever named Bullet, but she didn't give the dog much exercise. So when I'd take Nugget for a walk, I'd let Bullet join us. Later I found out the neighbor was also relocating and couldn't take Bullet with her. She just didn't know what to do. Some kid told her that if she paid him one hundred dollars, he would take the dog. The neighbor agreed to the deal. The kid took the money, and promptly turned Bullet over to the Orange County animal shelter. The woman got a call telling her that her dog was scheduled to be euthanized. She immediately telephoned me, in tears, stating, "They're going to kill Bullet. They're going to kill him." I went out to the shelter that night and rescued the sad retriever. I already had several canine pals living with me, so I started searching for a new home for Bullet. Finally, my good pal and colleague Judge McEachen gave him a home.

In recalling anecdotes about my dogs, I still laugh about an incident during a trial being prosecuted by a deputy D.A. named Ed Muñoz. I usually rode a bike to work, but sometimes drove an old car that I had used to take my dogs various places. Mr. Muñoz, who was arguing a murder case to the jury, needed to go somewhere at noon, and I let him borrow my car. When he got back, and resumed his speech to the jury, they kept giving him these funny looks and snickering. I finally realized what the problem was. The back of his navy blue suit was absolutely covered with dog hair.

I FINALLY DECIDED TO RETIRE from full-time work in 1993. A few days before the effective date, June 1, my colleagues and friends, along with my wife and family, held a "roast" for me. Over three hundred people gathered on May 19, in Department 1 on the second floor of the Central courthouse. Just to be ornery, I entered in a wheelchair, wearing a yellow, hip-length rain slicker, a sun visor, and white athletic shoes. To top it off, I carried a cane, as if I were blind. My golden retriever Mandy walked in beside me as my guide dog. She belonged there anyway because she had spent a lot of time in court with me, usually in my chambers. It used to startle people when they heard muffled barking through the wall.

Karen, looking lovely in a blue flowered dress, chose to sit in the front row, not at the head table with me. I don't blame her.

Judge David Sills, Presiding Justice of the Fourth District Court of Appeals, acted as master of ceremonies. He had reviewed quite a few of my trials and offered a few humorous comments about them.

Judge Don Smallwood came to the lectern. He said he had been asked if he could tell what he thought of Don McCartin in five minutes. "I could do it in five seconds, " he wisecracked. About contacts with me way back in 1962, he recalled, "I'm going to tell you a little bit about Don in those days. He was quite rude and genuinely offensive, and efficient. . . . I've watched his growth in the last thirty–one years as a lawyer, a judge, and a human being, and I'm happy to report that he is now rude, genuinely offensive, and efficient." He had seen part of the Randy Kraft trial down the hall, and watched "the pain I inflicted daily on both the prosecutors and the defenders." My versatility, he said, was evident in the fact that I was a Goldwater Republican appointed to the bench by Gov. Jerry Brown. Smallwood concluded by saying I would be missed, and when they needed someone to conduct one of the nine-month death penalty trials, and do it in two weeks, I'd be hearing from them.

DEFENSE ATTORNEY GARY PROCTOR came forward to needle me. He spoke of being invited to my Bass Lake home, probably because I didn't have any other friends. While thinking about it, he said, he rode a bicycle nearly thirty miles up a mountain against a stiff wind in his face, and it occurred to him that was like trying cases in my courtroom. He told the audience that one time he had entered my court during a trial, and in front of everyone I had said, "Mr. Proctor! I thought you were disbarred." Proctor concluded by admitting he was going to miss that "colorful character" he'd had a lot of fun with over the years.

Judge Robert Fitzgerald spoke next and said he thought the meeting was for all of McCartin's friends. If so, it could have been held in chambers (where there was room for maybe two or three people). Comparing me to Judge Roy Bean, he said that I needed to retire before the Commission for Judicial Performance caught up with me.

The next "roaster," Mike Naughton, from the family-law contingent explained how I had been appointed by Jerry Brown. Appointees, he said, were usually lawyers who know the governor, but my case was different. In Naughton's version, Presiding Judge McMillan had told Tony Klein, Brown's appointment secretary, that what we really needed was a "caring, personable fellow in touch with his feelings as a family law judge, Mike said. "Up until that time, Judge McMillan had an excellent reputation for truth and veracity." He ended on a nice note. "I'm sorry to see Judge McCartin go and I think the judiciary loses by his absence."

Orange County Register crime reporter Larry Welborn stepped up to say the press "loved being in Judge McCartin's courtroom because it was a gold mine."

In the style of David Letterman, Welborn presented a top ten list of quotes from the mouth of Judge Don McCartin:

10–On leniency: When Rodney Alcala asked for mercy, McCartin said, "Hogwash. You're as guilty as anyone who has ever been in my courtroom."

9–On politics: "I'm probably to the right of Attila the Hun." Welborn questioned the word "probably."

8–On attorneys: "An attorney with an IQ of nine, which is higher than most attorneys, could cross-examine this witness. Even I could cross examine this witness."

7–On fashion sense—as he pointed to my sun visor and yellow rain slicker: "McCartin loaned a convicted rapist a necktie then said, 'You look like a hobo in my tie.'

6–On respect for higher courts: "Screw the higher courts. I'm sick and tired of [them]. I'm not going to tip-toe through the tulips with the higher courts on this case."

5–On being convinced by false arguments—this was also to the convicted rapist: "You are a delusional liar. You are a pathological liar. In fact you are the biggest liar I've had in this court in ten years."

4–On self-assessment: "I've seen it all. I've done it all. Unfortunately, maybe I've done too much."

3–On successful marriage—after a defendant allegedly threatened to kill his wife: "So what, I feel like killing my wife sometimes too."

2–On being outspoken (Larry said my picture was in the dictionary next to that word): "I don't mean them, I just say them."

1–And number one—On media relations and his own tendency to speak out: "Some of my comments may have been ill-advised."

When Larry concluded, he gave me a water-color sketch of the Randy Kraft trial, on which was printed another one of my quotes: "If you don't keep your sense of humor in this business, you'll lose your mind." Maybe that one sums up my attitude best of all.

I WAS HAPPY TO SEE defense attorney Gary Pohlson come forward to speak. He was one of the best defense attorneys I've ever worked around, along with John Barnett who defended Rodney Alcala in the first trial, then years later represented one of the officers charged with beating Rodney King.

Pohlson said, "I've been waiting for this a long time." In an animated, good-humored talk, he reminded everyone that I had once advised him, in court, not to wear double-breasted suits because they made him "look chubby." I had also teased him about hair loss in front of a jury when he looked down at his notes. "Put your head up," I had said, "You're blinding me."

He drew a huge laugh when he held up a book of evidence codes and said, "This is a book I know McCartin has never read."

Gary did a terrific job of entertaining the folks in attendance. He imitated my "ferocious stare" and "growling voice" when I supposedly said to one of his clients, "You know, if you didn't have such a good attorney, I would have given you the death penalty, 'cause that's what you deserve." Gary looked at me and added, "And this was a CIVIL case."

Winding up his hilarious tirade, Pohlson sounded sentimental in saying, "It's been a lot of fun, it really has. It's been more interesting than anything else I could imagine." With a big grin, he added, "And I'm glad I don't have to do it anymore."

My idol and mentor, Justice Robert Gardner came forward. His distinguished appearance—standing tall in an elegant suit, ramrod-straight posture, crowned by a shock of pure white hair—commanded respect. Noting that he'd spent twelve "miserable" years on the court of appeals, he said, "Anyone who would take that job should have his head examined. The only reason I stayed is because we were reviewing McCartin's records."

GARDNER HAD A GREAT SPEAKING VOICE, slow and clear. He said, "Every court should have a curmudgeon. In my day on the Superior Court, which is before most of you were born, Howard Cameron was our house curmudgeon." I listened with admiration as my old friend spoke of my other role model. "The position of being the curmudgeon of the court is one which carries with it great dignity and allows appreciation from the practitioners who appear before you." He recalled Howard Cameron's retirement in which the "curmudgeon" had stood up after all the speeches. Gardner quoted Cameron's very brief response: "You said if I came here tonight, you would say nice things about me and I could get drunk. You did, and I am."

Turning toward me, Gardner finished with, "I commend that to you, when it comes your opportunity to respond." The audience showed their respect with deafening applause for this grand old man.

Judge Sills finally introduced the last "roaster," my son, Mike McCartin. Still a lawyer at the time, Mike began his spiel by giving his reason for representing the family. He said it was because he had been the only one "dumb enough to go into law," and that he had been cut out of my will, replaced by "this thing lying on the floor . . . " He pointed to my dog, Mandy, snoozing peacefully near my feet under the table. I interrupted to tell him that his speech had put Mandy to sleep. Mike said, "You usually have that effect on people."

With a certain amount of pride, I thought Mike sounded a lot like John F. Kennedy's barely suppressed mirth, calm voice and short pauses. He informed the assembly that many people had mixed emotions about my upcoming retirement. "I know Karen's quite concerned. He's going to be around quite a bit and she's been expressing her fears and feelings of despair. . . . Also, I've noticed around the courthouse lately, public defenders, district attorneys and defense attorneys with huge smiles on their faces when they say, 'I heard your dad is retiring.' . . . The court of appeals is quite excited, I'm sure, about all the spare time they're going to have."

Mike told of a case in which he and attorney Jack Mandel were opposing parties in a divorce case. They were told that no other courtroom was available except Judge Don McCartin's. Mike discussed the problem with Mandel. According to Mike, he asked Mandel if he felt comfortable with me as the trial judge. "Sure," said his opponent. "I've known Judge McCartin almost as long as you have, and I think he probably likes me better."

When Mike turned over the lectern to me, my dog rose and followed. Everyone applauded, and I said, "I noticed Mandy was the only one who stood up."

Now it was my turn to have some fun, so I teased some of the judges and gave them gift-wrapped T-shirts imprinted with personalized messages, told them about a few courtroom incidents along with one of my favorite jokes, and showed them a framed collage my staff had given me. It pictured the nine men I've sentenced to death with a photo of the gas chamber in the center.

The event took only about an hour and a half, but will stay in my memory as long as I live.

AFTER RETIRING FROM ORANGE COUNTY, I continued to sit as an appointed judge on a number of cases in various counties. I even found myself temporarily involved in the notorious Charles Ng trial in Calaveras County, north of Bass Lake. Ng was accused of murdering twelve people near the small town of Wilseyville, as an accomplice to Leonard Lake, who killed himself with cyanide. I recommended that we refer the matter to the Judicial Council for a change of venue. The council agreed and selected Orange County. Ng was eventually tried and convicted in my old Santa Ana courtroom, on eleven counts of murder. He's now on death row in San Quentin.

I PRESIDED OVER A DIFFERENT TRIAL in Madera County. They had a D.A. prosecuting who didn't seem too bright to me. He was trying a burglary case, involving a defendant who threw a brick through a warehouse window. It was the worst case of "breaking and entering" that I had ever heard. I suggested charging him with trespass. The more so-called evidence the D.A. put on, the more aggravated I was getting. The court was an old school room. My clerk was right next to me, penned in by the desk and me. I would have to get out of my chair for her to exit. I was bored, and said to the jury, "The only fun I'm going to have today is when the clerk tries to get out of the courtroom and has to climb over me."

I thought it was kind of funny. But at the recess, I was called in to face a grim tribunal. There were the presiding judge and a couple of officious-looking women. One of them said, "Judge, we're disturbed about this comment you made about having fun when the young lady, the clerk, would climb over you."

I said, "Now, give me a break. Don't you have any sense of humor?" I paused a minute, then said, "Look, let's do this. I'll get rid of this one case, then this will be the last time you will ever see me in Madera County. Is that fair enough?"

They squirmed around, muttering with frowns on their faces and said they felt they really should file a harassment case. Finally, they relented.

I made up my mind that incident was going to be my last experience with the judicial system.

KAREN AND I SETTLED in Bass Lake with our dogs. Anyone who knows me realizes the importance of dogs to me. My courtroom and chambers were filled with photos of them. The license plate on my van is 4DNSDGS. The interior of my other car, an older Honda, has been chewed to shreds by my various dog passengers. I wish people had the same qualities dogs have; unconditional love, forgiveness, loyalty. Of course, they can be pests, too, just like people.

KONA LOOKS SORT OF LIKE a chocolate lab, but she's a mixed breed. She originally belonged to my son Mike, but came to visit in Bass Lake and decided to stay. We got Camper in 1993 when she was lost in a campground and we rescued her. Nugget rounds out our family.

My son Duffy had three canine pals, Dali, Lama, and Buddha. Those names came from Duffy's travels in Tibet and China for four years after he graduated from Pomona College. He left China just before the Beijing rebellion in 1980.

Mark, my son who is an E.R. physician, sometimes leaves his big, black rascal named Chaos with us. He's the one who inflicted most of the damage to my Honda. Dogs are always welcome in the McCartin home, as are my human friends. Judge Don Smallwood, who spoke at my retirement roast, and is kinda of a formal guy, was having dinner with us one evening. With four of us at the table, he was in the midst of telling a story and glanced down at his plate. Nugget was eagerly lapping up his remaining food. Slurp, slurp. We gave the judge a replacement plate and food, but I think his appetite was spoiled.

WITH RETIREMENT, AND CESSATION of appointed work, I thought my career as a judge and as a lawyer had come to an end. However, my son Duffy, who teaches school in Coarsegold, not far from Bass Lake, caused me to change my mind. He owns a home on scenic mountain property. He originally acquired 5½ acres, then bought ten contiguous acres from a neighbor. The transaction required a survey.

Afterward, another neighbor said Duffy was encroaching on their land, by two feet. He filed a lawsuit, to wit: a quiet title action over the two feet of disputed land. "Quiet title" refers to a court action brought to establish title and to remove a cloud on disputed ownership. I attempted to resolve the matter amicably.

However, the opposing attorney refused to speak to me because my active bar membership had expired. On February 6, 2004, I sent a check for $390 to the State Bar Association; the fee required for renewal of my right to practice law. I am going to defend my son in court, against his wishes. He has told me if I lose this case — and I know nothing about quiet title action — that he will sue me for malpractice. I think he may still dislike his father for allowing his youthful class to come and observe in my court during the showing of grisly body parts. I think he is serious, and I have no malpractice insurance (just like my ancestor who wouldn't insure the family flour mill) as the premium is over twenty–thousand dollars.

If I can still afford to, I will retire for good after this case

God bless.

* * *

During Judge Don McCartin's tenure with Orange County Superior Court, he sentenced nine men to death, including Rodney James Alcala. The other eight were William Payton, Robert Thompson, Richard Ramirez, Martin Kipp, Randy Kraft, Gregory Sturm, James Marlow, and Richard Boyer.

They have been called "McCartin's Gallery of Rogues."

PART III

McCARTIN'S
DEATH ROW

William Payton

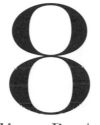

The William Payton Story

On March 5, 1982, the day after comedian John Belushi died of a drug overdose in a bungalow of Hollywood's Chateau Marmont Hotel, Judge Don McCartin faced a decision about another man's life. For the first time since being appointed to the bench, McCartin had presided over a murder trial involving the death penalty. It had been a prolonged affair starting with jury selection on November 2, 1981, and extending through the holiday season. After the jury found William Payton guilty of murder, they reassembled to hear evidence in the penalty phase and eventually arrived at a verdict of death.

Before handing down the sentence for Payton, McCartin would have to make a tough choice. California law gives a judge final authority to change a jury's verdict of death. If evidence supports it, in the judge's opinion, he or she may reduce the sentence to life in prison without the possibility of parole. While this option is seldom applied, it is still a ponderous decision.

In the assembled court, McCartin invited both the defense attorney, James Merwin, and the prosecutor, Michael Jacobs, to make any final statements.

Merwin used the opportunity to introduce a motion for McCartin to strike the special circumstances, reasoning that "defective legislation violated due process of law." The penal code, he said, contained "fatal flaws."

He also requested a new trial and asked permission for William Payton to speak on the subject. Payton stood, faced the judge, and began to ramble. "I'm not really that educated in the law — so the only thing I can really use is just basic common sense that I have. When the situation first arised [sic] in May of 1980, the confusion that was involved with myself was awfully extreme because of the fact that — that I didn't realize what had happened, and the fact that I wasn't sure of which way to turn or what to do to turn myself in. You know, after I read it in the paper — I really didn't know what had happened until I read it in the paper.

"And so I ran. But the thing is, eventually I was caught. I was brought to trial, to arraignment." He referred to the first court proceedings in which another judge had decided that enough evidence existed for Payton to face a murder trial. "And I remember, you know, that I was in front of Judge McBride, I believe. The thing that put peace in me was the fact that he promised me that I would be given a fair and just trial and defense. And, you know, I been brought up in a—that we just been raised to believe that this is the way the judicial system is. And so I relaxed. And because of the fact of the way I looked at it was if I was guilty of a premeditated murder, consciously, then I was deserving of the penalty of the law. And this makes it difficult for me—it was a big decision for me because I'm pro-death penalty myself. I'm not—I support the law is what I'm trying to say.

"But the thing is, I wasn't conscious at the time of the crime. This is something I know. It hasn't been proven. It hasn't even been attempted to be proven. The thing that affects me the highest, is that we've now gone through—I've gone through two lawyers.

"The first lawyer I lost because of the fact that a jailhouse informant decided that he wanted to get a deal and so he made up some information. And that particular informant happens to be in jail with me now and has told me the whole story of how it all came about.

"But the thing is, also, after that, I was given Mr. Merwin who, I as a person, enjoy completely. I think he's a delightful guy. But at the same time I think, because of the involvement he has with other cases, the intense schedule that he has, that they didn't have the time or the investigative support— maybe it's financial too—but it all added up that I— that the defense I proposed to him, which was the truth—and regardless of what the circumstances were at—after finding out the truth, I was going to live with them."

He expressed belief that his conviction had been based on lies. "And here, in the back of my mind—the whole idea is I thought we were going to shoot for the truth. . . . It's not, gee, the death penalty or the life without . . . the life imprisonment doesn't bother me in the slightest. Compared to the trial, or the defense   I guess the judicial system is fair. It's just the defense and the prosecution, the way they were formulated. It's not a fair system the way it's working right now.

Rewarding jailhouse informants for false testimony wasn't fair, he protested. "One of the guys that testified against me slit a guy's throat and robbed him, and they are giving him a year. The majority of the information that he told to the courts was false.

"The whole trial has had me in kind of a turmoil. And I don't think I've had a fair chance to prove my defense. I really don't. I think that if Mr. Merwin really searched his heart that he'd really have to agree with me that he hasn't put full effort into my defense.

"I think that if anybody was in my shoes, that if they really tried to look at it from my side, they wouldn't think that they had a fair defense either. . . . To be honest with you, it saddens me, the way the whole system is—That's about it."

Payton sank back into his chair at the defense table.

Court observers had listened carefully to every word and realized that Payton had not once expressed remorse about the death of Pamela Montgomery. Judge McCartin noticed the same thing.

He wasted no time in responding to the motions.

"First, with regard to Mr. Merwin, your motion to strike the special circumstances will be denied, for the record . . . . With regard to Mr. Payton's motion for a new trial in the guilt phase, the court will make a few comments."

McCartin's face showed none of the usual sly humor. Deadly serious now, he spoke. "Mr. Payton, the change of attorneys came about and Mr. Merwin was appointed. For the record, I feel he does an outstanding job. He has tried death penalty cases . . . before and I'm not going to spend time going into the pros and cons of Mr. Merwin. But in this particular case, certain things stand out. Number one, there was no financial restraint. I signed orders for many expenses including payment for psychiatrists and various tests. There were no unreasonable limitations.

"As far as you indicating you were unconscious during the time of these particular acts and that you didn't recall what occurred—of course I'm not privy to the discussions between you and Mr. Merwin—I do recall signing at least four orders for psychiatrists to perform all sorts of scans and tests."

None of them, he noted, had shown any corroboration for Payton's complaints. "As I recall, Mr. Merwin felt that calling these psychiatrists, and using that kind of defense, was not in your best interests. I'm not in a position to say whether that decision was right or wrong, but he is an experienced attorney and well versed in these matters."

Further, McCartin reminded the defendant, rules of discovery allowed him and his attorney to see, in advance, all evidence the prosecution planned to introduce in court.

"So I would have difficulty granting a new trial based on those particular issues you've indicated."

Turning his attention to the defense attorney, McCartin said, "Mr. Merwin, before I rule, do you have any additional comments to put on the record?" Merwin declined, citing potential violation of attorney-client privilege or concern that his words might not "assist Mr. Payton's motion."

THE JUDGE EXTENDED ONE MORE CHANCE for Payton to speak. Words tumbled again from the man who faced a bleak future. He may have sensed the need to express remorse. "I think only of the sadness over what happened in 1980. . . . It's greater than anybody has ever imagined. Regardless of whether I was conscious or unconscious, the responsibility of having helped someone to their demise, or cause their demise, or been responsible, or afflicted the victims the way I did, is a horrible thing to imagine, much less to live with.

"My sorrow for the people that were involved is great. And the trial that I had only extends that sorrow to be even fuller because of the fact that I hoped the truth would come out, basically for my benefit, but also for theirs. . . . Like I told you before, I'm more than willing to face the responsibilities that are rightfully mine. . . ."

Payton dropped his gaze to the floor. Observers weren't sure exactly what he had been trying to say. Certainly, the expression "helped someone to their demise" was a different way of defining a murder. To some, the speech sounded memorized and inconsistent with Payton's previous use of language. It fell short of credible remorse.

McCartin's voice cut short these speculations. "All right, sir. Motion for a new trial with regard to the guilt phase will be denied at this time." But he wasn't finished. The law required, he said, that some explanation for his decision be stated.

"Gentlemen, I don't propose to review the entire trial record, but I do have in mind certain things that leap out to the court. This was a murder, and a rape, and an attempted double murder. It's difficult for the court to imagine a more heinous crime. This is the type of tragedy that shocks the public consciousness. It was only by chance . . . that we didn't have a triple slaying. The murder weapon became blunted by multiple stab wounds inflicted on all the victims. Miraculously, two of the victims survived. The defendant took advantage of a prior friendship with the landlady and killed a tenant in her residence whom he had never seen until that particular evening. And that was just momentarily.

"Certainly, the reasonable inference to be drawn by the attacks on the woman and her son was that the defendant had no intention on leaving any witnesses. The rape and killing of Miss Montgomery was for no apparent reason except, as [he] related to fellow inmates while in custody, that he liked to stab and rape women. . . ."

Payton's voice cut in. "Your honor, can I interrupt for a second?"

McCartin, displaying remarkable patience, said, "Surely."

"Is that—are you saying that the motive for the crime was the fact that I enjoy—that it enticed me to go out and stab and rape?"

Like a father exercising calm while chastising an errant son, McCartin explained, "I'm indicating, as I said Mr. Payton, the witness who came in on the penalty phase, and testified that while you were in custody, there was a discussion about why these crimes were committed. And that was your statement, as related to the jury by this witness." The judge stated that he was simply reviewing testimony the jury had heard.

Payton responded in disjointed phrases. "Is that—so the intent based on the idea that—that the informant from the jail—he said that the motives that I—that I related to him, that's the basis for the intent that were—"

McCartin intervened, referring again to the need for examining the factors relating to mitigating and aggravating circumstances. "But it doesn't stop there, Mr. Payton. The court has to determine whether there's a presence or absence of criminal activity involving violence. We have a young lady who testified during the penalty phase that she was your girlfriend in October 1973. She was awakened by you, and at that time you were stabbing her with a knife. [You] were convicted of misdemeanor assault with a deadly weapon. . . . That is a crime similar in circumstances to what we have here. And the court certainly feels that it is an aggravating factor."

With apologies for interrupting again, Payton asked, "Doesn't it create some curiosity in your mind about why? Once again, here I was asleep. I had spent the night with my girlfriend—and I'm talking about having all the normal relations, I guess, and I don't consider them normal, but all the relations that are of the world." Court watchers in the gallery wondered just what sort of abnormal relations he meant. They would never know.

If McCartin's patience was thinning, he hid it well. "The court is under a duty to determine whether the offense was committed while the defendant was under extreme mental or emotional disturbance. There's no testimony . . . nor any doctor's reports submitted which would show evidence of this type of influence that would cause the defendant to undertake a project such as we have here."

The presence of prior convictions must also be considered, explained McCartin. He reminded the defendant of a 1976 felony rape conviction in Oregon.

Rising again, Payton asked, "Are you familiar with the contents of that case . . . that it was third degree rape which is similar to the statutory rape law in this state?" His question revealed a knowledge of the law that probably came from long hours of study while behind bars.

"Yes sir," McCartin answered. "But it still relates to the presence or absence of prior felony convictions, Mr. Payton, which are part of the record I have to make for the appellate courts so they can see if what I am doing is correct."

A question hung heavily in McCartin's courtroom. Would this, along with Payton's arguments about a fair trial, influence the judge to spare his life?

* * *

THE SEQUENCE OF UNHAPPY EVENTS that led William Payton to face this life and death decision began on a chilly night almost two years earlier, in Garden Grove, just a few miles from "the happiest place on Earth," Disneyland.

Georgia Lester tossed and turned all night, unable to sleep. Finally, at about four in the morning, she rose, and crept quietly into the kitchen, careful not to wake her three sleeping sons or a new boarder who had moved in just two days before, on May 24, 1980. Georgia poured a cup of coffee, and picked up a pencil to complete an unfinished crossword puzzle. As she lifted her cup, a sudden noise caused her heart to leap almost through her chest. Someone had opened the back door and stepped into her kitchen.

With a relieved sigh, Georgia recognized Bill Payton who had recently been one of several boarders in her home. She had always thought the twenty–six-year-old man was rather handsome with his blue eyes, square jaws, curly blond hair barely touching his collar, and an athletic physique. She asked what in the world he was doing. Payton said he'd had car trouble just up the street and didn't know where else to go. Besides, he added, he wanted to talk to her.

Payton accepted Georgia's offer of a beer and joined her at the kitchen table. While they chatted, the new boarder, Pamela Montgomery, a young, attractive, dark-haired woman, came in for a drink of water. Georgia introduced her to Payton and explained to him that Pam would be living there while her husband was away on duty with the National Guard.

After Pam returned to bed, Payton asked if he could "sack out for awhile" on the living room couch. Of course he could, Georgia replied. She gave him a blanket, then returned to her own bed. Her ten-year-old son, who had vacated his own room for the new tenant, slept soundly beside her.

On the couch, Payton waited in silence, still sipping from a bottle of beer, his third one. A rumbling fury boiled within him like the bowels of Mount St. Helens, the Washington volcano that had erupted exactly one week earlier.

Shortly after Georgia finally dozed off, two sharp blows to her back jerked her instantly awake. She rolled over just in time to see Bill Payton land on top of her. Shock rippled through Georgia's whole body as Payton raised a small knife and plunged it down to her neck, again and again. Each shallow puncture delivered pain but no lethal wounds.

The boy next to her screamed and tried to grab the weapon from Payton, only to suffer several bloody injuries himself. Georgia yelled, "Take me. Leave my son!"

The wild-eyed assailant began thrusting the knife at Georgia's abdomen, but the blade had bent and wouldn't penetrate her flesh. Frustrated, he leaped off the bed, growled, "I'm leaving now," and headed to the kitchen.

Fearful that he would return and kill them, Georgia's maternal instinct to protect her son took over. She ordered him to escape while she kept Payton busy, then staggered into the kitchen. On the counter, she notice the bent and bloody knife the assailant had used. Payton glared at her and snatched up a large knife. Gripping the handle in his fist, he lunged just as she turned around. The sharp point punctured her back. Her son, still in the bedroom, heard her scream and dashed in to her rescue. Payton slashed at him as he passed, and inflicted several wounds. The commotion roused another son from sleep. He heard his mother's voice imploring him to wake up a male boarder who might help.

Payton stopped, spun around and stumbled out the back door.

Georgia collapsed into a chair and pulled her two boys close. She had suffered forty stab wounds to her face and neck, while her youngest son had endured twenty–three similar injuries. They telephoned for police and paramedics.

Orange County sheriff's deputies arrived, questioned the victims, two other sons, and a couple of boarders, then asked if anyone else was in the house. Yes, said Georgia, Pamela Montgomery was in a guest bedroom. An officer suggested to the older son that he check to see if the woman was okay. The youth rushed to the bedroom, opened the door, and stood in frozen horror.

"Oh my God!" he yelled. "Someone come quick."

Pamela lay on the floor in a gory heap surrounded by a pool of blood. Her only garment, a flimsy nightgown, was open in the front. Twelve deep stab wounds extending from her navel to the pubic area had bled profusely. More punctures marked her hip, abdomen, lower rib cage, and upper thigh. She had apparently tried warding off the attack with her hands and arms only to suffer numerous slash injuries.

More police and emergency medical technicians soon arrived at the Garden Grove home, followed by homicide detectives and forensic experts. Examination of the body and the crime scene revealed that Pamela had been dead between fifteen and thirty minutes before discovery of her death. Blood spatters in various places throughout the bedroom evoked images of a violent attack against a desperately frightened victim. On the bed, her underpants were entwined with a man's pair of shorts. A technician used swabs to collect samples of saliva from the dead woman's breasts and semen from her vagina. A fingerprint was lifted from a beer bottle in the room.

Georgia Lester told investigators of the terrifying events that morning, and named William Payton, her former boarder, as the man who had attacked her and her son. Detectives pulled his rap sheet, and arranged an arrest warrant. But when police arrived at Payton's residence, they found he had skipped town.

When they examined his criminal record, they found two previous felony convictions, both in 1976. One was in Idaho for possession of more than three ounces of marijuana, and the other, in Oregon, was for unlawful consensual sexual intercourse with a minor under the age of eighteen.

WHEN PAYTON LEFT GEORGIA'S KITCHEN, he fled to his own residence. His wife would later describe her shock at his condition.

She said he arrived a little after six o'clock, at about sunrise. His face, hands, and shirt were covered with blood, the soaked clothing clinging to his body. When he stripped off, she could see his genitals were also messy with blood as were his legs, chest, and other sections of his body. Payton's wife notice scarlet scratches in his flesh that looked like "fingernail digs," as if "somebody had applied quite a bit of pressure with fingernails."

After Payton cleaned himself and changed his clothing, he and his wife hurriedly packed up and left. They stayed one night in Palm Springs and departed the next morning for Florida. The cross-country getaway did him no good. Investigators traced him and, with the help of Southeastern officials, extradited Payton back to California to face charges of rape, murder, and attempted murder.

While the accused killer waited in the Orange County Jail, he allegedly confided in fellow inmates. At least one of them informed. He said Payton admitted raping and stabbing a woman, and attacking a boy and his mother with a knife, all driven by "an urge to kill," and that he spoke of a "severe problem with sex and women." According to the snitch, "All women on the street that he seen was a potential victim, regardless of age or looks."

SOMETHING ELSE REPORTEDLY HAPPENED during Payton's incarceration in Orange County. He adopted religion. His mother stated that he was completely "immersed" in the Lord. A minister who had known Payton for years expressed belief that his "commitment to the Lord" was sincere. Fellow inmates attended Bible classes founded by Payton, who announced a wish to form a ministry within the prison system. Several officers spoke of his beneficial influence on other prisoners.

By all appearances, Payton's turn to religion seemed genuine. Sceptics pointed to an unusually high incidence of jail and prison inmates suddenly becoming devout in their theological beliefs, many of whom lose the call as soon as they are back on the streets.

The major question looming over the entire tragic event remained unanswered. What had driven William Payton into a bloody frenzy of rape and murder? One possible answer suggested by behaviorists lay in the defendant's Vietnam combat experience. Three doctors, working from statements made by Payton, offered opinions that he suffered from posttraumatic stress disorder (PTSD) at the time of the murder and stabbings, and that this disease, combined with other personality dys-functions, caused him to commit the crimes while in a "dissociative state." The doctors spoke of Payton's early childhood, identity prob-lems, and successful military careers of both his father and stepfather. They made reference to Payton being sent to Vietnam at age seventeen, being subjected to a rocket and mortar attack on the first day, and uti-lizing heroin on that same day. He had continued using heroin, experi-enced pressures of potentially being assigned to a combat helicopter, was subjected to gruesome war stories, all of which damaged his frag-ile personality. The result, they opined, caused him to suffer PTSD.

AT THE MURDER TRIAL in Judge Don McCartin's courtroom, the guilt phase evidence left the jury with no reasonable doubt that Payton had raped and slain Pamela Montgomery. Defense attorney Merwin found minimal evidence to refute the charges, but did contest the rape. He suggested that semen discovered in the victim wasn't necessarily from the defendant. (This was a few years before the acceptance of DNA as forensic evidence in courts.) But the jury believed evidence supported the rape charge. The defense centered its penalty phase efforts on avoiding a death sentence.

The prosecution, in presenting aggravating circumstances, brought in a woman who had lived with Payton in 1973. The witness told jurors that on a terrible September night, after she and Payton had sexual relations, she fell asleep. She woke suddenly to find Payton pressing a knife to her throat. When she screamed for him to stop, he stabbed her three or four times in the chest and right arm. She survived, but the relationship didn't.

Payton's previous felony convictions also came before the jury.

Most of the defense's case focused on Payton's reported religious propensities. Merwin did not present evidence of posttraumatic stress disorder related to Vietnam experiences as mitigation for the crimes.

AT McCARTIN'S SENTENCING HEARING, the question remained—would he have the will, for the very first time in his career, to order a convicted killer to face death?

McCartin answered it unequivocally. "None of these witnesses Mr. Payton called could offer any explanation or any circumstances that would extenuate the gravity of the crime. . . . In conclusion, I'm satisfied that the jury's verdict imposing the penalty of death is consistent with the law, and that the factors in aggravation, beyond all reasonable doubt, outweigh factors in mitigation. The motion to modify the penalty is denied."

McCartin said, "William Payton shall suffer the death penalty, and said penalty to be inflicted within the walls of the appropriate Department of Corrections facility in the manner prescribed by law and at a time to be affixed by this court in the warrant of execution." Within ten days, McCartin, ordered, Payton was to be transported to San Quentin's death row.

After the trial and sentencing, Payton appealed to the California Supreme Court, claiming ineffective defense by his lawyer. His complaint included Merwin's failure to inform juries about the effect of combat horrors in Vietnam.

In pondering the appeal, the state court sent representatives to interview McCartin about Payton's complaints against Merwin, but the judge offered nothing to substantiate them.

Eventually, the high court found that "Counsel for the defendant did not render ineffective assistance by failing to investigate or present evidence of posttraumatic stress disorder caused by defendant's combat experience in Vietnam, as there was no such evidence prior to the trial, and the later evidence of defendant's combat experience had been fabricated."

Payton also included in his appeals an objection to Judge McCartin's handling of testimony from a jailhouse informant who told of alleged confessions by the defendant. The California Supreme Court replied that "the defendant was given full opportunity to explore in front of the jury any motive to cooperate, or any other bias, on the part of all witnesses, including the informant. The standard instructions on judging the credibility of witnesses adequately guided the jury's assessment of the testimony." The justices concluded, "The trial court did not err."

TWELVE YEARS AFTER Judge McCartin sentenced Payton to die for his crimes, the inmate faced execution on December 6, 1994. But, as with so many other inhabitants of death row, an appeals court ordered a "temporary" stay of execution.

IN AUGUST 2002, the U.S. 9th Circuit Court of Appeals reexamined Payton's motion for reversal of the death penalty. The jurists stunned Orange County officials with a decision that Judge McCartin had erred by not considering the defendant's conversion to Christianity and his good conduct in jail. The conviction remain intact, but the death penalty was overturned. The U.S. Supreme Court disagreed and rebuked the 9th Circuit Court with an order to reconsider its findings.

An eleven-member panel took up the case again and announced their decision on October 22, 2003. By a narrow majority of six to five, the panel stubbornly insisted on overturning Payton's death sentence. In their infinite wisdom, the six judges criticized prosecutor Mike Jacobs for telling jurors he had heard nothing in mitigation of Payton's crimes, which ignored the defendant's religious conversion. Judge McCartin, they ruled, hadn't reacted to this "oversight" by ordering a mistrial.

As of spring, 2004, pending action is in the hands of California's attorney general, who is considering a request for the 9th Circuit Court to hold an en banc (full court) hearing. If appeals fail all the way through the U.S. Supreme Court, the Orange County district attorney will either retry the penalty phase, or settle for re-sentencing Payton to life without the possibility of parole.

Robert Thompson

The Robert Thompson Story

When a child disappears, there are no words to adequately describe how parents suffer. The pain inevitably clouds the lives of other relatives, friends and neighbors. But for parents, the trauma is virtually unbearable.

Benjamin Brenneman,12, didn't return home from his newspaper delivery route on Tuesday, August 25, 1981. His absence wouldn't make headlines, though. In that same time frame, news media thundered with reports of crimes that had caught the national interest. The man who shot President Ronald Reagan, John Hinckley Jr., pleaded not guilty to charges of attempted assassination. Another shooter, Mark David Chapman, stood defiantly before a judge who handed down a sentence of twenty years to life for killing Beatles icon John Lennon.

IN ANAHEIM, CALIFORNIA, Benjamin's parents and neighbors waited in agony, unable to think of anything but the missing youngster who had left astride his bicycle shortly after school. People who knew him admired the boy's dedication to his afternoon job delivering The Orange County Register, and his sense of responsibility. He used his earnings to help pay for the bike. Usually, he returned home at about five–thirty, no later than six. On this Tuesday, though, when he was nearly an hour late, and the dinner hour had passed, his dad went searching for him. As the sun dropped into the Pacific, his father's heart sank when he found his son's bicycle abandoned in an apartment complex. He immediately called the police. Within a short time, officers fanned out in several directions, knocking on doors and canvassing the apartments. The sprawling, three-story complex included more than seven hundred units.

By eleven o'clock, they found a lead.

A middle-aged woman responded to the police rapping at her door. Yes, she said, she had seen the boy at about six o'clock that evening. He had been talking to the occupant of apartment L-106. The guy's name was Thompson and he worked in Redondo Beach, about twenty–five miles away.

Investigators rushed to the apartment, but could raise no one inside. Anxious to move as fast as possible in case the boy had been abducted and lay injured somewhere, they needed to find Thompson right away. He might be the only person who could give them any useful information. One of the officers asked the apartment manager to open apartment L-106 so they could look for the telephone number of Thompson's workplace. Inside the residence, they found several numbers, copied them, and left. No other search was conducted inside Thompson's dwelling.

Any need to telephone the absent resident evaporated at the moment officers stepped out into the hallway. Robert Thompson, returning home, had entered the passage, spotted the police, and stopped in his tracks. When he identified himself to the officers, they asked about Benjamin Brenneman. Thompson denied any knowledge of the boy and volunteered to help search for him. At the nearby command post he spoke with Sergeant Larry Flynn, a sixteen-year-veteran of the Anaheim Police Department, and admitted chatting with the missing youngster at about five or five–thirty Tuesday afternoon.

Thompson mentioned something else that grabbed Flynn's attention. Without being asked, he said he had recently been released from Vacaville State Prison after serving a sentence for molesting a fourteen-year-old boy! Thompson said he was volunteering this information because he wanted to help find Brenneman and avert any suspicions about himself.

Flynn studied Thompson, who had passed his thirty–fifth birthday just eleven days earlier. He stood about five–ten with a slim, athletic build. A stubble of beard covered his dimpled chin, and a mustache bristled atop his full lips. Deep, close-set brown eyes stared intently at the officer. The sun had bleached a streak into his long brown hair which extended well below the collar.

The sergeant asked Thompson if he had any objection to the police entering his apartment and searching it. It would be no problem at all, said Thompson. As they entered, Flynn double-checked, and got the same answer, this time with an invitation to come in.

Benjamin Brenneman's parents had described clothing the boy wore when he left. It included a pair of thong-type sandals. In Thompson's bedroom, Flynn spotted footwear that seemed to match that description.

"Where did those thongs come from?" Flynn asked Thompson.

"They belong to my girlfriend," he responded.

Flynn, now a little more assertive, said they looked like thongs the missing boy had been wearing, according to a parent's description.

Thompson visibly flinched. Flynn would later describe his reaction. "It was like I had slapped him in the face. He just recoiled back . . . ."

Thompson groped for words. Maybe they weren't his girlfriend's sandals, he muttered, and suddenly recalled that he had found the footwear in the hallway just outside his apartment. He couldn't explain why he'd brought them inside. To Flynn's questions, Thompson insisted that he had spoken to the lad only a few minutes about subscribing to the newspaper. Twice, he insisted that the boy had not been inside the apartment. Thompson adamantly denied any knowledge of where Benjamin might be.

"Do you mind if I bring in a fingerprint technician to verify there are none of Benjamin's prints inside?" Flynn asked.

Thompson stroked his chin in the pose of deep thought, as if trying to remember something, then changed his story. "You know, I had to go in the back bedroom to find some one-dollar bills, and when I got back the boy was standing about five feet inside the door and I don't know whether he touched anything or not."

When Flynn asked if Thompson had a car, he led the officer outside to a dirty, white Buick station wagon. With the owner's permission, Flynn looked inside and noticed a large blue trunk, partially open and empty.

Flynn summoned Detective David Tuttle and introduced him to Thompson. Tuttle asked the nervous man if he'd be willing to go to police headquarters and talk about the missing boy. Thompson said he'd "be happy" to. A short time later, they sat in an interview room with a tape recorder running.

Recognizing that he had no probable cause to arrest the suspect, Tuttle simply wanted to learn as much as he could without scaring him away. Thompson repeated his earlier statement that he had seen the boy at about five–thirty or six and said they had talked about a newspaper subscription. He recalled not having the right change to pay for the paper, so he borrowed three dollars from a neighbor, the woman who had directed police to his apartment. Again, he admitted that the boy had stepped inside the apartment. After the youngster had left, Thompson had "found" the thongs out in the hallway and brought them inside. Soon afterwards, he had gone to the beach area and cruised around look-ing for a woman "to pick up." While he was driving around, the muffler on his car had given him some trouble, so he stopped to repair it.

As they continued to talk into the predawn hours of Wednesday, Thompson stifled several yawns and said he was getting tired. Tuttle nodded his understanding, and asked Thompson if he would return at three–thirty that Wednesday afternoon to answer a few more questions. He said he would.

Without taking a break for any sleep himself, Tuttle contacted Thompson's parole agent. He learned that the convict had been released from Vacaville on May 5, 1981, and was considered a "high risk to society." Thompson had been out of prison nearly four months. Even more interesting to Tuttle, the felon had failed to register his residency in Anaheim as required by law.

When Thompson showed up at three–thirty, as agreed, Tuttle asked him to take a ride. The detective wanted to retrace the purported route taken by the suspect on the previous day while looking for woman to "pick up." En route, Tuttle asked where the muffler difficulty had taken place. The trip did nothing to quell his growing suspicions. When they parted, the detective asked Thompson to give him a call at 4 p.m. the next day.

AT TEN FORTY–FIVE THAT NIGHT, Tuttle received a telephone call he had been dreading. Benjamin Brenneman had been found. A trio of farm workers had discovered his dead body in a rural culvert, near a dirt road. Investigators sped to the scene, in the mountainous Palos Verdes Peninsula, overlooking the Pacific Coastline between San Pedro and Redondo Beach.

The battered and abused corpse, with blood staining the ruined face, lay on its side surrounded by brush and leaves. Someone had hogtied the boy, binding his wrists together with rope, pulled them to his groin, lashed the rope several times around the ankles which caused the knees to draw upward, then looped the other end around the boy's throat at least four times. A subsequent autopsy revealed the boy had died from ligature strangulation, probably from the rope. He had been brutally sodomized. Sperm was found in the anal canal.

HOMICIDE INVESTIGATORS SEE so much savage death, they develop thick skins to ward off emotional reaction. But a murdered child is something else entirely, and it penetrates even the tough shell cops cultivate.

When Thompson failed to call at the appointed time, Tuttle started looking for him. He'd had the foresight to collect from Thompson telephone numbers of his cronies. It took only one call to find him in Santa Monica, forty miles from the Anaheim apartment. But, as soon as Tuttle identified himself, Thompson instantly dropped the phone and ran. His flight gave the officer reason to request the Santa Monica Police Department to find and detain the fugitive.

It took only one day to track him down. On Thursday, August 27, they spotted Thompson in a car being driven by his pregnant girlfriend, Glenda Norris. She accelerated and sped recklessly through traffic, attempting to evade the police. It worked, but only for a short while. Patrol officers took both of them into custody inside a Santa Monica mall, at five o'clock that afternoon.

This time, Thompson wasn't at all cooperative. He refused to speak to Tuttle without the presence of an attorney. A public defender came to his aid and advised him not to answer any questions.

He sat in jail three days before undergoing another change of heart. Expressing concern about Glenda Norris' welfare, Thompson spoke to a jail trustee and said he wanted to see Detective Tuttle.

Tuttle made contact and asked if Thompson wanted to talk. Yes, said the suspect, but only about "certain aspects" of the case. Tuttle realized he might be able to use some leverage by hinting of charges against the girlfriend.

Later, in an interview room, joined by detective Larry Johnson, Tuttle started a tape recorder, reiterated the Miranda warning and began the session by suggesting to Thompson that his girlfriend may have suffered a miscarriage due to stress and mental strain over the arrests. He wondered aloud how involved Glenda might be in any crimes Thompson had committed.

"Bobby, you know I'm not totally convinced that she doesn't know something about this. You know, I'll have to present the case to the D.A.'s office and it's going to be up to them to make the determination as to whether or not she stays or whether she is released."

Thompson's voice quivered with emotion. "I just love her so much. . . . I can't see her at all?" No, said the officers.

"I love that girl," Thompson repeated. "I've never loved a girl in my life. I've always just played with them, loved them for just, you know . . . . At first I felt sorry for her, then I thought—about having a good time . . . just having a couple of one-night stands with her, or whatever. But every day—I don't know what it was—it was just something about her that I loved her more and more every day that I've known her. I wasn't looking to fall in love. I wasn't looking for it."

Tuttle's voice took on a sympathetic tone. "Well, I'll tell you this . . . . Bobby, I think she truly loves you too. . . . And she thinks that you wouldn't willingly hurt her. And yet she's still in jail, Bobby, just 'cause of something that you know that happened. I think if you truly loved her, you wouldn't allow her to sit here in jail if you knew information that would help her. See what I'm saying?"

"Yes," he nodded.

"If she's found guilty of this—if the D.A. decides to prosecute and she's found guilty, that could really push her over the edge. . . . She's really committed herself to you, you know. You're more important to her than anything else in the world. And I think in actuality, if she's incarcerated, or whatever, it could really break her. Up to this point, I really don't have any reason to release her. . . ."

A nearly inaudible groan escaped from Thompson.

It would be helpful, Tuttle suggested, if something could come out to clear Glenda. Thompson said he wanted to write her a "little note," and added, "I was told by the public defender not to talk at all . . . I don't even think I should be talking now . . . I was told not to say nothin' about the case or anything unless I had a lawyer present . . . and I agreed with him."

"Yeah, I can appreciate that," the detective said. Thompson had not yet asked for the presence of an attorney, but was simply informing Tuttle of what he had been told. Until he asked for one, Tuttle figured, the interview could continue.

Detective Johnson decided to turn up the heat. "Well, the only thing I'm telling you right now, partner, we have given you every opportunity to explain how it happened. [Maybe] I could buy the theory that it was an accident. You don't care to tell how it happened. Hey, man, that's your right. But don't just sit here—You've heard the old saying, 'You can't bullshit a bullshitter.' "

"Yeah, I've heard that."

"All right. It's not remorse you're showing. . . . You're scared 'cause you know exactly what I'm talking about, and you know that your ass has been had. . . . I'm going to let you finish writing your letter to Glenda, and we'll see you in court. And I can tell you we're going with the theory that you killed [the boy] so you wouldn't get identified. But I want you to remember, you made too many mistakes along the line, okay?"

A resident of the apartment complex had mentioned an interesting incident to one of the investigators. The witness had seen Thompson carry a large blue trunk out to his car that Tuesday evening. Johnson asked the suspect what that was about. Answering too quickly, he said he was moving some clothing to his mother's house in Los Angeles County.

Now perspiring, Thompson protested. "I didn't kill that kid, that I remember. I did not. I do not remember."

Johnson snapped back, "Wait a minute. I know your whole history. You remember everything you do. The only question is whether you want to talk about it. And obviously you don't. So I'm wasting my time and I'm wasting your time."

If there had been any question that Thompson didn't want to speak without a lawyer present, his next words settled the issue. "I'd rather continue."

The officer playing the role of "bad cop" growled, "Well, I'm not going to sit in here and listen to any more bullshit. I would really like to know whether it was an accident or not."

At that moment, Tuttle returned to the room, placed a photograph of the victim on the table, and, "Take a look at that."

Still spewing anger, Detective Johnson said, "That's what I would like to know — whether it's an accident or not; or whether you just cold-bloodedly killed that kid so he couldn't identify you."

Tuttle shoved the gruesome photo under Thompson's nose. "Take a look at that, Bobby."

The suspect turned his head away. "I don't want to see what it looks like. I don't want to see the kid, please."

Said Johnson, "It's quite obvious you don't . . . we know how it happened; we know where it happened . . . we can tie the kid into your apartment, tie him into your automobile, tie him into the trunk, disprove your alibi about being over at Glenda's. . . . We're going to argue that you did it because in the past you got caught . . . . I just can't see wasting my time. We'll just do what we have to do and that can be very unfortunate for you." He gave the suspect a disgusted look, spun around, and stalked out of the room.

NOW THE "GOOD" COP took over. Tuttle said, "I can't see any more we can do for you, Bobby. I'm telling you, you'd better come forward on this. You're nailed. We've got evidence." Tears welled in

Thompson's brown eyes, and he wiped fingers under his nose as the flood opened. Tuttle bore in."Why did you do it, Bob? Lay it out. Tell me what happened."

"I don't trust this room," Thompson wailed. He objected to the tape recorder running. "You want to step someplace else, I'll say something, other than right here."

Tuttle agreed to move the conversation into the hallway.

With Johnson as a witness, Thompson told Flynn he had killed Benjamin Brenneman, but claimed he "didn't mean to do it." Flynn would later quote words Thompson used: "When I left him, he was alive. He came into my apartment. I made sexual advances and he got scared. I didn't know what to do."

Flynn asked, "Did you put him in that blue trunk?"

"Yes," Thompson sobbed. "God forgive me. He was alive when I dropped him off."

Later, according to Flynn, Thompson admitted more. Inside the apartment, the boy was frightened, wanted to leave, and started to scream. Thompson slapped him and said if he would cooperate he wouldn't be harmed. The sexual acts inside the apartment included, in the suspect's words, "oral copulation."

Thompson was formally charged with murder, kidnapping, and child molestation.

Larry Johnson went to the home of Thompson's parents and recovered a blue steamer trunk that had been observed inside the luggage compartment of the suspect's car.

A GRAND JURY CONVENED to consider an indictment of Thompson for murder. At the hearing, Kay Brenneman, Benjamin's mother, choked back tears as she testified about her son. He had turned twelve just three months before his death and would have been entering junior high school in the fall. Several times, she had helped him deliver newspapers in the apartment complex where he disappeared. Both parents had expected him home no later than six that afternoon. "He had been at the beach that day and it was so hot it may have taken a little longer if he was tired. . . . Her voice trailed off, knowing she would never hear her child's apology for being late.

Assistant District Attorney James Enright brought out the thongs recovered from Thompson's residence. The mother explained that he had owned them a couple of years. Due to the boy's minor back trouble, a chiropractor adjusted them for maximum comfort. When he had left that afternoon, wearing the thongs, a tank top, and light-colored yellow shorts, she had waved to him and said, "Goodbye. Hurry home." But he never made it home.

The woman who had told police of seeing the boy talking to Thompson testified next. She revealed a certain irony in the stream of events. Her reason for going into the hallway, where she overheard the conversation, was to deliver a message for Thompson. He had lived there only a few weeks and didn't yet have a telephone. His girlfriend had called the woman's number and asked her to let him know she was trying to reach him. Glenda, the person for whom Thompson later expressed so much love and desire to protect, had made a call that turned out to be the first link in a chain leading to his arrest.

The grand jury issued an indictment charging Robert Thompson with first degree murder. Special circumstances including kidnapping, sodomy, and lewd conduct with a child under fourteen, made the defendant eligible for the death penalty if a jury found him guilty.

In the modern, twelve-story Orange County central courthouse, Superior Court Judge Donald McCartin conducted the trial; his second capital punishment case.

Enright handled the prosecution duties while a local appointed attorney, Ronald Brower, defended Thompson. Proceedings began in the spring of 1983.

A succession of law enforcement personnel presented evidence to the jury, including the admissions Thompson made to a pair of detectives. Enright presented a powerful case while Brower faced an uphill battle.

Most defendants in murder trials, on the suggestion of defense attorneys, do not testify in the guilt phase. Generally, the lawyers fear defendants will say something that might open up a Pandora's box of cross-examination by the prosecutor and damage the defense case. Robert Thompson decided to take that risk.

In the witness chair, wearing better clothing than he had ever owned, clean shaven, hair arranged neatly, he spoke clearly, and recanted the confession he had made to Tuttle and Johnson. He said he had been drinking heavily on the day Benjamin disappeared, and had injected himself twice with "downers." The newsboy, he said, was selling subscriptions for three dollars. Thompson wanted to buy one, but Benjamin didn't have change for a five, so Thompson ran downstairs, borrowed three dollars from the neighbor woman, and returned. He admitted putting his arms around the boy's shoulders and asking him if he would like a sexual relationship. Benjamin, had said "no" and rushed out of the apartment. According to Thompson's testimony, he never saw the youngster again.

After the newsboy left, said Thompson, he found the thongs in the hallway, picked them up, and kept them because they were "in good condition." He testified he took the empty blue trunk to his car, as seen by a witness, simply because he was returning it to his mother who owned it.

When questioned by the police, he had lied because he feared getting in trouble as a result of his sexual advances toward the victim. Then later, from his jail cell, he had initiated conversation with detectives Tuttle and Johnson because he hoped he could say something that might get his girlfriend, Glenda, released from custody.

The confessions? Those were the detectives' fault. They had repeatedly made references to his "darker" side and kept indicating they possessed all kinds of evidence that he had kidnapped and killed the victim. All of this confused Thompson and made him believe that he might actually have taken and bound the boy, but had somehow suppressed the memory.

The jury didn't believe very much of his testimony. They found him not guilty on the kidnapping charge, but brought in a guilty verdict of first degree murder with special circumstances of forcible sodomy. Regarding their choice to exonerate him on kidnapping, jurors explained that it was unclear whether or not Thompson had killed the victim in his apartment or at the body discovery site. If it had happened in the apartment, the charge could not apply. You can not kidnap a dead body.

In the penalty phase of the trial, to determine if Thompson should be executed or sentenced to life in prison without parole, the prosecution introduced records showing Thompson had entered a plea of guilty in 1978 to charges of forcible sodomy and oral copulation with a thirteen-year-old boy.

The defense brought in an expert to testify that the defendant, an "aggressive pedophile," had not received adequate psychological treatment while in prison. Another doctor told jurors how drug and alcohol abuse can cause blackouts and loss of ability to control one's own behavior.

Again, Thompson took the witness stand in his own behalf. He spoke of his childhood in which his own father insisted they drink alcohol together and forced him to engage in sexual acts. A minister told the jury that he had heard about the father's sexual abuse of his son.

THE "ABUSE EXCUSE" CONVINCED THREE JURORS that Thompson should not die for killing Benjamin Brenneman. Judge

McCartin was forced to declare a mistrial of the penalty phase due to the deadlocked jury.

Before a new penalty trial could begin, defender Ronald Brower asked for a hearing in Judge McCartin's chambers. He told McCartin he wanted to be relieved as counsel for the defendant. When the judge asked why, Brower said he had developed such an intense dislike of the defendant that he could not properly represent him. McCartin accepted the resignation, and appointed public defender Michael Maron to take over the duties.

In the retrial, Enright brought more ammunition to the battle. Not only did he reveal Thompson's 1978 conviction, but the prosecutor also let the victim tell jurors exactly what took place. Now eighteen, but only thirteen when the crime occurred, the witness described how Thompson drove him to a park, offered him a beer, then put knife to his neck and demanded oral copulation and acts of sodomy.

The same expert doctors who had testified in the first penalty trial spoke again for the defense. Remarkably, Thompson chose not to testify. It might have been a fatal error.

The jury returned with a verdict of death.

ON DECEMBER 6, 1983, Judge McCartin, for the second time, sentenced a convicted murderer to death. In a packed courtroom, he explained that he had carefully weighed all the evidence and considered mitigating versus aggravating factors. Recognizing that Thompson had psychological difficulties involving "violent sexual tendencies with young children," McCartin said, "I do not feel that the mental problem impaired his ability to recognize what is right from wrong, to understand the requirements of basic human decency or the ability to conform his conduct to the requirements of law."

About the innocent victim, McCartin explained, "I considered that this is a child; that the child was particularly vulnerable . . . that there was no provocation on the part of the child; that there has been no remorse or regret on the part of the defendant; that there has been a pattern of violent misconduct; that he has demonstrated violent sexual tendencies toward children; that his act and the way he took a life show a high degree of cruelty; and that there are no extenuating circumstances for what he did."

After sentencing Thompson to numerous prison sentences related to corollary convictions, McCartin dealt with the primary matter. "It is the order of this court that the defendant, Robert Jackson Thompson, shall suffer the death penalty, and said penalty to be inflicted within the wall of the appropriate Department of Corrections facility in the manner prescribed by law and at a time to be affixed by this court in the warrant of execution."

Robert Thompson entered San Quentin's death row one week later.

On February 8, 1990, the California Supreme Court affirmed his conviction and verdict. A warrant was signed to carry out his execution in August 1990, but appeals courts granted a "temporary" stay.

Fourteen years later, in 2004, Thompson is still waiting.

Richard Ramirez

10

The Richard Ramirez Story

"Hi. My name is Richy Ramirez: black hair, brown eyes, 5' 4" (5' 5" on a good day!). I have been on death row 19 years. I have a good sense of humor—enjoy music: Classic Rock-Oldies, Blues, and I am a serious artist. I spend a good portion of my day drawing; mostly wildlife. I also exercise daily; keeping my body and mind fit is important to me. I'm not seeking romance, but a good friend, and maybe some that might act as an outlet for my artwork. Please reach me direct:R. Ramirez"

This little note appears on an Internet web site featuring numerous requests from prison inmates for pen pals. At the bottom, Richard Ramirez includes a mailing address. He does not include any mention of the crime that sent him to death row.

Richard Raymond Ramirez is sometimes confused with the notorious "Night Stalker," the other Richard Ramirez on death row. The more notorious of the two invaded a series of Los Angeles homes to rape and murder during a satanic reign of terror in 1984. A jury convicted him of savagely killing thirteen victims; men and women.

The Orange County Ramirez tried by Judge Donald McCartin for a single slaying was born in 1959, eight months before the Night Stalker.

Interestingly, he committed murder at about the same interval, seven months earlier than the L.A. County killer with the same name. His one victim was an innocent young woman in search of love.

FOR KIMBERLY GONZALEZ, 23, the path to romance was full of pitfalls and heartbreak. Like her old, battered Honda, love failed Gonzalez when she most needed it. One former boyfriend had recently made threats to beat her up. Kimberly didn't understand why men mistreated her. She did everything she could to please guys and even went on diets to make herself look prettier. With a flawless round face, liquid brown eyes, full lips, waist-length black hair, and full curves, she certainly attracted the attention of men, but usually the wrong kind. Still, she kept trying.

On Sunday evening, November 20, 1983, Kim needed to have some fun. She had never before gone to a bar alone, but the girlfriend who usually accompanied her had made other plans. Kim just didn't want to sit at home and mope. She put on her most attractive pants and sweater and carefully applied exactly the right amount of makeup. She loved gold jewelry—her ring, chain necklace, and watch were all gold. After checking herself out in a mirror, Kim stuffed her wallet into a black purse, and gave her sister a goodnight hug. Outside her parents' home, she tried to start her own reluctant vehicle, with no success. So she borrowed her father's pickup and left at about seven o'clock.

After stopping at a couple of nightspots and finding no one she knew, Kim arrived at a Garden Grove bar where she and her girlfriend had sometimes found dancing partners. It was located in a section of town with a less than sterling reputation, so she parked under street lights near a neighboring doughnut shop. Kim chatted with the bartender, played a game of pool with the bouncer, then ordered a Bloody Mary. She sat by herself, sipping the drink, wondering if the entire night was going to be another dull waste of time. The place was too quiet until a guy named Richy walked in.

RICHARD "RICHY" RAMIREZ, accompanied by his sister and a couple of her girlfriends, made their grand entry at about ten o'clock, laughing and ready for a good time. Wearing green pants and a colorful poncho over his T-shirt, he seemed carefree and friendly. There was something about him that attracted Kimberly. Maybe the self—confident expression, perhaps the neat little goatee and mustache, or the look of mystery in his dark eyes.

According to one person in the bar, Kim invited Ramirez to dance. Another patron said Ramirez noticed Kimberly sitting by herself, and invited her to play some pool with him. She smiled and accepted. Ramirez ordered a bottle of Budweiser and racked up the balls.

They played, joked, and drank. Ramirez asked about her music preferences and led her to the jukebox. She selected her favorite music and they danced to it. Near the front door, he pointed out a late-model Buick Rivera parked at the curb in which he and his group had arrived, but didn't bother to mention that it belonged to his mother. When Ramirez leaned forward to steal a little kiss, the smiling girl didn't resist. One kiss led to another, and more.

The time passed swiftly as they drank, danced, and flirted for about three hours. At close to 1 a.m., he carried a bottle of Budweiser with him while escorting her out the back door toward a parking lot used by most of the customers. The couple disappeared into darkness.

No one ever saw Kimberly Gonzalez alive again.

GARDEN GROVE POLICE ROUTINELY PATROL the high crime region in which the bar was located. At about 6:30 the next morning, a patrol officer made a grisly discovery behind the establishment. The

cold, blood-covered body of Kimberly lay about seventy–five feet from
the back door. Shrubbery nearby had been crushed and twigs broken
off. Her blouse and sweater were pushed up around her breasts. Her
pants had been partially taken off, baring one leg, and her underpants
were pulled down to her knees. Investigators searched the area but
failed to find any of her possessions; no purse, car keys, wallet, or identification of any kind.

Whoever had taken her purse hadn't bothered to steal Kimberly's
gold watch, necklace, or ring. Several yards from the body, a Budweiser
bottle sat upright on the pavement.

An autopsy of Kimberly's body revealed knife wounds to the back,
face, and neck. Her arms and hands were slashed with "defensive"
injuries.

The pathologist found traces of semen in her vagina and anus, but
no injuries. The time of death could only be estimated as between one
and three in the morning. Seven of the stab wounds at the base of the
victim's skull had severed her spine, leaving her completely paralyzed
during the rape.

Questioning of customers who had patronized the bar turned up no
witnesses to the crime, but several people had seen Richard Ramirez
and Kimberly Gonzalez together over a period of three hours. The word
circulated that the Garden Grove police were looking for Ramirez.
When he heard the news, he voluntarily surrendered. Ramirez acknowledged his presence at the bar that night, but claimed to know nothing
about the victim's death. He had very little to say.

The long-necked beer bottle said more than he did when a fingerprint expert found his fingerprints on it. Also, the semen found in her
body was consistent with his blood type. DNA evidence couldn't yet be
used. It wouldn't make its entry into the world of forensics until a year
or two later.

* * *

A WOMAN WHO SHARED LIVING QUARTERS with Ramirez and was pregnant with his child answered detective's questions. She had seen him come home at about one–thirty in the morning. No, she said, she didn't see any blood on his green pants, poncho, T-shirt, or brown shoes. He had not seemed the least bit upset. As a matter of fact, she explained, Richy didn't even take a bath or shower when he arrived. He just climbed in bed with her. The woman candidly admitted that they had sexual intercourse later that morning. Asked if Ramirez owned or carried a knife, she said that he did not.

Using statements from witnesses who had seen Kim leave with Ramirez, plus blood-type evidence and fingerprints on the beer bottle found near her body, the Orange County district attorney pressed charges of first degree murder. The prosecution, he said, would seek the death penalty.

While Ramirez waited in jail, across Flower Street from the Orange County Central Court, he shared space with other inmates in the protective custody section. One of them, a Blackfoot Indian accused of murder, seemed quite friendly. Martin Kipp expressed interest in Ramirez and asked quite a few questions.

An investigator would later reveal that Kipp offered to inform on Ramirez as barter to avoid a death penalty. But he couldn't find any takers. Kipp would also face trial in Judge Don McCartin's courtroom.

The Ramirez trial opened in January 1983. News headlines of that week focused on upbeat stories such as President Ronald Reagan being sworn in for his second term, and the San Francisco Forty-Niners beating the Miami Dolphins in the Super Bowl.

In Judge Donald McCartin's Santa Ana courtroom, lawyers, court watchers, and family member focused on the death of Kimberly Gonzalez. Deputy District Attorney Thomas Goethals, who would prosecute Rodney Alcala the following year, presented evidence for the people. Deputy Public Defender Ramon Ortiz spoke for the defendant, Richard Ramirez.

CUSTOMERS AT THE BAR on the night of November 20, testified that Kim had a little too much to drink. By 1 a.m., said a witness, Kim and the defendant were sitting by themselves at a table near the jukebox, and close to the back door. At about that time, they exited together. He was carrying a long-neck bottle of Budweiser beer. A fingerprint expert told jurors that prints on the beer bottle found not far from Kim's body were made by Richard Ramirez.

Semen found in the victim's body, according to a forensics expert, was consistent with fluid samples taken from the defendant, although that same conclusion would apply to a rather large number of the general population. The witness also said that tiny spots of blood had been found on the poncho Ramirez wore that night.

Jury duty, particularly in a murder case, is a heavy responsibility. Most jurors treat it as such by listening to the judge's instructions and admonition, and obeying the rules. Repeatedly, throughout the entire process, judges admonish jurors not to speak to anyone about the trial. But all too often, certain individuals decide they are exceptions. Sometimes they cause appeals courts to overturn the verdicts.

IN THE RAMIREZ TRIAL, Judge McCartin noticed a female juror behaving oddly. He held a bench conference with the lawyers, and said, "She was leaning forward, holding her head in her hands. Her eyes look strange, and the way she's walking out of this courtroom bothers me. I'm concerned whether or not she's taking drugs and so forth."

McCartin also said he had received a call from the woman's doctor who said his patient had complained of hysterical feelings and doubts about being able to continue as a juror due to her own experience of being mugged at gunpoint. McCartin recalled that she had mentioned the incident during voir dire, in the jury selection proceedings, but had said it would not have any effect on her ability to be a juror.

Prosecutor Tom Goethals reported that he had been informed by two witnesses, who had already testified, that the juror spoke to them in the hallway. She had said, "I thought you guys did a great job. If I had been up on the witness stand, I would have probably broke down crying."

JUDGE MCCARTIN SUMMONED THE WOMAN to the conference and asked for an explanation of her situation. She stated that she had been very upset and suffered from headaches and stomach pains. When asked about speaking to the witnesses, she admitted it.

The following morning, McCartin received another call from the woman's doctor to report her extreme discomfort. The judge decided to excuse her and fill the vacant seat with an alternate juror.

When the defense attorney put Ramirez on the stand, he agreed with the witness who had said Kim approached him and asked for a dance. He recalled the dancing and kissing, and said that afterward he told Kim he planned to leave soon. She offered to walk him out to his car. They left together through the rear exit.

That raised a big question. Anyone familiar with the facts knew that Ramirez had parked the Buick in front of the bar. Why did he leave with her through the back door?

Ramirez's rationale left skeptics wondering. He explained that he had turned around to tell his sister something, and by the time he looked back at Kim, she was already heading out toward the back. So he just "simply followed her."

Did he plan to have sex with her? Ramirez denied it, stating that as far as he was concerned, when they left the bar he was not interested in pursuing "any further sexual activity" with Kim. He testified that when they got outside, they kissed again briefly and then walked around the building to his car parked in the front. "I was carrying a bottle of beer at the time," he admitted, and was "feeling kind of drunk." When he arrived at his car, Ramirez claimed, he gave the bottle, which was about half full, to Kim. He last saw her, he claimed, moving toward the bar's front entry. He had never even been on the back walkway where her body was found, he told jurors, and adamantly denied sexually assaulting or killing the victim.

Asked what he did after leaving, Ramirez said he drove directly to his girlfriend's home, arrived at about one–thirty, went to bed, and fell asleep. When he learned a few days later that the police were looking for him, he voluntarily went to the station and was arrested.

THE DEFENSE PRESENTED A THEORY that Kim could have been killed by someone else. Witnesses testified that the bar was located in a neighborhood plagued with crime and that the rear alley was especially dark and dangerous at night. Anyone lingering in that vicinity, particularly a woman by herself, would be vulnerable. Also, the rear exit of another bar, frequented by "low rider" types, opened up to the same parking lot.

After both lawyers, Goethals and Ortiz, summarized their cases to the jury in final arguments, the five women and seven men retired to deliberate. Observers realized the evidence was primarily circumstantial. Physical evidence consisted of fingerprints on a beer bottle, semen that could be from the defendant, and minuscule blood spots on his poncho. Was this enough to convict Ramirez? Did his story of escorting her out the back door, when his car was in front, make sense? Would they really have walked all the way around the building in a dark, dangerous alley to get to his car, rather then re-enter the bar and exit through the front door?

The jurors deliberated three full days before coming out with a verdict on February 13. Judge McCartin examined the signed form, then handed it to his clerk, Gail Carpenter. She read it aloud. "We the jury, in the above entitled action find the defendant, Richard Raymond Ramirez, guilty. . . ." The defendant was convicted of rape, sodomy, and murder, with special circumstances.

The same jurors would now hear penalty phase evidence and deliberate again to decide his fate: life in prison without parole or the death penalty.

THEY SOON LEARNED that Richard Ramirez was not an innocent, law-abiding citizen with a clean record. On the contrary, his rap sheet was a mile long. Between 1977 and 1982, he had been charged with driving under the influence, assault on a peace officer, rape by threat, burglary, crimes against children / lewd acts, assault with a deadly weapon, burglary, receiving stolen property, drug violations, possession of burglary tools, petty theft, and another burglary. All of this was in addition to lesser violations such as possession of drug paraphernalia. As a teenager, he had served time in California Youth Authority (CYA) facilities. If legislation later enacted in California, called the "three strikes law," had been in effect, Ramirez might already have been serving a life sentence before he met Kimberly Gonzalez.

The most serious crime had taken place in Merced, located in California's central valley. The victim testified in Judge McCartin's court to tell exactly what had happened back in October 1977.

She stated that she had met Ramirez, age 18, very casually on two occasions a few days prior to being raped by him; once when she was standing in the front yard of her apartment building, and once when he came to the door of her residence to borrow cigarettes for his girlfriend. On the night he assaulted her, Ramirez, armed with a knife, entered her apartment while she was asleep on the couch. She woke up to find him on top of her, holding the knife to her throat with one hand, and the other hand tightly covering her mouth. At one point, she broke loose and ran toward her door, but he grabbed her and wrestled her to the floor. Ramirez threatened not only to kill her, but also to harm her one-year-old son, who was asleep in another room. If she didn't submit to having intercourse with him, she said, he told her he would cut off the child's legs!

EVEN AFTER FIVE YEARS, the woman had difficulty controlling her emotions as she spoke. She recalled that Ramirez had demanded she take off her night gown. While she started to remove it, he had grabbed the garment and ripped it apart. He forcibly raped her several times. During the course of the attack, he took her into the bathroom, grabbed a hair spray can, and forced it into her vagina. The pain, she said, was almost unbearable. While in the bathroom, he compelled her to perform other sexual acts. The victim had begged for Ramirez to stop, but he refused. He paused in the assault long enough to ransack her purse, and even asked where the child's piggy bank was. She endured everything until the assailant headed for her little boy's bedroom. She ran outside screaming at the top of her lungs for someone to help her. This must have frightened Ramirez because he sprinted out of the apartment.

The brutal attack had torn her uterus, the witness said, and after four unsuccessful operations, a hysterectomy became necessary. She was only twenty–three years old.

Caught soon afterward and convicted of rape, Ramirez was sent to a California Youth Authority facility. Incredibly, he was on the streets again fourteen months later when he was arrested for possession of a deadly weapon. Within the next two years, he was picked up five times on charges of drug possession, burglary, theft, and receiving stolen property.

Now facing a possible death penalty for killing Kim Gonzalez, Ramirez listened as his mother testified for him. She told jurors of his troubled childhood, his father's alcoholism, and of illnesses the boy had suffered. The family had been poverty-stricken and the parents went through a divorce, after which Ramirez's father passed away.

Several psychologists testified, revealing that Ramirez had a lower-than-average IQ. With his learning disabilities, they said, the public education system had failed him. One of the experts pointed out that CYA had not provided proper sex-offender counseling for the young inmate.

ALL THE DEFENSE NEEDED was one juror who would resist voting for the death penalty. And that's exactly what they got. After intense deliberations, the jury was hopelessly deadlocked, 11 to 1 for death. The holdout would not budge.

Years later, Judge McCartin was asked if there was any solution to the problem of a single juror blocking the strong majority of eleven other members. It occurs with remarkable frequency, especially in the penalty phase of murder trials. A few jurors have even confessed afterward to giving false statements in order to be accepted on a death penalty jury so they would be able to impose their personal values regarding capital punishment. McCartin shook his head. "It's an integral part of the jury system. It happens. There have been proposals to change it, to allow a majority decision rather than a unanimous one. But I don't agree with that. When jurors are literally deciding life or death, that's much too important to allow just a majority vote."

The judge declared a mistrial in the penalty phase, and set a date for a new trial.

A SECOND PENALTY TRIAL IS FAR MORE EXTENSIVE than the first one because the new jury must hear a reprise of the guilt phase so they can understand what led to the verdict. It's very much like conducting a mini-trial of the guilt phase, and then a full hearing to determine the punishment.

On May 18, 1985, a new panel of jurors heard of Kimberly Gonzalez and how she died. They listened as the crimes of Richard Ramirez were laid out before them. Once more, twelve people deliberated to decide whether Ramirez should spend the rest of his life in prison, or die in the execution chamber at San Quentin.

It took them only one day.

The verdict was death.

IN HANDING DOWN THE SENTENCE on August 8, 1985, Judge McCartin called the murder and rape of Kimberly Gonzalez "cruel and inhuman" and told Ramirez he posed a danger to society. Noting that he had spent ten years incarcerated in various juvenile and adult facilities, McCartin said, "Society did the best it could under the circumstances, but it did no good." Not once had the judge been able to detect any sign of remorse in Ramirez. Regarding the victim who was raped in Merced, McCartin said, "It's not hard to imagine what would have happened to this young lady if she hadn't escaped."

The judge ordered Ramirez sent to San Quentin to be confined until a warrant was issued for his execution.

Appeals to the California Supreme Court are automatic in death penalty cases. The justices examined several motions brought forth by the defense. First, they weighed the possibility of a reversal due to misconduct of the female juror who had spoken to witnesses. The high court's written opinion stated, "The defendant does not argue that it was improper to excuse the juror, but contends that the trial court erred in failing to inquire whether other jurors were improperly affected by her conduct."

This issue was dismissed by the high court. "There is absolutely no indication in the record that other jurors may have been affected by her 'anxiety attack' or misconduct." Judge McCartin had properly explained her absence to the other eleven panelists.

A second question involved the sodomy conviction. Defense attorneys claimed there was not enough evidence to support the charge "because it does not adequately prove that the victim was alive at the time of the penetration."

DOES THIS SUGGEST that if a rapist kills the victim first, then sodomy is within the law? The high court offered an interesting discourse on the subject. First, they defined the act. "Sodomy is sexual conduct consisting of contact between the penis of one person and the anus of another person." It may come as a surprise to some people that sodomy, according to section 286 of the California Penal Code, is indeed a crime. Further, "any sexual penetration, no matter how slight, is sufficient to complete the crime of sodomy"

The court, though, had to dig deep regarding the issue raised; was it still a crime if the victim was dead? In the court's decision, they wrote, "Although we have found no case that discusses the question of whether the offense of sodomy requires that the victim be alive at the time of penetration, with respect to the analogous crime of rape the California authorities uniformly hold that the victim "must be alive at the moment of penetration in order to support a conviction of rape. . . . Because the sodomy statute, like the rape statute, defines the crime as sexual contact with another person rather than with a body," we conclude that the offense of sodomy requires that the victim be alive at the time of penetration."

SO, HAD THE RAMIREZ LAWYERS won their case on that issue?

The high court's decision continued. "Nonetheless, we cannot agree with the defendant's contention that the evidence presented in this case was insufficient to support a sodomy conviction. Although the prosecution's pathologist may not have been able to determine clinically whether penetration occurred shortly prior to death, at death, or just after death, in the absence of any evidence suggesting that the victim's assailant intended to have sexual contact with a corpse, we believe that the jury could reasonably have inferred from the evidence that the assailant engaged in sexual conduct with the victim while she was still alive rather than after she was already dead. . . . We conclude that a reasonable trier of fact could have found the essential elements of sodomy beyond a reasonable doubt.

"Accordingly, we reject the defendant's claim that the evidence is insufficient to support the sodomy conviction or the sodomy-murder special circumstance."

JUST BEFORE A JURY RETIRES to deliberate a verdict, the judge is required to read to them a list of specific instructions formulated from the California Jury Instruction Codes. These are intended to provide the jurors legal guidelines regarding the issues they must consider.

The defense team for Ramirez included several arguments regarding jury instructions provided at the end of his trial. The Supreme court gave due consideration to these issues, too, but found no errors.

Other points in the defense petition to overturn conviction included objections to admitting into evidence, during the penalty phase, prior criminal conduct. This included the Merced rape and specific objection to allowing testimony about the sexual assault with a hair spray can. The high court disagreed.

In a decision written by Justice Allen Broussard, and concurred by Justices Malcolm Lucas, David Eagleson, Edward Panelli, Armand Arabian, and Joyce Kennard, the California Supreme Court said. "The judgement is affirmed in all respects."

On May 31, 1991, Judge Don McCartin signed a warrant ordering Ramirez to be executed on July 26, that same year.

Appeals courts granted a stay of execution, the resolution of which is still pending in 2004.

Richard Ramirez spends his time on death row creating artwork, listening to music, exercising, and corresponding with people who answer his Internet request.

Martin Kipp

The Martin Kipp Story

J ames Martin Kipp, who preferred to be called by his middle name, shared a fourth-floor Orange County Jail cell with Richard Ramirez while they waited for their murder trials. Kipp faced charges of killing two young women, one in nearby Huntington Beach, and one in Long Beach, Los Angeles County. If convicted of both, he could go to San Quentin facing two separate penalties of death. Of course, state officials couldn't kill him twice, but the double rap would reduce his chance of relief through courts of appeal.

A former member of the U.S. Marine Corps, Kipp, 29, stood husky, tall, and straight. His features and bearing left no doubt of his heritage as an American Indian, a member of the Blackfoot tribe of Montana. Long, black braided hair hung down between his shoulder blades. Prominent cheekbones, a broad, jutting face with a high bridge to his nose, and intense brown eyes gave him a certain look of nobility. With no facial hair, he contrasted sharply to the diminutive, goateed Ramirez.

TO KIPP, RAMIREZ REPRESENTED a potential bartering chip. If he could convince "Richy" to divulge details about killing a young woman named Kimberly Gonzalez, Kipp might be able to snitch out his cellmate and negotiate a deal to avoid a death sentence. His plan didn't work though. The D.A. didn't even reply to his offer and the jail-wise Ramirez spoke very little about himself. So Kipp turned to something a little more drastic—escape. His wife and stepson would provide the "get out of jail free" tools and assistance he needed. Once free, Kipp could flee to Canada, north of his Montana roots.

When his wife and her teenage son came for their next visit, Kipp told her of his idea. Her job as a paralegal, working with several of the inmates, made the plot even more feasible. His two-year-old marriage just might pay dividends. Kipp had met the paralegal while in jail, convinced her to leave her husband and proposed to her. They were wed in a jailhouse ceremony.

During several subsequent visits, while the son distracted guards, Kipp whispered details of his plans to his mate. It would require her to buy a screwdriver, wire cutters, tin snips, hacksaw blades, bolt cutters, rope, and towels, then bring a change of clothing for Kipp. He would also need a Taser stun gun, a .38 caliber handgun, and ammunition.

Roughly, the scheme would require the woman's slim son to climb through a trap door in the ceiling of a visitor's restroom, enter the ventilation system, and crawl toward the cellblock. The boy would periodically say, "Hey, dude." As soon as Kipp heard the signal, he would reply, "Rapunzel."

Within the next few days, Mrs. Kipp acquired everything her husband had listed. She even found an ally who said he would help. The friendly fellow told her he had been in county jail, and knew details of its layout. Grateful for his assistance, she met him at a restaurant and joined him in a scouting trip, walking around the jail perimeter. She even introduced her son to the generous volunteer.

The escape was scheduled to take place on Saturday, April 19, 1987.

Everything seemed to be falling into place until that Saturday, when it all fell apart. Sheriff's deputies arrested Mrs. Kipp and her son for conspiracy to assist in an escape.

The helpful ally had been an undercover cop.

Kipp hadn't been as clever as he thought. A jailhouse deputy who was being "distracted" by the teenage boy visiting Kipp had noticed something fishy. While Kipp's wife spoke to him in hushed tones, the inmate appeared to be drawing diagrams of the jail.

Also, another inmate had reported hearing that a female paralegal was trying to figure out a way to help one of the prisoners escape. He knew only her first name. Investigators checked the visitation log and found the paralegal was Mrs. Kipp. A quick look at Martin Kipp's records indicated that he was an escape risk; he had once tried to climb out through air ducts in a Los Angeles County jail. Officials sent the undercover agent to ingratiate himself with the errant wife.

When she was arrested, she had $5,000 in her possession, apparently for Martin Kipp's run to Canada. A search of her residence turned up the escape tools, material, clothing, and weapons she had assembled.

Sheriff's spokesman Lt. Richard Olsen reported the foiled plot at a news conference. He stated that the boy would never have reached Kipp's cell through the ventilation ducts. The hare-brained scheme "would never would have worked anyway," he said.

Mrs. Kipp eventually entered into a plea deal. In exchange for her promise not to see her husband again, she was given probation. Her son was released from a juvenile facility to rejoin his embarrassed mother.

Under secure incarceration, James Martin Kipp faced trial in Judge Don McCartin's court for the murder of nineteen-year-old Antaya Yvette Howard.

YVETTE IS WHAT SHE PREFERRED TO BE CALLED during her years at Marina High School in north Huntington Beach. She liked the school, located at one corner of a triangle formed by two shopping malls and the campus. Yvette Howard's good looks, combined with her intelligence and athletic skills, made her one of the most popular girls at Marina. Tall and graceful, she participated in track, volleyball, and starred on the basketball team.

Life for Yvette had changed several years earlier when her mother and stepfather decided to move from a Los Angeles neighborhood to Huntington beach so she and her two siblings could attend better schools. Her grades and social life gave the teenager a new sense of confidence.

After graduation she took a job in a photography studio and commuted from her parents' home in a bright orange Datsun. Yvette also enrolled at Golden West College. Certainly, most teenagers have their little personality quirks, but Yvette's mother could see few faults. "She was always smiling, very happy all the time, just a happy-go-lucky kind of person with a real zest for life."

A few days after the family celebrated Christmas, the promising future for Yvette came to a sudden end.

Maxine Britton would never forget the last time she spoke to her daughter on the night of December 29, 1983. Just before going to bed, Mrs. Britton reminded Yvette that a favorite television program called "Knots Landing" had just started at ten o'clock.

The next morning, Yvette's bed was empty. It seemed strange to Maxine Britton because her daughter seldom left the house without telling her mother. When Yvette failed to come home later that day, fear enveloped the household like a toxic fog. Telephone calls to her workplace and friends produced nothing. The parents filed a missing-person report with the Huntington Beach Police Department.

Painful hours crawled by and stretched into miserable days. While the world celebrated New Year's Eve and cheerful crowds attended a sparkling Rose Parade in Pasadena thirty miles away, the Britton family huddled in desperation, praying for Yvette to return safely.

ON JANUARY 3, 1984, a traffic officer observed an orange Datsun parked illegally in a Huntington Beach alley and placed a citation on the windshield. The next morning, a woman strolling by the car noticed a strong odor. She had seen the vehicle in the alley on the last day of December and wondered why no one had moved it. She notified the police.

A patrol officer responded, opened an unlocked door, and made a horrifying discovery. Behind the front seat, covered by a yellow blanket, lay the still body of Yvette Howard.

Detective Richard "Dick" Hooper, 42, one of the most experienced investigators with the P.D, had been chasing bad guys for fifteen years. Husky, light complected, and still wearing a flat-top haircut from his U.S. Navy days, Hooper could scare the hell out of a suspect or lull him with a disarming manner of speaking. He and a team of forensic investigators soon arrived at the cordoned-off scene. When the blanket was removed, they photographed the body and the vehicle's interior.

The victim's blouse, missing a button, had been pulled apart revealing a still clasped bra twisted above her breasts. Blue jeans and panties were pulled down around her ankles. Mud and dirt caked her knees, her left side, and the back of her clothing.

After the body had been removed and sent to a laboratory for autopsy, a fingerprint technician brushed black powder on nearly every surface of the Datsun to test for prints. He lifted several clear images, mostly from the driver's and passenger windows. Of particular interest were the whorls and ridges found on an empty beer can retrieved from the car's interior.

A PATHOLOGIST CONCLUDED that Yvette Howard had died from asphyxiation due to strangulation, with blunt force injury to the head as a contributing factor. Abrasions could be seen on her forehead over the left eyebrow and on the left thigh. Deep bruises marked her face, legs, and back. A sharp blow to the head had not only fractured her skull, but had caused subarachnoid hemorrhage, bleeding below the brain lining, that "could have been fatal had she not died first of strangulation."

Tests for semen and sperm were inconclusive due to decomposition.

Dick Hooper and his partner, Sgt. Ed McErlain, found several witnesses whose stories helped retrace the path Yvette had taken on her last night of life.

At a little after ten o'clock, Yvette had parked her Datsun outside a Huntington Beach bar called The Bee Hive. No one would ever know why she left her home without a word to anyone and drove directly to the bar. Inside, she took a stool next to Martin Kipp. The bartender had served both of them on previous occasions, but had never before seen them together. The issue of Yvette Howard's age, nineteen, never came up. She either had a fake ID, or wasn't asked to show one.

Detective Dick Hooper

The couple was seen chatting and drinking beer, perhaps cocktails too, over a period exceeding three hours. When they left together, at about 1:15 the next morning, both Yvette and Kipp "showed the effects of alcohol," but neither of them appeared to be sloppy drunk. If anything, Kipp seemed "less impaired" than the woman.

Just before 1:45, they turned up again inside The Bee Hive. They ordered more beer, but the bartender refused, having already announced "last call" in preparation for closing. Once again, they departed together.

Yvette and Kipp were next seen at a small, all-night restaurant near the Newport Beach Pier, just a few miles down the coast from Huntington Beach. Between two o'clock and four o'clock, in company with a "sandy-haired man," they sat in a booth and drank a bottle of champagne. When they left, Yvette discovered that she had locked her keys inside the Datsun. She borrowed a butter knife from the restaurant, and managed to open her car door. The man with them was seen driving away by himself. According to another customer, Kipp and Yvette climbed into the Datsun, and he drove it out of the parking space. But another patron of the restaurant thought they had walked toward the beach together. That was the last time anyone, other than her killer, saw Yvette Howard alive.

* * *

MARTIN KIPP HAD BEEN TEMPORARILY STAYING in a Huntington Beach apartment with Gabe Leonard, an old childhood friend. A warrant had been issued for Kipp's arrest due to accumulated traffic citations in Laguna Beach, twelve miles down Pacific Coast Highway.

At about ten o'clock on the night of December 29, Kipp had borrowed his buddy's sweater and headed to The Bee Hive bar.

When Leonard left for work at six the next morning, Kipp had not returned. Late that afternoon, though, when Leonard arrived home, Kipp was in the shower. The sweater he had borrowed lay on the floor, dirty and stained. A sour, strong body odor permeated the bedroom in which Kipp had slept. When asked why it smelled so bad, Kipp offered no explanation. He moved out that day and took a hotel room for a single night.

On January 6, Kipp went to Laguna Beach and surrendered to police on the traffic warrants. He was transported to Laguna Niguel and held pending a hearing. Meanwhile, two other police agencies had developed a strong interest in Martin Kipp,

Detective Dick Hooper in Huntington Beach had entered fingerprints collected from the orange Datsun into a new statewide identification system. Some of the prints belonged to Kipp. His rap sheet showed that he had served time in prison for rape.

IN LONG BEACH, fifteen miles to the northwest in Los Angeles County, investigators wanted to interview Kipp in relation to the rape-murder of nineteen-year-old Tiffany Frizzell. She had flown from Seattle-Tacoma International Airport on September 15, 1983, checked into a motel, and telephoned her mother to tell her of a safe arrival. Tiffany's body was found two days later sprawled on the bed of her motel room. A belt someone had used to strangle her still encircled her neck. The only clothing on Tiffany was a sweater pulled up over her face. The bed had apparently not been slept in, but the bedspread had been folded over the body. Semen and sperm were found in her vagina and on the external genital area. Investigators had located a fingerprint on a telephone in the room, and it matched Martin Kipp's prints in the state computer.

Two days after discovery of the body, a canvas bag was recovered from shrubbery in a Long Beach residential neighborhood. Among the contents were a woman's wet bathing suit, panties, a book in which Tiffany had written her name, and other personal items. Kipp's fingerprints turned up on the book's cover. Detectives located a female acquaintance of Martin Kipp who said she had seen the canvas bag and its contents in a van used by Kipp.

Another item of evidence turned up when detectives canvassed pawnshops in the city. On October 13, Kipp had pawned a radio. When a technician dismantled it, he found Tiffany Frizzell's fingerprint on a battery.

BOTH DICK HOOPER AND THE LONG BEACH homicide team found good reasons for wanting Martin Kipp when they examined his criminal history.

In June 1981, inside a Long Beach bar late at night, Kip had met Betty Young, age 22. She accepted his invitation to sit in his truck parked outside and listen to music on the stereo system. As she settled into the passenger seat, he drove away to a dark residential area. Frightened, Betty reached for the door to escape, but found the handle missing. Kipp just laughed when she demanded that he return her to the bar. He parked, forced her into the back of the truck, ripped off her clothing, and clapped a powerful hand over her mouth when she tried to scream. Terrified and struggling, she bit his palm. Kipp reacted by encircling her throat, squeezing so hard she nearly passed out. Betty felt her entire body go limp, convincing her she was going to die. In her helpless state, Kipp raped her. As she started to revive, he forced her to orally copulate him. Again, she gasped for air and nearly strangled. At last, when he relaxed, she managed to scramble away and escape into the darkness.

It didn't take the police long to track her assailant down. Kipp pleaded guilty to forcible rape and served a year in prison.

In August 1983, Kipp began traveling with a girlfriend. While they moved from town to town in a nomadic existence, he sometimes slapped or punched her. At a Coos Bay, Oregon, motel in October, Kipp insisted that she have sex with him and began removing her clothes. When she resisted, he slapped and choked her. About to pass out, she agreed to do what he wanted if she could use the bathroom first. He gave permission. She locked the door, escaped through a window, and begged the motel manager to call the police.

Later though, the woman refused to press charges. Eventually she explained her reluctance. Kipp had allegedly threatened to harm her three-year-old son if she testified against him.

He drifted back to Orange County in early September.

DETECTIVE HOOPER AND SGT. MCERLAIN, on January 10, 1984, drove to Laguna Niguel where Kipp was being held on traffic warrant charges. Officers brought the suspect to a jury deliberation room in the local courthouse. After introducing himself and his partner, Hooper mentioned that they were investigating a homicide. A witness, said the detective, had seen a guy with long hair, so they were routinely interviewing several people who fit that description.

In his soft-spoken manner, Hooper advised Kipp of his Miranda rights, then said, "What I'm wondering is, what you have been doing the last couple of weeks. Can you give me some kind of agenda, what you've been doing and where you've been?"

Kipp immediately started trapping himself with lies. "For the past couple of weeks? Oh, I just got back from Oregon, about a week ago . . . somewhere about, uh, December 31st to, uh, right now."

"Okay, this December 31st date. Is there some way you remember that?"

"Uh, just uh, basically, I don't know if that's for sure, but that's when I rode a bus from Roseburg . . . that's when I went by a friend's house."

"Where did you get off the bus, Martin?"

"Uh, Los Angeles." After a few moments he changed his mind. "It was Santa Ana."

"What time did you arrive?"

"I guess we got down there about eight o'clock in the morning."

"Do you remember what day it was? Thursday, Friday, Saturday?"

"I believe it was Thursday." December 31, 1983, was a Saturday.

In answer to Hooper's request for a few more details, Kipp mentioned that he'd met a guy on the bus, and when they arrived, the fellow's girlfriend had given them a ride to Newport Beach. Kipp couldn't seem to remember any names or addresses and could give only a vague description of the people. His activities afer arrival were just as foggy. He'd walked from Newport to Huntington Beach, stayed a few days with a friend, then spent some time in Laguna Beach, ". . . in a Motel 6 or something. . . ." There was no Motel 6 in Laguna Beach.

Kipp was able to recall that he had spent some time with a pal named Gabe Leonard, and gave his Huntington Beach address Hooper leaped on it instantly. "Have you heard any news about a girl being murdered near there? You see, coincidentally, she lived right there in that area." Kipp denied having heard about it.

HOOPER WANTED TO KNOW how Kipp traveled to Laguna on New Year's Eve. Did he walk, hitch a ride, or what? The suspect said he had taken a public transportation bus. Hooper asked for details but got fuzzy answers with mention of spending some time in a nightclub.

Had he spoken to anyone at the club? Yes, the musicians. He had stayed until closing time, then gone to a friend's house. "That was New Year's Eve," said the detective. "Was there a big party at the nightclub?"

"Yeah, they had something like that going on. Yeah, basically, whatever each bar has going, you know, but the band was playing so you couldn't really tell." Hooper wondered why he always heard that word "basically" when suspects were lying.

Kipp said he had walked to the friend's house and found some people "partying." Among them was "Sherry," a woman he'd seen earlier at the nightclub. He gave a detailed description of her, but had no idea where the detectives could find Sherry because " . . . she's street people."

"Did you go to bed with her?"

"Yes." They had spent two nights together, he claimed.

"What did you do on the next day, January the second?"

"Her boyfriend came and exchanged some heated words with me." Kipp looked disgusted, saying that Sherry hadn't told him about a boyfriend. "She didn't let me know, you know, so I cooled that down. . . . Then I went to Long Beach. On a bus."

ANOTHER STRING OF QUESTIONS FOLLOWED, seeking exact details of what he did in Long Beach. Kipp said he got a room and slept there. On January 3, he had returned to Leonard's house in Huntington Beach to see if he had any mail. Then back to Laguna Beach on a bus, where he "just crashed on the beach."

Addressing McErlain, Hooper said, "Well, why don't we show him a picture of that girl just in case it might remind him of seeing her somewhere. . . . Let's see if I know where it is." The detective pretended to fumble around through a folder, located Yvette's photo and laid it on the table in Kipp's view. "You ever see her before, ever talked with her before, ever been around her before?"

"Not that I know of. No."

"No? Pretty sure?"

"Yeah. I'd know if I'd seen her."

"Okay. All right. That girl's name is Antaya Yvette Howard. Does that name sound familiar to you at all?"

"No. Like I said, I don't know her."

"Okay. The only reason—it's kind of a coincidence she lives right down the street from where you visited. . . . You never saw her down there or anything else, huh?"

"No."

Hooper made motions like he was starting to wrap things up, then said, "Okay. Well, guess . . . Oh, one more question." He shoved another picture across the table, of a bright orange Datsun. "Uh, this car. This is hers. Have you ever seen that car before?"

"No."

"Are you sure?"

"Yeah."

"You've never been around it?"

"No. I'm positive."

"Never been in it?"

"No."

"Well, shoot," said Hooper with a sigh. "I guess — well . . . " He pulled a soiled sweater from a paper bag. "Oh, do you recognize this sweater? Have you ever seen this sweater before?"

"No."

Hooper made an incredulous sound and his voice went up one octave. "You don't know this sweater?"

"No, I don't."

"That's, uh, Gabe's sweater. He gave it to us." Kipp croaked another denial. Hooper carefully returned the garment to the bag and asked, "Well . . . have you ever gone over to a little restaurant in Newport Beach?" He named the place where witnesses had last seen the victim with Kipp. ". . . Down there at the pier. You know where that is?"

At last Kipp gave an affirmative answer. "Uh, yes I have . . . but not anytime since I've been back from Oregon."

"So how long has it been? Maybe six or seven months?"

"I guess around October or November."

"Well, who were you with?" Kipp named the girlfriend who had been with him in Oregon.

"You know, that's strange," Hooper said. "Because a witness told us they saw someone matching your description get in this orange car. You sure you've never been in it?" Kipp was positive.

NOW WITH A SCOWL and his blue eyes turning cold, Hooper said, "Sometimes guys party with women they forget. Could that have happened?" Kipp said it couldn't have possibly happened.

"Well, what we've got, Martin, is — we've got your fingerprints all over that car. Okay?"

Kipp could only manage a strangled, "Uhmm."

"You got any idea how they'd get there?"

"No."

"And we've got people identifying you with her."

A sigh escaped Kipp's thin-lipped, down-turned mouth. "Beyond me."

A little louder now, and indignant, Hooper snapped, "Beyond you? You sure you don't just want to tell us about it and get it off your chest? I can see your eyes are starting to water up and you're—well, you're pretty upset. You want to just tell us about it?"

"I tell you, I don't know her, or anyone like her in Huntington Beach."

Putting on a sympathetic face, Hooper said, "I'm sorry this whole thing has happened," and made another appeal for Kipp to confess.

"I ain't got nothin' to tell you. I don't know what to tell you about." Kipp continued to deny ever seeing Yvette Howard or her car.

"Well," said Hooper, "you know we're going to charge you with murder. You seem like a pretty calm, mellow guy. I know it's got to be a big burden to live with something like that. Sometimes it helps just to talk about it."

Sgt. McErlain leaned forward and stated, "Okay, we know that you killed her."

The direct accusation seemed to jolt Kipp. "I killed her?" Quickly regaining his composure, he reiterated the litany of denials.

HOOPER SWITCHED THE SUBJECT to Kipp's background on the Indian reservation in northwest Montana where his late father had owned a ranch. Kipp spoke of money he regularly received by mail from a fund set up by his father's will. When asked how much, he replied,

"Uh, it varies. Five thousand dollars, sometimes two thousand, some-times ten thousand. . . . He passed away, and made it clear in the will that I would receive money from the people who run the ranch. I was-n't going to run it. I told him that. So he made it clear in the will that I was going to get money." He hadn't been in Montana for at least five or six months, he said.

The brief break from the subject of murder didn't change Kipp's reluctance to admit anything. The detectives showed him a "six-pack" photo lineup, six mugshots of men, including the suspect. Hooper asked, "Why are these witnesses consistently picking your picture and saying you were the person they saw with Yvette Howard?" Kipp didn't know.

"Do you have a twin?"

"No . . . I don't have no twin brother."

Both detectives implored Kipp to explain the fingerprints and wit-nesses. "We're truth seekers. That's our job as detectives."

He maintained his innocence. "Well, as far as I know, I'm telling you the truth. Everything I've said so far.

The interview lasted thirty more minutes during which the same ground was covered repeatedly, with the same results.

Martin Kipp, in the face of overwhelming evidence, would not con-fess to anything.

THE TRIAL IN THE COURT of Judge Donald A. McCartin com-menced in June 1987. Jurors heard evidence from witnesses who had seen Yvette Howard with Martin Kipp on December 30, 1983. Experts presented evidence of his fingerprints in her car and on a beer can found inside it. Detective Hooper testified about the lies Kipp told during an interview. The defendant also faced charges in Long Beach of murder-ing Tiffany Frizzell. Because the two crimes were similar enough to show a pattern of behavior, Judge McCartin allowed facts about the Frizzell murder into the guilt phase of Kipp's Orange County trial.

The jury came back on August 14 with a verdict of guilty on the charges of murder and attempted rape, plus a special circumstance of attempted rape in connection with the murder. At the completion of the penalty phase ten days later, they recommended that Martin Kipp be put to death.

Judge McCartin, before formalizing the sentence, delivered a few comments. "This is a young man who is highly educated in the Indian culture from the tribe he belongs to. The court was impressed with what he had to say. . . . I am sure there is a good side to Mr. Kipp, and a sick side that I must deal with in this particular instance. I feel that the jury made a just and rational decision. Where do I go in weighing the aggravating versus the mitigating circumstances? It certainly is difficult. I have to look at actual killings and circumstances of crimes. I do have sympathy and pity for the defendant, his age, drugs, alcohol, and loss of parents. The court thinks he is a bright person. He doesn't have mental or physical problems that explains his violent sexual tendencies, or impaired ability to recognize right from wrong. He doesn't lack a formal education which would cause him to not conform to the requirements of society. Aggravation included a past history of violence against vulnerable victims. He was on parole at the time of the offense.

"THEN THERE WAS A YOUNG LADY in Long Beach who had her demise at the hands of this defendant. . . . His past and present behavior over the last four years show all these violent tendencies toward females, basically to satisfy his own sexual desires. He took a life-it's hard to imagine someone who can choke the life out of another human being. It doesn't appear that there is anyplace in a civilized society for the likes of Mr. Kipp. Unfortunately his conduct couldn't be condoned by his Indian culture or any other civilized culture. It's a horrendous case, one of the worst this court has ever heard. The court has feelings for Mr. Kipp as far as his good side, but can't overlook what has been presented . . . . It is the judgment, sentence, and order of this court that the defendant shall suffer the penalty of death. . . ."

Kipp was also found guilty in Los Angeles County of raping and murdering Tiffany Frizzell. He received a second death sentence.

The California Supreme Court has twice affirmed the Orange County trial and sentence.

In 1999, an execution date was signed by Judge McCartin, but a federal court granted a stay. In 2004, Martin Kipp still sits with more that six hundred other men on San Quentin's death row

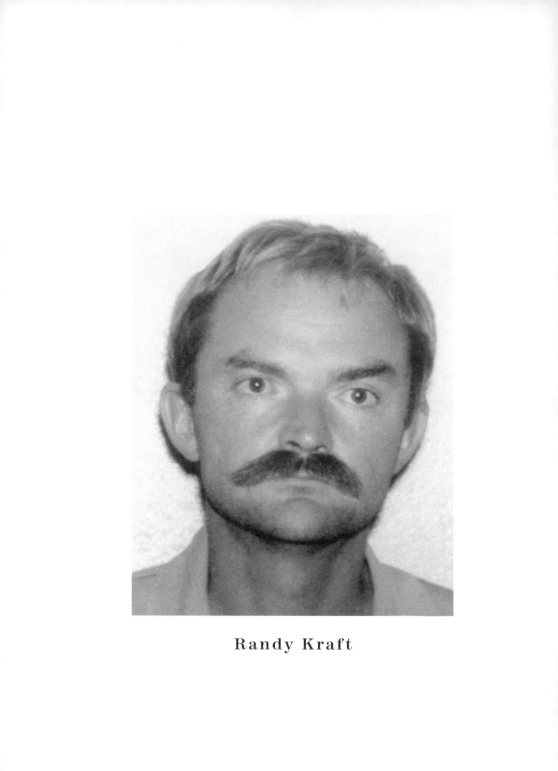

Randy Kraft

The Randy Kraft Story

Randy Steven Kraft is perhaps the most diabolical serial killer in U.S. history. In the sheer numbers of human lives snuffed out, he ranks with the confessed "Green River Killer," Gary L. Ridgway; John Wayne Gacy; and the notorious Ted Bundy. Ridgway and Bundy victimized only women, while Gacy and Kraft targeted males in their hunger for homosexual lust killing. Kraft was convicted of killing and sexually mutilating sixteen young men, but suspected of more than sixty murders.

In the early morning of Saturday, May 14, 1983, just one hour after midnight, a pair of California Highway Patrol officers followed an erratic motorist. Traveling north on the San Diego Freeway, Interstate 5, near Orange County's southern border, they watched a brown Toyota Celica weaving along in the right lane. It edged several times onto the shoulder and swerved back as if the driver might be intoxicated. Sgt. Michael Howard switched on flashing blue lights, signaling the car to pull over and stop. The driver only slowed, then appeared to grab something from behind him and toss it onto the adjacent passenger seat.

When the officer used a spotlight and issued a loudspeaker command, the Toyota finally halted. Howard would later describe the events to *Orange Counter Register* reporter Larry Welborn. "The driver began to yield to the right shoulder but he continued to drive very slowly at about five miles per hour . . . until he pulled up to a guardrail. He stopped so close to the rail that we couldn't approach the car from the passenger side."

The driver jumped briskly from the Celica and headed toward the officers. A beer bottle fell on the ground at his feet. Said Howard, "It still had some foam in it. That wasn't good for him. He was wearing those 501 button-type jeans, and all but the top one were unbuttoned. My partner made contact with the individual and directed him to the front of the Toyota, to a position of safety . . . . That's when I noticed a passenger in the reclining front seat with a jacket over his lap. He appeared to be either sleeping or passed out."

A driver's license identified the driver as Randy Steven Kraft, age 39, a resident of Long Beach, California. Patrol officer Mike Sterling put Kraft through a field sobriety test. Howard recalled, "Mr. Kraft failed, barely . . . My partner advised Kraft he was under arrest on suspicion of driving while intoxicated. He . . . handcuffed him. We asked him about the other person in the car . . . to see if he was sober enough to drive the Toyota home so Kraft wouldn't have to pay storage. Kraft said he didn't really know the guy, that he just picked him up hitchhiking."

Kraft hadn't really answered the question, so Sgt. Howard squeezed himself between the guardrail and the passenger door. "I knocked on the passenger-side window [but] got no response. I walked over to the driver's side and noticed that there was a pill vial on the floor." Howard removed the vial along with several beer bottles and placed them on the Celica's roof. "Then I saw a buck-type knife on the seat cushion. I leaned over to the passenger and I shook him. I noticed he wasn't breathing. His skin was cold and kind of clammy. There were marks on his wrists, looked like he had been bound. His pants were down around his knees and a coat covered his lap. I went back and told Mike to make sure that Randy Kraft was secured inside the patrol car, and secured well."

The routine traffic stop had opened the door to a panorama of events that would hit headlines and inspire effusive television newscasts across the country for months. Sgt. Howard knew he had an unusual situation, but did not yet realize the magnitude of it. "I told Mike Sterling, 'I think we have a dead body up there and this is either a drug overdose or the guy who is killing people and dumping their bodies all over the freeways. I was sure Kraft was watching us but he didn't make any indications. He did not bat an eye."

While they waited for the arrival of paramedics and sheriff's officers, Kraft asked Howard one question. "How's my friend?"

His "friend," slumped down in the passenger seat, a twenty–five-year-old U.S. Marine named Terry Lee Gambrel, was virtually dead. Someone had apparently tied his wrists together with the victim's own shoestrings, them removed them leaving deep ligature marks. A reddened band of skin around Gambrel's neck matched the width of his belt found in the back seat. His jeans were open and pulled down, exposing his genitals.

Frantic efforts by the paramedics, including pumping stimulants into this bloodstream and using electroshock paddles, could not revive Gambrel. He was transported to a hospital where he was pronounced dead a little after two o'clock that morning.

Randy Kraft was arrested and taken to the Orange County jail. He would never again see a day of freedom.

BORN ON MARCH 19, 1945, to a middle-class family in Long Beach, Kraft lived in loving comfort with his three older sisters. After his third birthday, the family moved to Westminster in Orange County, when citrus groves still covered most of the fields that are now industrial or residential tracts. He earned high academic marks and became profoundly interested in politics at an early age. He didn't mix well socially, though, preferring the company of a small group of intellectuals. During high school summers, he worked flipping burgers near the Huntington Beach Pier.

Pretending to admire the hordes of bikini-clad beach girls, Kraft later said he knew quite early that he was homosexual. Openly admitting it in the early 1960s, though, was just not done and could be dangerous.

Kraft graduated from Westminster High School in June 1963 near the top of his class, and worked at Disneyland that summer before enrolling at Claremont Men's College in northeast Los Angeles. There, he was isolated from the social and sexual revolution sweeping other campuses in the decade of hippies and flower power. Kraft joined the ROTC but quit when Vietnam heated up. During summer vacation from college, he made love with an African American youth, whom he awkwardly introduced to his unsuspecting family. They still didn't make the connection. At night, Kraft tended bar in a gay tavern.

Back in school, he also began to suffer from migraine headaches and stomach problems. The following summer, during nocturnal cruising of beach restrooms, he inadvertently solicited a vice cop, but lucked out with just a warning. Afterward, Kraft made a show of dating women and mixing socially. He learned to play bridge and mastered the game to an exceptional level.

IN 1968, AFTER EARNING HIS DEGREE, Kraft enlisted in the U.S. Air Force. Picturing himself as climbing the ranks to become a glamorous officer, he was disillusioned by a lesser assignment; painting aircraft and weathered buildings in the dusty, desert heat of Edwards Air Force Base. Now more openly gay while off duty, he spent weekends visiting homosexual hangouts in Los Angeles. His family tried to hide their embarrassment when Kraft's behavior caused the Air Force to dump him. He departed with a stigmatic general discharge for "medical" reasons after only thirteen months of military service.

In civilian life, Kraft bounced from job to job, dissatisfied with the routine of meaningless work. His masculine behavior and rejection of effeminate posturing affected by many gay men gave no hint of Kraft's sexual orientation. He shared an apartment with a gay roommate in a Long Beach neighborhood called Belmont Shore. In March 1970, Kraft convinced a runaway boy, age 13, to accompany him home. The humiliated youth later reported being drugged, but failed to say anything about being used sexually. Police investigators filed the case without taking any action against Kraft.

Bodies of sexually brutalized young men, many of them nude, began turning up along Southern California freeways, most of them emasculated and strangled with a wire ligature. Some remained nameless and valueless, written off as street bums who solicited the wrong homosexual trick. One anonymous victim had been carved into multiple pieces and scattered for miles.

Bored with ordinary jobs, Kraft discovered the burgeoning field of computer technology. He sharpened his natural aptitude by taking classes at California State University, Long Beach, and thereafter was easily employable in a high-tech career. At night and on weekends, he discovered the added pleasure of picking up young Marines from three bases in the region; El Toro and Tustin Marine Corps Air stations in Orange County and the massive Camp Pendleton near San Diego. It was no coincidence that one of the dead and mutilated servicemen turned up near the Cal State campus in Long Beach.

IN MARCH 1975, KRAFT GAVE A RIDE to two high school boys, drugged them, and dumped one out. The other one's severed and decomposed head was found in a marina jetty. The rattled survivor described Kraft and a classic Ford Mustang he drove. Detectives spotted it in the parking lot where Kraft had picked up the boys. They questioned Kraft, who admitted giving the dead victim a ride but insisted that he had dropped the lad off unharmed. A deputy D.A. decided that the surviving boy's word was inadequate evidence to support prosecution.

After a brief hiatus, the body count accelerated again in 1976. The first one, in January, turned up in the Saddleback Mountains of south Orange County, with an extremely high blood alcohol level. The victim's mouth and throat had been packed with muddy leaves which suffocated him. Round burns from an automobile cigarette lighter left marks all over his nude body, including his eyes. After sodomizing him, the killer had sliced off the victim's genitals and stuffed them into the anus.

The new crop, extending into 1977 and 1978, included not only Marines, transients, and gay prostitutes, but younger boys who had been shot instead of garroted. The killer, or killers, expanded the selection of disposal sites into the southern California desert. More than a dozen sexually mutilated young men were found in 1979. In June 1980, William Bonin, dubbed "The Freeway Killer," was arrested and later convicted for fourteen of the murders.

Investigators knew, though, that another predator remained at large.

Kraft acquired a new Toyota Celica in 1980. He also found another employer who utilized Kraft's computer skills in a job that required travel to other states. During these business trips, bodies kept turning up in places where Kraft spent time. At least a dozen victims died in Oregon. The killer also struck in Michigan, Connecticut, and central California. And, when Randy Kraft stayed in Long Beach, more violated bodies were discovered in the region.

In May 1983, Kraft made the mistake of driving erratically after midnight, with a dying Marine seated beside him.

A SEARCH OF THE BROWN TOYOTA Celica produced evidence that would eventually be used in court. It included a substance advertised to be an aphrodisiac for gay lovers, numerous vials of prescription drugs, most of which would induce sleep or unconsciousness, and a stack of photographs picturing nude young men, several of whom appeared to be dead. In the vehicle's trunk, investigators found a piece of yellow lined paper from a legal pad. On it were sixty–one neatly lettered, short, cryptic entries in two columns. Column one began with, "STABLE," "ANGEL," " EDM," "HARI KARI," and "AIRPLANE HILL," In between were lines reading "HAWTH OFF HEAD," "TEEN TRUCKER," and "2 IN 1 HITCH." The second column ended with, "ENGLAND," "OIL," "DART 405," and "WHAT YOU GOT."

It didn't take investigators long to realize they had stumbled on a coded list itemizing at least sixty–one of Randy Kraft's conquests, and they figured that all of them had been murdered.

FROM THE MOMENT OF KRAFT'S ARREST, an epic struggle began, a series of legal battles that would be astronomically expensive and frustrating to lawyers on both sides, and to the general public. The war of litigation would stretch over a period of five years.

Kraft filed a federal lawsuit complaining of conditions in his jail cell. He demanded that he be allowed to keep an inventory of personal bathroom supplies plus more access to television, radio, and hobby materials. In addition, he requested to have food in his cell, to receive a package of personal-use items every three months, to receive any printed material that could be legally sent through the U.S. mail, including X-rated items, a cell with electrical outlets and a television antenna, a cassette-compact disc player, plus the right to receive cassettes or CDs without censorship. He wrote, "What is tolerable detention or justifiable punishment for the overwhelming majority of jail inmates has become the petitioner's (his) entire life. . . . It is not enough for long-term human survival."

A federal judge apparently thought Kraft's lawsuit meritorious. U.S. Magistrate Ronald Rose criticized Orange County officials for not taking Kraft's complaints seriously. He called the county's arguments "inane objections." The suit was never settled to Kraft's satisfaction.

After incessant legal wrangling, motions, denials, hearings, and delays, the trial at last began on September 26, 1988, more than five years after Kraft was arrested.

Author Dennis McDougal, in his riveting book about the case, *Angel of Darkness* (Warner Books, 1991) described the setting and the key players. About Judge Donald A. McCartin, he wrote, "McCartin waited at his chamber door until everyone had a seat before making his own entrance. His gaunt, gray figure wrapped in black robes made him look a little like an absentminded grim reaper who'd misplaced his scythe. McCartin . . . speaks in a slow, graveled drawl that matches his cranky grandfatherly appearance. His sunken cheeks, wavy steel-gray hair, thin nose, and stiff, deliberate stride make him look more like an aging gunfighter than a jurist. . . . Beneath his robes, he wears rumpled shirts and casual slacks and thin, dark ties, if he wears them at all. Occasionally he shows up for court in blue jeans and bolo tie. McCartin radiates a tired competence: the day-in, day-out moodiness of a man who has assumed the tedious responsibility of meting out punishment to too many men and women who probably deserve to be punished but routinely deny that they ever broke the law."

McDougal also points out a notable record. "Of the fifty–four Superior Court judges in Orange County, McCartin had sent more convicted murderers to the gas chamber than any other—six condemned men." The judge would later mete out the death sentence to three more. As of mid-2004, none of the killers sentenced to capital punishment by McCartin have been executed.

The Randy Kraft trial would take a staggering thirteen months to complete.

PROSECUTOR BRYAN BROWN PRESENTED the state's case against Kraft. Among the scores of witnesses and hundreds of exhibits admitted was the cryptically coded death list found in his Toyota. Of the sixteen Orange County murders for which Kraft was charged, fourteen were purportedly on the list. All of the victims except Keith Crotwell, whose remains were too decomposed for analysis, had been drugged and sexually mutilated.

Those fourteen were:

"EDM": The initials of Edward Daniel Moore, 20, a Camp Pendleton Marine whose body was found near the I-605 Freeway in Seal Beach.

"AIRPLANE HILL": An unidentified body was found on a rise in Huntington Beach known locally as Airplane Hill.

"7TH St.": The body of Ronnie Wiebe, 20, was found at the 7th Street on-ramp to the I-5 (San Diego Freeway) in Seal Beach.

"PARKING LOT": Keith Crotwell, 19, had met Kraft in a parking lot not far from where the victim's head was found floating in a Long Beach marina. His skeleton turned up in Orange County.

"NEW YEARS EVE": Mark H. Hall, 22, vanished on December 31, 1975. His body was found in the Santa Ana Mountains four days later.

"EUCLID": Scott Hughes, 18, another Marine, was found dead on the Euclid Street on-ramp to a freeway intersecting Anaheim.

"JAIL OUT": Roland G. Young, 23, had been bailed out of jail the day before he disappeared. His body was found in Irvine.

"MARINE CARSON": Richard A. Keith, 20, a Camp Pendleton Marine was last seen alive leaving his girlfriend's house in Carson, Los Angeles County. His body was found in Laguna Hills, Orange County.

"HIKE OUT LB BOOTS": The body of Keith Klingbeil, 23, found near the I-5 (San Diego Freeway) in Mission Viejo, still wore hiking boots. A matchbook in his pocket was from Long Beach.

"DART 405": Michael Inderbieten, 21, was found on the shoulder of an on-ramp to the I-405 Freeway in Seal Beach.

"MARINE DRUNK OVERNIGHT SHORTS": Donnie H. Crisel, 20, a Marine from Tustin M.C. Air Station, was drunk at the time of his death and wore boxer shorts when his body was found near a freeway on-ramp in Irvine, Orange County.

"MC HB TATTOO": Robert Loggins Jr., 19, a Marine from Tustin M.C.Air Station, had tattoos and was last seen in Huntington Beach..

"2 IN 1 BEACH": Geoffrey Nelson, 18, was with Rodger De Vaul Jr. when they vanished from a beach. Nelson's castrated body was found near an on-ramp to the S-22 (Garden Grove Freeway) De Vaul was found in local mountains, with beach sand on his face.

Kraft hadn't yet entered a code on the list for Terry Lee Gambrel when he was stopped by the Highway Patrol and arrested. No code could be positively associated with the remaining Orange County victim, Eric Church, 21, whose mutilated body was found near the I-605 Freeway in Seal Beach.

Jurors watched and listened, through October and November, to Bryan Brown's presentation of facts relating to sixteen hideous, sadistic murders.

WHEN THE PARADE of more than one hundred fifty witnesses had testified, and the evidence, including 1,000-plus exhibits, were all a part of the record, Brown summarized the case for jurors. He graphically described the defendant's modus operandi. Kraft would befriend a targeted youth, in a bar, on the beach, or by picking up hitchhikers. He would offer free beer, laced with strong sedatives. When the victim was incapacitated, Kraft would bind them, sometimes using the helpless person's own shoelaces. The young men could only recline in horror as Kraft used a cigarette lighter from his car, a broken vodka bottle, or a buck knife to torture, maim, and mutilate them. From the location of burn marks, Kraft always seemed to administer his nightmare from the victim's left side. Jurors could easily visualize Kraft in the driver's seat turning to torture his passenger.

One victim, said Brown, was castrated before the drugs could even knock him out. The killings always took place in the predawn hours, often on weekends or holidays. Victim Mark Hall had suffered terribly on New Year's Day. Lighter burns were found on his eyes, chest, and genitals. A swizzle stick was driven into the length of his penis, penetrating his bladder, before he was castrated. Hall died choking on dirt and leaves jammed into his mouth. Cigarette butts around the victims' bodies told a horrific story of Kraft stopping for a smoke while he admired his work. The killer photographed many of his victims so he would have mementos. But those pictures and his coded death list were his undoing.

THE PROSECUTION'S CASE LASTED until the final day of November. The defense team, James Merwin and C. Thomas McDonald, requested a hiatus until January 30, 1989, to prepare their case. They used nine weeks attempting to persuade jurors that Kraft had killed no one. Much of their strategy revolved around theories of alternate predator. The notorious "Freeway Killer," William Bonin had been working his horror: kidnapping, raping, and killing young males in 1979 through 1980. Los Angeles County had convicted him in 1982 of ten murders. Orange County slapped him with a second death penalty in 1983 for murdering four youths. Kraft's defenders suggested that Bonin may have been responsible for more than a few of the murders charged to their client. Other known or unknown homicidal maniacs could be responsible for pre-1979 slayings. Randy Kraft, they contended, hadn't killed any of them. The defendant did not testify.

Although the subject matter was grim, McCartin managed to lighten moods periodically with his off-the-cuff humor. During consideration for sequestering the jury, McCartin quipped that he might send them to the Bates Motel, referring to Anthony Perkins' decrepit inn where Janet Leigh's character in the classic horror film "Psycho," was stabbed to death in a shower.

Always pushing for full use of the court's time and trying to avoid excessive waste, McCartin grew impatient when lawyers frequently asked to end proceedings in mid-afternoon. He barked at the defense, "If we go any slower, we'll stop." And he aimed his barbs at the prosecution as well. Bryan Brown reciprocated by using a metaphorical reference to McCartin's known affection for dogs. The prosecutor said that if McCartin was a dog, Brown was a fire hydrant.

After the defense rested, and passionate final arguments faded away, the jury retired to consider verdicts in sixteen counts of murder with special circumstances plus assorted charges of sex perversion. On May, 12, their decisions were announced. They acquitted Kraft on the charge of sodomizing victim Rodger De Vaul Jr. It took clerk Gail Carpenter thirty minutes to read the remaining litany of guilty verdicts, all sixteen murders plus one count of sodomy and one count of mayhem in the gory castration of Geoffrey Nelson.

Now, the same jury would be required to hear penalty phase evidence and arguments.

FOR THE FIRST TIME, they heard that Kraft was suspected of killing perhaps forty–five additional victims across the country. A man who had been only thirteen-years-old when Kraft raped him told of the humiliation and life-long trauma it has caused.

The defense brought out an Episcopal priest who got carried away and started lecturing the jury about the evils of execution. McCartin put an instant halt to it. "The evidence should focus on the offenders and the offense," he scolded. Defender McDonald strenuously objected, but to no avail. McCartin came right to the point. "It's silly. It's so far afield it's stupid," he railed. "I've heard all I want to hear."

The priest asked, "Your honor, may I just add one thing?"

"No, sir, you may not!" McCartin snarled, and ordered the jury to disregard the witness's comments.

It only took one day of deliberating before a decision was reached. On August 11, 1989, the jury delivered a verdict of death.

Judge McCartin waited until November 29 before handing down the sentence. At the final hearing, he said, "Normally, this court has dealt with people who have shot, killed, or raped in passion. But here we're dealing with a man who put these victims through a long, torturous death for what some of the evidence indicates may have been possibly over as long a period of time as a weekend. They were made helpless, manipulated . . . this was sophisticated killing.

He read a few details of the savage torture and castration endured by one of the victims. "I don't know of any type of person who could do that to another human being. . . . That's the tip of the iceberg. . . ." He guessed that most people really didn't want to hear any more of the incomprehensible cruelty.

DEFENSE ATTORNEYS HAD PRESENTED speculation that Kraft may have suffered from mental disorders. "I'm a long way from reaching that conclusion," McCartin stated. "The mitigating circumstances equated against the enormity of the crime here doesn't meet the test by a long shot. In summary, unsuspecting victims were killed and mutilated. . . . Mr. Kraft demonstrated an unbelievable aggressive violent tendency toward humanity. It was done clearly to satisfy his own sexual desires. I can't imagine anyone who could do that, [even] in a scientific experiment-on a dead person, not a live person. It's unbelievable.

"I sat here for a year and I looked at Mr. Kraft and heard him ask a lot of questions. . . . I didn't see any remorse, any feelings of regret. It was like he was in another world while his trial was going on. He showed no emotion or breakdown, nothing." The judge mentioned previous death sentences he had delivered. "I can take all those aggravating circumstances in those other cases and they don't match Mr. Kraft's record. . . . If anyone ever deserved the death penalty, he's got it coming."

McCartin delivered the formal sentence that Randy Steven Kraft would be put to death in San Quentin State Prison.

Ordinarily, those words close death sentence hearings. But McCartin felt the need to say one more thing. He hoped that Kraft might at least apologize to victims' families in attendance.

"Mr. Kraft, this is probably your last chance in this courtroom to say anything."

Kraft responded. "I have few things to say. . . . I wanted to say a lot more, but Mr. McDonald has advised me not to. I take his advice. But just briefly, I would like to say I have not murdered anyone, and I believe that a full review of the record will show that. That's all."

McCartin shook his head. "I have no further comments." But he did. "Mr. Kraft, In—between you and me—and this has nothing to do with my sentencing. And it may not be proper. But now that the case is all over, I'm talking now not as a judge, but just as a person. I want to make it clear that there's nothing here that can influence my thinking on the record as far as your comments about not being guilty. That's your prerogative."

The judge said he had received two letters. "They were from the parents of children who were missing and they want to know if they are on the list. The famous list we've all referred to as containing sixty–one or sixty–five victims. There were so many unknown entries on there that have never been tied down. Somewhere down the line, with response to your legal grounds for appeals, maybe you might give some thought in your waning moments to helping these people out."

Both defense attorneys, Merwin and McDonald, leaped up, demanding the letters become a part of the record. McCartin ignored them. "One was from Corona Del Mar and the other was postmarked from somewhere in Iowa, and I didn't respond. I didn't think it would be proper and I didn't know if there was anything I could say to those boys' parents."

It was a touching appeal, to all but the defendant. Randy Kraft said nothing.

Three days later, he was on his way to San Quentin.

The trial was estimated to have cost taxpayers more than ten-million dollars.

REPORTS WERE PUBLISHED in 1990 that Randy Kraft spends his time on death row playing bridge with serial killers William Bonin, Douglas Clark, and Lawrence Bittaker. The foursome was broken up in February 1996 when Bonin was executed. No information has come forth about Bonin's replacement in Kraft's bridge circle.

Kraft is reportedly handling his own appeals through the federal courts after the California Supreme Court affirmed his conviction and death sentence.

With the ponderously slow procedures of higher courts, and the paucity of executions in California, it is not likely that Randy Kraft harbors any fear of ever facing lethal injection in San Quentin's apple-green death chamber.

James Gregory Marlow

The James Gregory Marlow Story

Author's Note

Shortly after James Gregory Marlow was convicted of murder and sentenced to death in 1992, I interviewed him in the Orange County jail . A few days later, my telephone rang. I answered, "Hello."

The voice at the other end said, "Hey, Don, this is Jim. I'm down at the corner convenience store. Can you come pick me up?" I recognized the gravelly tones. It was Marlow!

I faltered in my answer, uttering a confused, "What?"

A burst of laughter assaulted my ear. "Gotcha, didn't I?"

The practical joke had, indeed, "got" me. Here was a man waiting for a judge to hand down a death sentence now playing a little prank on someone who had visited him. I had some trouble coming to grips with it. I hadn't given him my telephone number, but it was in the directory.

Marlow corresponded with me from San Quentin during the next year. His handprinted letters expressed fear that he would be murdered by guards or other inmates, and spoke of health problems. He often addressed me as "friend." That changed after Property of the Folsom Wolf was published, detailing three murders he and his lover, Cynthia Coffman, perpetrated. I had warned him in a letter I sent on June 3,

1993, that he wouldn't like what I wrote: "I wonder if you will still call me friend when the book comes out. I have tried to be as objective and fair as possible, yet tell a compelling story that will appeal to the emotions of readers. Obviously, you are not going to come out as a choir boy in it, nor is Coffman going to look like an angel. I have written it as factually as possible, but of course I can only go by what is documented, what was covered in the trials, and what was revealed to me in interviews." Eventually, his letters tapered off, then stopped altogether.

My research had revealed a remarkably complex person in James Marlow. It's jolting to speak with an individual convicted of savagely raping and murdering two innocent young women, in addition to shooting a man to death, then find the killer intelligent, personable and humorous. An internal conflict sets in. I had visited the families of all three victims, and felt not only sympathy, but deep affection for them. They were generous, wonderful people who hadn't deserved to suffer because of the selfish, brutal acts committed against their loved ones. All during the trial I had watched Marlow and loathed him. After the interview, it was a struggle to keep from liking his personality while hating his deeds.

I really didn't regret the end of our correspondence.

The relationship between James Gregory Marlow and Cynthia Lynn Coffman began with incarceration in jail, and ended with confinement in prison.

In April 1986, just a few months after being released from Folsom State Prison in California, where he had served a term for armed robbery, Marlow, then 29, argued with this third wife, beat her up and stole a limousine she had owned before their marriage. In Barstow, halfway between Los Angeles and Las Vegas, the police grabbed Marlow and tossed him into the slammer.

While fuming in his cell, Marlow could hear loud cursing in a woman's voice echoing from down the hall. He thought it was funny. So did Marlow's cellmate who said the shouter was his girlfriend, Cyndi Coffman. Cyndi had been arrested on suspicion of drug possession. Her boyfriend was taken in on a DUI charge, but his stay in jail would be extended when officials discovered arrest warrants for his failure to pay child support.

In the cell he shared with Marlow, the boyfriend described his lustful relationship with "Cynful," and indicated he might someday marry her. They lived over on Crook Street, he said. Both men could hear her angry voice a couple of days later when she was released. Marlow, too, walked out in less than a week.

His curiosity had been aroused by the fiery sound of Coffman. He located the residence, roused her out of bed, and told her that he had promised his cellmate to visit and see if she needed anything. She did. She needed a new relationship and Marlow seemed like a good candidate. His muscles were buffed up from his time in Folsom, and his engaging personality intrigued her. Coffman might even have admired the artful tattoos she saw on his body the first time they bedded together. A flaming swastika decorated the center of his chest, and dramatic portraits of vikings covered both shoulders. The pièce de résistance was a snarling wolf tattooed on his left side. From it, he had been dubbed "Folsom Wolf" during his stay in the California prison.

Before long, Marlow and Coffman embarked on a journey together that would cost three lives and end in abject misery.

CYNTHIA COFFMAN HAD LEFT her young son with his middle-class grandparents in a decent St. Louis, Missouri, home in order to escape the humdrum life of working in a factory. A mother at age eighteen, she had afterward married the child's father, a high-school dropout fry cook. She left him two years later, worked at various jobs, and decided she needed a complete change in her life. In the spring of 1983, Coffman drove her Pontiac Trans-Am to Page, Arizona, and found a job as a bartender. Somehow, she couldn't escape the "wrong crowd" syndrome, and wound up in a shabby Barstow flea trap where her relationship with Marlow began.

James Marlow had endured a horrendous childhood. Born on May 11, 1956, in rural Kentucky to a beautiful but amoral hillbilly, he was neither loved nor wanted. His mother moved to California, where she became a drug-addicted prostitute and later reclaimed her boy and his little sister. As a young child, Marlow was taught to steal. One of his mother's boyfriends even found a way to use the lad by lowering him on a rope through holes cut in the ceilings of business establishments so he could unlock the doors. His mother took him to "parties" at which she would service men, and coax the boy to steal from their coats while she performed her business. The most horrifying tale of all came when Marlow told of an event when he was thirteen. His own mother injected him with heroin, then sexually seduced him.

Barstow held no promise for Marlow and Coffman, so they drove cross-country in a pickup she helped him steal from a friend of hers. Marlow boasted to Coffman that his father had left him an inheritance in Pine Knot, Kentucky, a little town where he had spent part of his youth. When they arrived, there was no inheritance nor anything else of value. They hooked up with a group of bikers, pals from his teen years. Drugs and booze cost them everything, including the stolen vehicle.

After Marlow had spent their last cent, a thug called "Killer" offered him a way to fill his pockets again. A man named Greg "Wildman" Hill, said the biker, had cheated him on a drug deal and needed to be dealt with. If Marlow would take care of the problem, he would be well paid.

CYNDI ACTED AS THE BAIT. Wearing revealing clothing, she knocked on Wildman's cabin door and whimpered about her car stalling at the top of an adjacent hill. Could he help her? He gallantly agreed, but slipped a pistol in the back of his jeans before leaving his cabin. They hiked up a steep slope where Marlow had concealed himself in brush near the pickup. As soon as Hill raised the hood, Marlow charged out yelling, "What the hell are you doing up here with my sister?" Angry words and gunshots echoed across the canyon. Hill, mortally wounded, dropped to the ground and was left there bleeding to death.

Cynthia Coffman

That night, Marlow and Coffman counted the payoff, $5,015. He used it to buy a Harley-Davidson "hog." It broke down, and Marlow traded it for a beat-up old Cadillac. Tensions grew between the penniless couple. She would later complain of several incidents in which he slapped and punched her.

They hit the road again, migrating to Georgia, where he found temporary work. One night, during a pool game in a bar, Cyndi's behavior with Marlow's coworkers made him jealous. Back in their motel, according to her recollection, he chopped off all of her hair, threatened to kill her, then stripped her naked and threw her outside. After a few minutes, he let her back in, and sodomized her.

Marlow lost his job. He and Coffman drifted back to Kentucky, sold the car, stole another one, and headed west. Halfway to California, in another seedy motel, he unpacked a tattoo needle, asked her to remove her underwear, and inscribed in blue letters on her left buttock, "Property of Folsom Wolf."

NEAR SAN BERNARDINO, they lived temporarily with his sister and her husband. As usual, a shortage of money plagued them. They wore out their welcome with his brother-in-law and sought a night's shelter in Fontana, with a friend of Marlow's who lived in a squalid apartment that had once been a Route 66 auto court. The next day, November 7, 1986, they both dressed in their best clothing, Marlow in an ill-fitting suit, and Coffman in a blue dress, purportedly to look for employment. They rode with his sister to her job at a mall in Redlands, southeast of San Bernardino. While the sister worked, Marlow and Coffman wandered around aimlessly most of the day. Back at the mall, they loafed away more time sitting in the vehicle. A new, white Honda CRX nosed into the parking place opposite them and a beautiful young woman exited.

Marlow could see dollar signs written all over her, reasoning that a girl driving such a new car must have money. He and Coffman immediately hatched a plan in which Cyndi would ask the Honda owner for a ride when she returned. Fifteen minutes later, Coffman said to Corinna Novis, "Excuse me. You look like a student. Are you going over to the college? Our car is broken down and we sure could use a ride over there." It would later be debated whether Novis willingly allowed them into her car, or was forced.

Corinna, 20, had moved from Gooding, Idaho the previous year to attend Redlands University. A high school cheerleader in her hometown, Corinna had grown up in a wholesome, rural community where people never locked doors and everyone knew each other. Her parents were hard-working, decent, middle-income people. After completing one year of junior college, Corinna arranged a transfer to Redlands University. By working at a State Farm Insurance agency, and attending college classes in the remaining hours, Corinna was able to pay a down payment on the Honda CRX. If the predatory couple thought they had targeted a rich college girl, they were badly mistaken.

With Coffman sitting on Marlow's lap in one of the car's two bucket seats, and Corinna driving, they traveled several miles before Marlow jammed a gun into Corinna's ribs. He ordered her to stop so Cyndi could take over at the wheel. "Please," Corinna begged, "don't hurt my car. It's new and I'm really trying to take care of it. Please don't wreck it or anything."

WITHIN A HALF-HOUR, they arrived at the grungy apartment where they had spent the previous night. Marlow handcuffed Corinna to a bed, rifled her purse until he found an ATM card, and began grilling her for the personal identification number. Coffman helped persuade her to surrender it. Then, according to Coffman, Marlow stripped the captive's clothing off and forced her into a mildewed shower. Later accounts by both Coffman and Marlow were contradictory, each one blaming the other for initiating and acting out a sexual assault against the victim. According to Marlow's resident buddy, who had parked himself in front of a television set the whole time, both "Greg" and Cyndi emerged from the bedroom with wet hair.

After dark, Marlow escorted Corinna from the bedroom and out to the Honda. His buddy noticed that the captive's mouth was covered with gray duct tape, her hands cuffed behind her back, and a green jacket draped over her shoulders. Marlow pushed her into a space behind the vehicle's seats, made her crouch down, and covered her with a sleeping bag. With Coffman driving again, they eventually wound up in a deserted rural grape vineyard on the lower slope of a hill. It would be several days before anyone knew what happened to Corinna Novis.

At nine o'clock that same night, Coffman inserted Corinna's ATM card into a slot outside a bank, and punched in the PIN number. Nothing happened. "The bitch gave us a phony number," Coffman howled. Marlow searched the car's glove box and found Corinna's apartment address, near the campus. A little later, the scavenging couple broke into Corinna's residence, rummaged around until they located her bank book with the PIN neatly printed in it, stole a few other items, and rushed back to the bank. The number worked this time, but frustrated the two thieves. Corinna had a balance of fifteen dollars, not even enough for a withdrawal since the machine dispensed only twenty–dollar bills.

The greedy plan to kidnap a wealthy girl and gain riches had failed miserably.

THE NEXT DAY, Saturday, they drove about seventy miles to Huntington Beach and cruised up and down Pacific Coast Highway all afternoon. Uncomfortable and hungry, they dozed in a sleeping bag on the beach that night and in the car Sunday night.

On Monday, when Corinna failed to show up at her State Farm job, her boss tried to contact her. Failing to reach her by telephone, she drove to the apartment, entered, and found it ransacked. She called the Redlands police.

Meanwhile, that same morning, Cynthia Coffman walked into a branch of Corinna's bank, produced the account book, a driver's license, and wrote a check for fifteen dollars. She and Marlow ate their first meal in two days at a Laguna Beach Taco Bell. When they had finished, Marlow stuffed Corinna's identification papers, including her driver's license and checkbook, into the empty bag, and then asked Coffman for her ID. He added his own cards, bundled the whole package, and tossed it in a trash bin behind the restaurant. When Coffman asked why, he explained that if they were stopped in a stolen car, they certainly didn't want the cops to be able to identify them. They could lie and give fake names. It probably wasn't what a cunning, master criminal would have done, but to Marlow, it seemed a good idea at the time.

On the following morning an employee of the neighboring Kentucky Fried Chicken restaurant picked up some debris that had blown over from Taco Bell. Some papers fell out of a bag, and he took them inside to his boss who made a quick examination and called the police.

DESPERATE AGAIN FOR MONEY, Marlow and Coffman pried open a soft-drink dispenser in the Huntington Inn, a three-story motel on Pacific Coast Highway, and raided the coin box. The loot paid for a couple of meals and some gas, which allowed them to continue drifting back and forth like flotsam in the pounding Pacific surf. On the afternoon of Wednesday, November 12, they parked near a dry cleaning store called Prime Cleaners. Marlow figured they could rob it. Inside, an attractive nineteen-year-old employee, Lynel Murray, eagerly anticipated her plans for that evening.

Lynel's life had settled into a pleasant routine. Her mother, Nancy, admired Lynel's strong sense of responsibility manifested by her determination to not only attend school at Golden West College, but to be self-supportive by working at the cleaners. While still in high school, Lynel and her boyfriend had been the driving force behind the establishment of a peer counseling center for troubled students who needed a sympathetic ear and sound advice.

On that Wednesday, Lynel and her boyfriend planned to rent a couple of movies, order some pizza, and spend a cozy time in the condominium Lynel shared with her mother and sister. At 6:20 p.m., she spoke to him by phone and agreed to meet promptly at 6:45 near the video store.

Just before closing time, 6:30 p.m., Marlow and Coffman barged into Prime Cleaners. He carried his rumpled suit coat in his hands and told the courteous, smiling young woman he wanted it cleaned. Glancing around, he and Coffman made certain no one else was present. Marlow pulled out a handgun. After binding and gagging Lynel with handcuffs and duct tape, they extracted about two hundred dollars from the cash register. From customers' clean apparel hanging on racks, they selected clothing that would fit them. In a back room, they stripped and changed. Coffman, carrying Lynel's purse, exited and drove the Honda to a rear entrance, where Marlow forced Lynel into the car. They headed for the Huntington Inn. At the reception desk, Coffman used Lynel's credit card to register for a room. Big mistake.

Lynel's failure to show up at 6:45 made her boyfriend realize something must be wrong. When all efforts to locate Lynel failed, he and her family contacted the Huntington Beach police. Detective Dick Hooper was assigned to the case.

IN ROOM 307 AT THE HUNTINGTON INN, Marlow locked his captive in the bathroom. Furious with Coffman for using Lynel's credit card to check in, he criticized her, then finally suggested she go out and get them some food.

Coffman drove first to a Bank of America ATM and cleaned out Lynel's checking account, withdrawing one hundred and forty dollars. At a McDonald's restaurant she ordered hamburgers with french fries and drinks for three. Returning to the room, she noticed that both Marlow and Lynel had wet hair. Coffman later said, "I knew what had happened. He had done the same thing that he had done to the other girl."

While they ate, Lynel cringed in terror on the bed's corner. Coffman offered the trembling girl a Big Mac. Lynel couldn't eat, but tried to sip some of the soft drink. When Coffman had finished, she told Marlow she wanted to take a shower. He assented, but cautioned her to hurry. He wanted to leave the place soon, fearful that police would soon learn of their presence due to Coffman using Lynel's credit card to check in.

In Coffman's chilling subsequent account of what happened next, she quoted Marlow's order. "You are going to kill this one."

She said that he ripped a towel into long strips and used them to bind the captive. Coffman looped a strip around Lynel's neck ". . . like he told me, and I started to pull the towel. She was lying on her stomach, and I just . . . started to pull. Greg was standing there watching me. Well, I couldn't do it. And so he took one side and started pulling while I was on the other side. . . I stopped because my fingernails were digging in my hand and cutting the palms. . . . He pushed me out of the way and said, 'I'll do it. Get out of here.'"

ACCORDING TO COFFMAN, Marlow ordered her to run some water in the tub. She complied, filling it six inches deep. "He picked up Miss Murray and took her in the bathroom and put her head in the water and her legs were over the toilet. . . . We started getting ready to leave. And he went back in the bathroom. He urinated on her."

They scrambled around the room, picking up their few possessions, hurried to the Honda, and drove away in the gathering fog of a cold November night.

An hour later, Marlow and Coffman checked into a luxurious Ontario motel forty miles from Huntington Beach, again charging it to Lynel Murray's credit card. Dressed up in clothing they had stolen from the Prime Cleaners, they found a nearby all-night restaurant. A waitress would one day report that while they waited for a table, she saw them locked in a loving embrace, kissing passionately. When their table was ready, the waitress hesitated to notify them. "They were hugging so I had to wait until they were through."

During the meal, the table server said, Marlow seemed serious and glum. Coffman, though, was ebullient and smiling brightly while she ordered the "hearty steak and shrimp for two" followed by Chablis wine. Coffman paid for the meal with Lynel's credit card, and added a generous ten-dollar tip. Afterward, she again used the card to buy a bottle of champagne, which they took back to the hotel room. The next morning, Marlow and Coffman visited a drug dealer to buy methamphetamine, then returned to the home of a San Bernardino friend where they had previously stayed.

AT THE HUNTINGTON INN, an employee made a horrifying discovery in Room 307. Lynel Murray's partially clothed body sprawled face down over the bathtub's rim, with her right leg on the toilet seat, her left leg on the floor, and her face submerged in water. The black skirt she wore was twisted, the white blouse ripped open, and her maroon bra was missing. Deep bruises marked the victim's back, ribs, and face. Both of her eyes had been blackened. Her neck, scalp, and nose were battered and bruised, and her left hand was twisted behind her back.

When a drowsy James Marlow opened the morning newspaper, he snapped wide awake. A large picture of a white Honda CRX, next to photos of a missing college student named Corinna Novis, accompanied an article asking for the public's help to locate a car like the one depicted. "We gotta ditch the car!" Marlow shouted.

Fleeing into the San Bernardino Mountains, Marlow and Coffman pulled onto a dirt road, threw a few branches over the Honda, then hitchhiked to a town at Big Bear Lake. People who saw them would later report how peculiar they looked; Marlow in a suit with heavy boots, and Coffman wearing a lightweight black and white dress with high heels. In the icy mountain air, their garb attracted unwanted attention. After checking in at a lodge, they sauntered into a sporting goods store and bought bathing suits to use in the hotel's Jacuzzi. It took several minutes for approval to come through on Lynel Murray's credit card. A little while later, the couple shopped for more appropriate apparel at a clothing store. They piled their selections on a counter, and waited for another approval on Lynel's credit card for the $255 bill. A read-out panel on the authorization machine gave instructions to "Call in."

"What's taking so long?" Coffman asked. The suspicious clerk made an excuse. Coffman snatched the card and rushed outside where Marlow waited. They both ran.

Nancy Murray, Lynel's mother, received a call at her Huntington Beach home. She grabbed the telephone, desperately hoping for news about her missing daughter. Instead, it was a Bank of America representative reporting that someone in Big Bear was attempting to use a credit card in Lynel Murray's name, and asking if it should be authorized. Nancy's heart nearly stopped and she asked for a description of the user.

"Oh, she's medium height, thin, and has very short, dark hair." Nancy's first thought was to wonder, if someone had abducted Lynel, why they had cut her beautiful long hair off? In an instant, she knew that was wrong, and told the caller to notify the police.

Just a short time later, Dick Hooper and another detective performed one of the most difficult tasks associated with their job. They knocked on the condominium door where Lynel had lived with her mother. When Nancy answered, with her former husband, Don Murray, standing behind her, Hooper spoke softly. "I'm sorry, Mrs. Murray." She screamed and collapsed into Don's arms.

Marlow and Coffman, realizing they may have been detected by use of the credit card, decided not to use the room they had rented at the lodge. As the sun dropped, dragging down the temperature with it, they walked several miles to the site of a new home under construction. Behind it were massive boulders with a cave-like hollow between them, and a portable toilet that could be useful. The fugitives crawled between the boulders and squatted in the chilly cave, like two wild animals. They hadn't eaten for almost twenty–four hours. To ease their discomfort, they used the last of their methamphetamine, or "speed." Their final night of freedom was cold, sleepless, and miserable.

In the misty mountain dawn, with clouds threatening rain or snow, Marlow said, "We gotta get outta here. But we better not wear these clothes. The cops might have a description of them. We need to change."

"Into what?" Coffman asked.

"The bathing suits." It was another idea of his that defied logic. Yet, an hour later, they were seen marching down the main road, clad in bathing suits in chilly forty-degree weather. Marlow also wore his white shirt while Coffman had slipped a sweater on. They didn't notice when a shuttle bus driver glanced at them and picked up his two-way radio mike. A few minutes later, four San Bernardino sheriff's deputies pinned the two fugitives between two patrol cars, leaped out, and yelled "Freeze!" It was an appropriate command considering the temperature. James Marlow and Cynthia Coffman meekly complied, were hand-cuffed, and transported to jail in Redlands.

In separate interviews, they both asked for lawyers. Dick Hooper had raced across two counties to question Coffman. He ignored her request for legal representation. Hooper knew full well that anything she might say to him could never be used in court, due to his violation of the Miranda rights, but he didn't care. His primary goal, at that point, was to find out if Corinna Novis was still alive and where she was. Working with Redlands homicide detective Scotty Smith, Hooper pumped Coffman with questions and tried appealing to her compassion. When they showed her a photograph of Corinna, Smith later said, "She just stared at the picture and showed no outward visible signs." After several hours, Coffman began to open up and reveal details of both murders, blaming everything on Marlow.

When Marlow heard of her betrayal, he budged only enough to say the responsibility was "fifty–fifty."

Hooper, using an often successful interview technique, let Coffman think that Marlow had not only confessed, but had also blamed her for both murders. She later stated, "They said that he had already confessed and told them generally where [Novis] was, but I had been driving so that I would be able to show them better."

At about 3 a.m., November 15, Coffman sat in the back seat of an unmarked car with Scotty Smith beside her. Hooper drove with another detective seated beside him. A fourth officer followed in his car. Coffman gave directions to the deserted grape vineyard. They parked and left one member of the team to guard Coffman while the other three launched a search for Corinna.

Using flashlights in the eerie vineyard, they searched for signs of recent digging. One of the men yelled, "Hey, over here I think I've found it. Hooper sprinted over, dropped to his knees, and clawed at the sandy soil. Within a few moments, one of his hands came in contact with cold human flesh. They had located the shallow grave of Corinna Novis.

WHILE JAMES MARLOW and Cynthia Coffman waited for the legal process to begin in San Bernardino County, they wrote erotic letters to each other. Not once did either of them ever note any regret for taking three lives.

In 1989, at a joint trial in which each defendant testified, Marlow and Coffman were found guilty of murdering Corinna Novis, with special circumstances of kidnapping, rape, and sodomy.

The jury recommended the death penalty for both of them, and a judge agreed. Coffman was the first woman in California to be sentenced to capital punishment since the law was restored in the late 1970s. Only four women have been executed in the state's history.

In Orange County, Marlow and Coffman faced trial for murdering Lynel Murray. At first it appeared they would be tried together in the court of Judge Donald McCartin, but Coffman's attorney, Leonard Gumlia, was granted a separate trial for his client. With the insurmountable evidence, there was no doubt of her guilt, so Gumlia's primary goal was to save Coffman from a second death sentence.

He succeeded. After an arduous penalty phase, the jury returned with a recommendation of life without the possibility of parole. But the death sentence from San Bernardino County remained intact. Coffman was sent to a new facility near Chowchilla in central California, to begin populating the death row for women.

IN MARCH 1992, Marlow was tried in McCartin's court, represented by appointed defender George Peters. The affable Peters had once been a prosecutor with the Orange County District Attorney's Office. He recalled losing his first case to a brilliant defense attorney, Donald A. McCartin.

Addressing the jury in his opening statement, Peters said, "We are virtually conceding the guilt phase. I will cross-examine very little, and we may plead guilty." But, he explained, Marlow had experienced a "horrific" childhood that had sent him on a path of self-destruction, drug usage, and psychological problems. Thus, his life should be spared.

After prosecutor Bob Gannon presented the state's case through the voices of thirty–three witnesses, Peters stepped forward and changed Marlow's plea to guilty. The jury would not need to deliberate regarding guilt, but would hear penalty phase evidence of aggravation and mitigation, then decide on a penalty of life in prison or death.

In Coffman's trial, most of the evidence was pointed at Marlow's guilt. But Marlow, testifying outside the jury's presence in a special hearing, refused to implicate her. He said, "I can plead to my own participation. . . . I am guilty of murder." Pressed by Gannon, he wouldn't relent. "I strangled Lynel Murray and I plead guilty to that."

Peters informed the jury that Marlow's reluctance to implicate his former lover may have been motivated by fear for his own security in jail. Snitches were often treated harshly by fellow inmates.

Marlow's "chaotic" childhood was replayed for the jury with

emphasis on abuse he suffered, his mother's abominable treatment of the boy, and how these experiences scarred him for life. A doctor testified and revealed that Marlow had told him how Coffman, who claimed to have been forced by Marlow to participate in Lynel Murray's murder, had actually planted her knee in the middle of Lynel's back during the strangulation.

Marlow on the stand

The jury listened intently, and retired to deliberate. It took them only six hours. On March 30, McCartin's clerk, Gail Carpenter, read the verdict aloud. James Gregory Marlow should suffer the penalty of death.

ON FRIDAY, MAY 8, Marlow stood before the assembled court, dressed in the orange coveralls of inmates, trying to hold back his tears. He stammered, "I have been involved in some evil things. I am sorry is very inadequate. . . . If you gave me a thousand lifetimes, I couldn't . . . compensate for any part of this." He wondered aloud if he would live long enough to ever reach the gas chamber, feeling that he would probably be assassinated first by other inmates. "The fear of death has got to be worse than death itself. . . ." He apologized profusely and said, "I am sorry to God, and I am sorry to society, and I am very sorry to the Murray family. If I could give myself to the Murray family to torture me, I would do that."

JUDGE McCARTIN WAS IMPRESSED with Marlow's contrition. Very few murderers, he would later say, ever demonstrated convincing remorse. He believed Marlow truly meant what he said. In McCartin's preface to handing down the sentence, he stated, "This has been an extremely difficult case for me. It doesn't seem like the fellow sitting in front of me could have committed these crimes. He appears to be a changed person. I have no doubt that he is sincere and remorseful."

The volatile relationship between Marlow and Coffman, McCartin said, created a chemistry that made them a deadly team. "When these two people got together, a third person arose and did these horrendous crimes. Mr. Marlow would not have done these acts if he had not connected up with Miss Coffman. . . . It's a given that he's a victim of abuse."

It sounded as if McCartin was going to overrule the jury's recommendation of death and impose life without parole. But he stayed true to his beliefs. "The jury's verdict was proper," he stated, and approved the death sentence, ". . . as much as I would like to do otherwise."

LATER DISCUSSING HIS DECISION, McCartin said, "When it comes to whether you're going to set aside the death penalty, I didn't go through any special process. They were always so overwhelmingly deserving of it. With Marlow, though . . . he seemed to be kind of a regular guy who just went haywire somewhere. The others were sociopaths with no conscience. I didn't think Marlow was like that. I gave some consideration to setting aside the death penalty because he came forward and said 'I did it.' He is the only one out of all my death penalty cases who had that decency and did not maintain his innocence. . . . But in the end, there was not enough mitigation to set aside the death penalty."

Marlow and Coffman have been on death row twelve years.

Their automatic appeals to the California Supreme Court have yet to start.

Gregory Sturm

The Gregory Sturm Story

Two headline stories ran side by side in both the *Los Angeles Times* and *The Orange County Register* on May 9, 1992, reporting remarkable connections between two separate events. Both took place in a single courtroom on the previous day. Both articles were about killers named Gregory. Both Gregorys had murdered three people and were tried by the same judge, Donald A. McCartin. Both men wound up on San Quentin's death row. In both cases, the juries had deliberated six hours to arrive at verdicts.

One article presented details of James Gregory Marlow being sentenced to death.

The other article announced a jury verdict convicting Gregory Sturm of a triple murder.

JUST BEFORE NINE O'CLOCK ON MONDAY MORNING, August 20, 1990, a store manager opened the Super Shops auto parts outlet operated in Tustin, California. Everything at first appeared normal to him. He made a mental note to remove the "Grand Opening" signs painted on front windows three months earlier. The manager expected employees to show up soon, ready to take care of customers and keep the shelves properly stocked with a line of high-performance parts the chain store sold.

Inside, he headed for his office. Three of his young male employees had labored all day Sunday, but they were reliable workers and would no doubt show up any minute. Darrell Esgar, as assistant manager, should be the first to arrive in order to help with store-opening procedures.

AS THE MANAGER WALKED PAST the customer area, through endless shelves of stock, and toward the back of the building, he glanced into a storage room. His world momentarily went into a crazy spin like a merry-go-round gone berserk. A nightmarish scene vacuumed his breath away.

Darrell Esgar, 22, lay in a frozen position on his back, his head resting in a puddle of congealed blood, his ankles wrapped with transparent tape. His right hand still clutched the tape dispenser on his chest. Russel Williams, 21, reposed on his left side, bent at the waist into an L shape. Blood from his head pooled around Esgar's feet. Both his wrists and ankles had been bound with the same kind of tape. Chad Chadwick, 22, in a sitting position, leaned nearby against a pile of white cardboard boxes marked with streaks of red. His ankles had also been restrained. Blood and brain matter adhered to the right side of his head. Shreds of the clear tape remained on his left wrist, suggesting that he might have torn it loose before someone took his life.

All three had died from gunshot wounds to their heads. Investigators tentatively announced that robbery was the motive for the murders since approximately $1,100 had been stolen. The crime had taken place sometime after the store closed at 5 p.m. on Sunday.

Homicide investigators worked all day Monday and kept going all night. At about 1:45 Tuesday morning, Detective Nasario Solis caught sight of a young man pressing his face against a front window and peering in. He sent an officer to see who the person was and why he was so

curious. After a brief interrogation in which the voyeur presented identification, mentioned that he was a former store employee, and was just
wondering what had happened, he was allowed to leave.

DETECTIVE NANCY RIZZO of the Tustin Police Department interviewed customers who had been in the Super Shops prior to its 5 p.m.
closing on Sunday. One man who had left at 4:55 spoke of seeing a fellow who stood about six feet tall, had brown hair, was stocky, looked to
be in his mid-twenties, and wore a faded yellow T-shirt on which the
words "Super Shops" were printed. This description matched the
voyeur who had been trying to see what happened.

Another investigator, Ron Frazier, received a call from a friend. The
caller said her roommate, an employee at Super Shops, had loaned a
gun to a man named Gregory Sturm who had recently been fired from
the auto parts store. Frazier contacted the gun owner and learned that
the Taurus .38 caliber weapon had been given to Sturm on Sunday
morning.

The owner, acting on a request by Frazier, telephoned Sturm and
asked him to return the gun. On Monday, Sturm promptly complied,
after which an investigator retrieved the weapon for laboratory testing.
It had recently been fired.

EVERYTHING SO FAR POINTED to Gregory Sturm as a suspect in
the murders. Detective Solis learned that Sturm had worked nearly
three months at the Tustin store and had been terminated for theft on
August 10. Sturm, a manager said, had a cocaine addiction problem, was
a "hothead" who "flies off the handle easily," and had frequently failed
to show up at work.

Detective Ron Frazier of the Tustin Police Department, sent word
to Sturm asking him to come in voluntarily for an interview. Sturm con-
sented.

Frazier, with Lt. Harold Williams, began the questioning at 3:15 p.m. on Tuesday. Sturm acknowledged being a former employee of the Super Shops store. He had worked there until "four days ago in sales and service." He usually rode a bicycle to the store, but sometimes drove his girlfriend's blue four-door Nissan.

Frazier asked, "Did you quit or were you fired?"

"I was told to resign. . . ." His attendance had been unsatisfactory.

FRAZIER WANTED TO KNOW if Sturm had been in the store on Sunday, August 19. Sturm at first nodded and said he had been there at about five–thirty, then quickly asserted that he had not entered, but had only spoken to his friend, Darrell Esgar, just outside the door. After answering a number of other questions, Sturm revised his story. He had been inside, he admitted, but couldn't recall exactly how far into the showroom he had gone. He definitely hadn't passed behind the counter. Asked about the handgun, he admitted borrowing a shotgun from a buddy to use in shooting practice out in the desert. It was in a case. Possibly, said Sturm, a handgun could have been inside the case as well, but he hadn't seen it.

"You live in Riverside?" asked Frazier.

"Yeah, basically, but I stay at my girlfriend's place in Tustin a lot of the time." There was that word, "basically," the hallmark of suspects who are not telling the truth. His girlfriend's apartment was a short distance from the Super Shops store.

Frazier inquired, of the three slain men, which one had Sturm known best?

"Uh, probably Darrell. Darrell and Chad. I didn't know Russ."

"What do you think happened to them?"

"They were probably robbed." He added, "It sucks. I mean this—there's no reason why someone should kill three people in cold blood like that. . . . I'm not—I mean it's just pointless. If I hadn't lost my job,

I would have been there, and that's why I've been sick all day. . . . If I hadn't fucked up . . . I'd be dead now."

To Frazier's question about drugs, Sturm candidly admitted daily use of cocaine.

Before he was released, a police photographer took Sturm's picture. It portrays a smirking self-assuredness in a young man with thick, dark curly hair, a light mustache, and a growth of chin whiskers about two days old.

A few hours later, the witness who had seen a customer wearing a yellow Super Store T-shirt examined a photo lineup of six men. He eliminated all but the one of a smirking youth, but couldn't state with absolute certainty that it was the person he had seen.

Ballistic examination confirmed recent firing of the .38 caliber Taurus handgun Sturm had reportedly borrowed. Additional tests revealed that several slugs removed from the three victims, plus one that had lodged in a cardboard box, had been fired from the weapon.

On Wednesday, Detective Rizzo obtained a search warrant for an apartment rented by Sturm's girlfriend where the suspect had been living recently. Rizzo collected a yellow Super Shops T-shirt and blue shorts stained with what appeared to be blood spatters. She asked Sturm's girlfriend if she knew where he might be. The young woman said she had telephoned Sturm that morning at a friend's house in Riverside to let him know the police were looking for him.

It would later be reported that Sturm had dropped the phone, muttered that his father was ill, and ran from his buddy's residence. The next day, Thursday, the girlfriend's father found Sturm sleeping in his back yard. The police were summoned and took him into custody, this time as a primary suspect for murder.

GREGORY STURM, HUSKY at one inch over six feet, 220 pounds, had always been a rebel, even as a child. He lived with mother and stepfather until age fourteen, then ran away to Virginia to stay with his biological father whom he had never before met. He returned to California when he turned eighteen and worked in various non-skilled jobs until he landed a position with Super Shops.

A second interview, also conducted by Detectives Ron Frazier and Solis began shortlyafter noon, on Thursday, August 23.

AFTER THE OFFICERS allowed Sturm to make a couple of personal phone calls, and gave him the customary Miranda advisory, Sturm said he was willing to talk without a lawyer. He admitted he hadn't "told the complete truth before." Frazier asked the suspect to describe his activities on the previous Sunday.

Sturm said he had been at his girlfriend's apartment most of the morning. "Later that afternoon, she gave me a kiss and left." He spoke falteringly, as if trying to properly word his next comment. "After that, an acquaintance of mine—okay, a drug connection—I saw him all of a sudden like—and then I woke up Monday morning."

He had left a huge gap between meeting his drug supplier and waking up Monday morning, failing to account for his activities when the slayings took place.

Sturm's responses to several follow-up questions remained equally vague. Solis asked, "What do you know about the murders?"

"I didn't—I was told no one would get hurt."

Puzzled, the detective asked him to explain. Sturm began a rambling account in which he had been visited by an acquaintance named "John Davis, a Mexican" from an apartment complex called "the war zone" where drugs are sold. Sturm and "Davis" had "done a line of cocaine, about four–thirty in the afternoon, said the suspect. "He kind of made a reference, you know . . . there's a lot of money down there. I said, 'Yeah, there is. But it's in the safe.' Then, fuck it, I showed him the guns I had borrowed."

"Which guns?"

"A shotgun and a thirty–eight." Sturm at last admitted that the murder weapon had been in his possession. "Davis said, 'Let me use it.' I asked, 'What for?' He goes, 'Well, I want to get some money.' And I asked him how and he said, 'Well, I'll rob 'em.' "

"Rob who?" Solis asked.

"Super Shops." According to Sturm's maundering account, he rode his bicycle to the store while "Davis" drove a car. "I went down there and there was a little bit of gibberish back and forth. He talked, I talked. I went outside and Darrell was talking to him. and then I rode off and that's the last I heard." He insisted that he had left and knew nothing about how the three young men had died.

"What happened after that?"

Sturm claimed he had returned to the apartment. The mysterious drug dealer named Davis had shown up later. "He brought the thirty–eight and said he didn't use it." Sturm admitted handling the gun, perhaps thinking it would account for his fingerprints possibly found on the murder weapon.

DURING THE NEXT HALF HOUR, both detectives took turns interrogating Sturm about specific details of his visit to the shop. Solis then asked, "How can we find this drug dealer, John Davis?" Sturm advised they would have to check around the "war zone" apartments and look for a guy about five–eight or five–nine wearing a red corduroy hat who spoke with an accent.

Regarding his being fired from the store, Sturm explained he has been suspected of stealing money to feed his drug habit, but it had been a mistake. He denied stealing anything.

A series of questions about work procedures culminated with, "Who knew the combination to the safe?" Without hesitation, Sturm said Darrell Esgar and a manager both knew it. It surprised the interrogators when Sturm also admitted that he knew what the inside of the floor safe looked like. He had seen it several times when money was deposited at closing time.

Solis asked, "Did this John Davis ever see the safe?"

"No, he never went over there with me before." They had met only at the "war zone" and at the apartment Sturm shared with his girlfriend.

"Why did you give the gun to this John?"

Sturm claimed he handed it over in exchange for some cocaine.

In the early part of the questioning, Sturm made it sound as if he had gone to the store at the same time as Davis. Now, he decided he had gone earlier, and was just leaving when Davis arrived, between five and five–fifteen.

Masking skepticism, Frazier inquired, "When John arrived, weren't you concerned about your friends?"

"Yeah, but I wasn't going to go back and say something."

"Why not?"

"Because he's fuckin' stupid. . . . He's always wired out . . . I got the hell out of there."

"You just rode off? I don't understand."

"I got scared. I was on coke myself. Coke does weird things to people. I got scared and left." Sturm said he had felt guilty about "how I let it happen. . . . I knew he had a gun. I knew he was going there for a reason. I didn't think he'd kill anybody, but he did. I felt guilty for the simple fact that I could have stopped it if I would have said something. But I didn't . . . . "

Frazier paused, his face grim. "You know, Greg, we don't believe that you are telling us the truth. Now, do you want to talk to us and tell us what really happened?"

Sturm appeared calm. "Well, what happened—what do you guys think happened? I mean, can you guys tell me that?"

"Sure," said Solis. "We think you went to the store and we think that you shot and killed those people."

"For what reason?"

"For the money. Or whatever other reason you may have. You tell us."

"I didn't kill them."

Over the next thirty minutes, the detectives took Sturm through the entire sequence of events again, asking for details. Frazier mentioned that a search warrant had been executed at the girlfriend's apartment and police had found a few things of interest. He asked Sturm what he had been wearing on Sunday night. The suspect readily described blue shorts and a yellow "Super Shops" T-shirt.

Frazier held up a yellow shirt. "Is this yours? The one you were wearing?"

"Yeah."

Pointing to several dark spots on the material, the detective said, "Do you see this, Greg? It's called blood spatter. I just got this back from the lab. This blood spatter belongs to Esgar. See these shorts?"

Frowning, Sturm nodded, "Uh huh."

"See the blood spatter?"

Another nod and weak grunt.

"That blood belongs to Esgar, too. Just tell me when you want me to stop."

"Oh, go ahead," Sturm snorted. "I'd like to see what else you've got."

"We know you were at the murder scene."

Strum swallowed hard, and gritted his teeth. "I was there. But I didn't kill them."

Frazier spoke calmly. "We know you were. There is no explaining this away. . . . What happened, Greg? Just tell us what happened."

Now speaking rapidly and louder, Sturm responded. "I didn't kill them. . . ." In a defiant tone, he growled, "I was fuckin' there when they got shot. It's evidence right there, okay? I didn't fuckin' kill them." He spoke as if he could make the denials more convincing by coloring them with obscenity.

In contrast to Sturm's emotional outburst, Frazier kept his voice calm. "Who killed them?"

"John did. I let him in the fuckin' side door."

Patiently, the officers asked for the truth. Sturm, almost in a rant, said, "He told me to get the money. I got the fuckin' money. He told me to grab a tape gun, give it to Darrell, and Darrell could tie them up. I went back there—they were in the back. He already shot the two. I'm standin' there and he shoots Darrell. And we left. . . . I didn't shoot them—he did. And if you guys can find him, I'll point him out. I didn't kill them but I was there. I'm an accessory."

Sturm had given the officers powerful evidence. Information about the use of tape had not been released. Now the detectives wanted every detail. Did you see him pull the trigger? Which hand was the gun in? How close was John to the victims? How close were you?

Sturm said he was five or six feet away. Frazier pointed out that the blood spatter put him much closer. Chad had been shot first, said Sturm, then Russ, and finally Darrell. Regarding the last victim, Sturm said, "I saw the blood fly out of his fuckin' head."

"Where did you take the money from?" asked Solis. Sturm said it came from the cash register. They had split it. His share was about six hundred dollars.

After listening another ten minutes to obviously fabricated details, Frazier interrupted with a question. "Okay, did you two guys know you were going to kill them?"

"No. I wouldn't have given him the gun if I knew that."

Staring directly into Sturm's eyes, Frazier asked, "How did you figure the guys you knew, who you were robbing, wouldn't tell the police who you were?"

Sturm's expression showed confusion. It was a question he probably hadn't anticipated. He cleared his throat and tried to evade the question. "I, uh, figured there was going to be a little more money in the sa— in the cash drawer."

He had made an interesting slip.

Frazier kept the pressure on. "Okay, Greg . . . we have a strong belief that this John Davis doesn't exist and that you were by yourself. We have more than a strong suspicion."

Sturm could only manage, "Great."

"Greg," said Frazier, "remember that stuff we did on your fingers at the station? We call that a GSR." He referred to a forensic tool known as gun shot residue testing.

Solis explained, "It shows whether you've shot a weapon or not. . . . You know that you were in there by yourself." He suggested it was now time for Sturm to get it off his chest. "The truth is going to have to come out, Greg. Right now is as good a time as ever."

Sturm's eyes appeared moist. He dropped his gaze to the floor.

"It's hard. It's hard. I know that," said Solis. "Look at me, Greg."

"I can't." His resolve was melting like ice in a Santa Ana wind.

"C'mon. Just bring it out. Tell us the truth. It's here, Greg. I see it."

Gregory Sturm caved in.

"Okay. I killed those guys."

NOW THAT IT WAS ALL OVER, he spoke easily. "I went in there to get some money. There was no other guy, you know that. I got scared. I was just going to leave them, but I got scared—and I shot all three of them."

"Why did you have Esgar tape their hands and legs?"

"I was going to leave them there. Then, I started to take off. I said, 'Don't move, please don't move.' And they said, 'Just leave,' that they wouldn't say anything. They'd forget it ever happened. So I started to leave."

"Then what happened?"

"I started up a ramp, turned around, and went back and shot 'em."

"Who did you shoot first?"

"Chad."

"Why did you shoot him?"

"I don't remember."

"Who did you shoot next?"

"Russ, and then Darrell." Sturm had given the same sequence of execution when he said that the imaginary John Davis had killed the three young men. At least he remained consistent.

Why had it been necessary to kill the victims? Sturm's explanation was chillingly simple.

" 'Cause I knew they'd tell on me and I'd have to go to jail for a long time. I didn't want to go to jail. . . . I was scared and didn't think about nothin' else."

Had any of the victims said anything to Sturm? His answer raised goose bumps. "Chad asked me, 'What's the matter Greg?' I told him I had a cocaine problem. He said, 'You don't have to do this. . . . You can get help. Please, don't do this. Think about what you're doing.' I said I did think about it. He just kept pleading."

Sturm denied any recollection of how close he stood when he pulled the trigger on each victim. But he did have one terrible picture branded in his memory. "Darrell looked at me, and he was crying, and I started crying, and he put his head down and I remember shooting, pulling the trigger, and seeing the blood."

The interview had taken over three hours.

The two detectives might have felt exultant over a remarkable job of crime solving. Instead, they felt a dark sense of depression.

With the overwhelming evidence and the taped confession, there was little doubt about the outcome of the trial in Judge Donald McCartin's court. From the District Attorney's Office, one of the best prosecutors in the nation would present the state's case. Lew Rosenblum, whose impeccable appearance and articulate verbal skills rivaled any politician, would eventually try sixty–six murder cases, all of which resulted in convictions!

Sturm's defender, Bill Kelley, decided his primary goal was to save his client from the death penalty. He stated, "Greg Sturm is not here to offer excuses for his acts . . . . He is here to accept responsibility for what he did." The defense strategy focused on Sturm's cocaine habit and suggested that he was high during the murders, thus could not have formed the intent to kill.

Rosenblum countered, "Gregory Sturm made a choice to kill these three young men, and there's no way you can justify this."

On May 8, 1992, the jury deliberated only six hours before finding Sturm guilty of murder with special circumstances of robbery and multiple murder. But they had difficulty agreeing whether or not the slayings were premeditated.

In view of this, Judge McCartin made an extraordinary prediction about the upcoming penalty phase. "It's my feeling that the jury will not come back with the death penalty . . . and I've never been wrong on such matters." He realized that jurors would be swayed partly by the defendant's youth and good looks.

AFTER THE JURY HEARD TWO WEEKS of testimony, they began deliberations. At one point, the foreman sent McCartin a note asking, "If we come out with a verdict of life without the possibility of parole, and the law changes in the future, will the defendant have a possibility of release?"

The judge provided a handwritten answer. "The governor has the right to commute either a death sentence or a recommendation of life without parole. But his should not be a consideration in your decision. You should not speculate as to any change in the law that may occur in the future."

McCartin's prescience turned out to be perfectly on target. On June 10, 1992, the jurors announced they were deadlocked, ten to two for life imprisonment without the possibility of a parole.

Considering such a heavily tilted balance against the death penalty, the district attorney could not have been faulted if he had decided against a second penalty phase. But Rosenblum felt confident he could use a slightly different approach and convince a new panel to recommend that Sturm face capital punishment.

IN LATE NOVEMBER, after more than four weeks of trial, the new jury retired to deliberate. Rosenblum had presented a stronger case, partially because of access to pre-trial statements from defense witnesses who had previously been unavailable to him. In addition, he put Sturm's girlfriend on the stand, eliciting testimony that the defendant showed no remorse immediately after the murders. Also, other witnesses who had been in the auto parts store just before it closed said Sturm did not appear to be under the influence of drugs.

After spending only two hours considering the evidence, this jury delivered a verdict on November 23, 1992, that Gregory Sturm should be executed for his crimes.

WHEN JUDGE McCARTIN HANDED DOWN the sentence at the end of February 1993, he said, "The three victims trusted him; they let him into the store. . . . He had an ongoing relationship with them. . . . He took advantage of their friendship, of their vulnerability. He has ended their lives forever." The judge characterized the crime as "callous and motiveless" and called Sturm "self-indulgent."

Sturm arrived in San Quentin's death row on March 5, 1993. Eleven years later, his automatic appeals to the California Supreme Court had not yet even started.

Richard Delmer Boyer

The Richard Delmer Boyer Story

In a darkened movie theater near Fullerton, California, Richard Delmer Boyer, 25, sat riveted to a horrific sequence of violent gore splashed across the screen. "Halloween II," starring Jamie Lee Curtis, depicted a character who has escaped from a mental institution, returned to a small town and slaughtered a trio of teenagers. Boyer watched as the butchery unfolded. A knife slices a pretty babysitter's throat, a security guard's skull is crushed with a hammer, a nurse is burned and finished off by drowning in a boiling cauldron, the killer plunges a hypodermic needle into one victim's eye and another woman's neck, and a police officer's throat is slashed.

Transfixed, Boyer would later blame the movie for his own outburst of violence.

The Los Angeles native, often unemployed, straggled from job to job, seldom earning very much. His appearance, with unkempt hair stringing from his thinning pate and hanging below the collar, a Fu Manchu mustache framing pouty lips, glowering brown eyes, and a scrawny six–one frame, didn't inspire employers to want him around. Abundant visible tattoos didn't help either. Inked into the skin of both arms and his back were messages, some explicit, others cryptic, such as "Smoke It, Born to Raise Hell, Evil, Mean, Dirty White boy, Bad Co" and the symbol of Nazi evil, a swastika. Boyer was in constant need of money to finance his craving for cigarettes, liquor, and a spectrum of drugs including PCP, amphetamines, LSD, cocaine, and heroin. His estranged wife lived in Northern California while he drifted around Orange County.

TROUBLE HAD A WAY of finding Richard Boyer, or vice versa. In 1977 a witness saw him brutally kill a stray cat. He reportedly forced the cat into a shopping bag and stabbed it repeatedly. When the wounded animal scrambled out, Boyer caught it and finished it off with a buck knife he carried in a holster attached to his belt. He was arrested and sentenced to two years formal probation, violated it, and spent a few days in jail.

The same year, he stole a bottle of rum from a supermarket. Stopped by store security and arrested, he spent nine days in jail and was again sentenced to probation. In 1978 he migrated to Arkansas, and built a rap sheet including theft, assault, and disorderly conduct. Another short jail sentence and probation didn't seem to put him on a straight and narrow path, just the road back to California.

In Orange County again, Boyer added more criminal behavior to his record between 1979 and 1982, including drug charges, attempted burglary, assault with a screwdriver, DUI, and robbery. Most of his incarceration periods were relatively short.

The longest period of employment for Boyer took place in 1979 when he and his wife worked several months as assistant managers of an apartment complex in Fullerton. During that time, he befriended a few tenants including an older couple, Francis Harbitz, and his wife, Ailene. Their adult son, William, often visited and got to know Boyer pretty well. It wasn't a real friendship though. William Harbitz trusted Boyer about as much as he would a rattlesnake.

Boyer's marriage turned stormy, with frequent quarrels and separations, until his wife finally moved out. He was adrift again.

When Francis and Ailene Harbitz moved to a modest little house in Fullerton, Boyer kept in touch, and visited occasionally. The couple seemed to like Boyer well enough to give him odd jobs working in their yard and even loaned him money.

IN THE LATE EVENING of December 12, 1982, William Harbitz, had been unable to reach his mother or father on the phone all day. Concerned, he decide to drop by the house to assure himself they were okay. He used a spare garage door opener his father had given him. Harbitz entered the eerily still kitchen, calling out to his parents. Only silence greeted him. He turned into a hall and saw at the other end his father slumped in a sitting position on the floor. Thinking that his dad had probably fallen, he rushed to his aid, saying, "Dad, what happened?"

Harbitz's blood chilled as soon as he touched his father. "I realized he was dead. He was stiff and cold. I immediately became concerned for my mother. I jumped over him and ran to the bedroom."

Now frantic with both grief and dread, he searched the bedroom but found no sign of her. He careened back down the hall and into the den. Still nothing. In the dimly lit living room, near the fireplace, Harbitz's worst nightmare became a reality "She was lying on her back with her legs crossed, with one arm to the side, and all covered with blood. I went over and I hugged her and told her I loved her."

Using the kitchen phone, Harbitz called his brother. "I told him Mom and Dad were dead and to call the police right away and then to come over himself as soon as he could."

Within a short time, the Fullerton police homicide unit swarmed the Harbitz home, examined the bodies, searched for evidence, and interviewed the two brothers.

At the autopsies, Francis Harbitz, 67, was found to have a broken left arm and three fractured ribs on the same side. Deep stab wounds penetrated the left side of his neck. Twelve more punctures marked his chest and thirteen were found on his back. One of his lungs had been nicked from both front and back. His heart had been pierced, as had his carotid artery. According the coroner's report, he had died from "exsanguination," loss of blood resulting from wounds to the heart and artery.

Ailene Rose Harbitz, 68, had suffered three stab wounds to her throat, one behind her left ear, and thirteen between the neck and abdomen. Six more thrusts of a knife with a blade over a half-inch wide and no more than four inches long had punctured her back. The assailant had apparently withdrawn the weapon partially, then pushed it back into each of several wounds, causing compounded damage to internal organs. She, too, had died from exsanguination due to a severed aorta.

Fullerton homicide detectives Richard Lewis and Jim Allred looked over the crime scene, then took William Harbitz aside to ask a few questions. It didn't take long for the son to mention Richard Boyer and wonder if he might have had something to do with the crime. Boyer had recently borrowed some money from the parents, and never repaid it. Furthermore, said Harbitz, Boyer had called a few days before to ask for more money. "The guy tends to be very violent when he drinks, and he's a knife freak," said the grief-stricken son.

By tracing Boyer's phone number to an address in El Monte, the detectives had little trouble locating where he lived.

Lewis and Allred, accompanied by two El Monte officers, arrived at Boyer's residence. While the uniformed cops covered the back door, Lewis and his partner knocked on the front door. Someone parted the blinds, and they heard a female voice say, "Wait a minute." No more than a few seconds later, the two El Monte officers came striding around the house with Richard Boyer between them. He immediately told them he wasn't trying to escape, but had exited at the back because the front door was jammed. The detectives informed him they were investigating a Fullerton case and asked Boyer if he would come with them voluntarily. He said he would.

En route, Lewis told Boyer that the interview wouldn't begin until they reached the station. They engaged in a brief conversation in which Boyer mentioned that he had recently visited his own father. He had gone there in a white car driven by a friend of his named Vic Carter. Changing the subject, Lewis said the Fullerton case they were looking into involved a homicide. Boyer casually asked, "So someone's really been murdered, huh?"

In an interview room, Boyer was given the standard Miranda advisory. After a few moments, Boyer said he didn't want to talk anymore. The interview was terminated. He did, however, give his consent to search his residence. He also agreed to be fingerprinted. During the process, Boyer asked, "Am I under arrest?" The detective told him that he was not. Boyer pulled up a chair, still in the interview room and sat down. Again, Lewis informed him that no questions would be asked because of the request for an attorney, then commented that he had spoken with one of the Harbitz brothers who had recently seen Boyer in the victims' home.

Just as the detective headed out the door to arrange transportation for Boyer's return to El Monte, Boyer spoke. It was like surprise endings of old "Perry Mason" television episodes in which a witness breaks down and confesses to the crime. Boyer said, "Hey, wait a minute. Come back here and sit down. I can't live with it. I did it. I didn't mean to do it, but I did it."

Once again, to make certain Boyer understood his rights, Lewis read him the Miranda advisory. Then, with a tape recorder running, Richard Boyer gave a detailed confession of murdering Francis and Ailene Harbitz.

With unexpected clarity, he told the detectives about Mrs. Harbitz cordially admitting him into her home. According to Boyer's statement, they conversed briefly in the kitchen. At that point, he had started feeling faint. She wanted him to say hello to her husband who was watching television in the bedroom. While in there, Boyer said, he spotted a bill-fold on the dresser. He formed the "crazy" idea to ask for money and if they refused, to just take it. He emerged from the bedroom feeling more and more dizzy and encountered Mrs. Harbitz. As he followed her back down the hall toward the kitchen, he decided to take their wallets, but did not intend to harm them. But as he placed his hand over her mouth, colors and flashes exploded like fireworks in the room and everything started spinning, he said. He "freaked out" and started stabbing her, again and again. She broke free and screamed for her husband. Mr. Harbitz came in and started hitting Boyer with his cane. Boyer "tore into" the old man with his knife. During the melee, he somehow stabbed himself in the knee but didn't realize it at the time. When both of the victims were down, he grabbed the wallet from atop the dresser. Returning to the kitchen, he washed off his knife in the sink. On the counter, he saw Mrs. Harbitz's purse and took her wallet from it. He grabbed a towel to stem the blood flowing from his leg, and left through the front door.

After his remarkable confession, Boyer guided the detectives in a drive along the I-10 (San Bernardino Freeway) to the Temple City off-ramp. They stopped at the curb and were able to recover a wallet Boyer had tossed into the gutter. It contained a driver's license belonging to Ailene Harbitz.

In Boyer's statement, he told the detectives that he had been driven to the Harbitz home by his friend Vic Carter. Lewis and his partner had Carter arrested and brought in for an interview. He agreed to tell everything he knew.

Carter's words flowed like water from a broken fire hydrant. Calling Boyer by a nickname, Rick, Carter said, "On that night, we went to Rick's mother first to get some money. I was driving and I had to wait outside. When he came back . . . he had some tires and a mattress we put in my car. It's a white Plymouth; actually my mother's car. Then he wanted to go to some friend's house."

They went to an apartment, he said, but found no one home. Boyer directed him to the residence of someone named Bill, where they also struck out.

According to Carter, "Rick got back in the car and he said, 'Well, let's go to Bill's parents' house because he might have moved in with them.' We went there, to Fullerton, and I decided to stay out in the car again. . . . I waited about forty–five minutes and started honking the horn. He still didn't show up for about another ten minutes. A police car passed at the same time he came out. Rick walked around behind the Plymouth and wiped off the window with a towel. He had something under his blue jacket. Then he got in the car and we left."

"Had he taken the towel in with him?"

"No, he brought it out of the house . . . . We headed up the I-605 Freeway, and he told me that he had got stabbed. He put the towel around his left leg, around the knee. I asked him what happened and he told me that some people started jumping . . ." Carter paused, trying to form his words. Detective Lewis told him to just slow down and take his time.

"He told me he got stabbed, then he said, 'Vic, I had to hurt 'em.' "

A pained expression creased Carter's face. "I asked what he had done to them. He said he had beat them. He said, you know, like he had 'hussled' them up, beat them up a little."

They had turned onto the San Bernardino Freeway, I-10, said Carter. "He threw a wallet out the passenger window between Dunphy Avenue and Santa Anita. And then he threw a second wallet into a drain on Temple City Boulevard. And from there we drove to his girlfriend's house about seven–thirty at night. He went in the bathroom to talk to her. And I called my brother and said, 'Come over here 'cause I need to talk to you about something.' He came over, and from there, me and my brother went home."

Lewis asked a series of questions to clarify a few points. "When you were parked outside the house where Rick got stabbed, did you see him go in?"

"No. I was parked around a corner and couldn't see the front of the house."

"Did you hear any screaming?"

"No, I didn't hear nothing at all. There was no noise whatsoever."

"Did either you or Richard take any kind of dope or drugs at all before he went in that house?"

"No, sir."

"Did Richard appear at any time that night to be high?"

"No, he just looked scared."

Boyer, he said, had been wearing a blue jacket, Levis, and tennis shoes. Carter didn't know whether Boyer had carried a knife into the Harbitz home. But Boyer did have a "buck knife" in a holster attached to his belt on the way home. At the end of the interview, Detective Lewis placed Carter under arrest for his complicity in the murders of two innocent victims.

While waiting for trial, Boyer spoke with a psychiatrist and provided supplemental information as well as embellishment about his state of mind at the time. In the follow-up report, the doctor said, "He was cooperative and had no obvious signs of emotional distress. . . . Mr. Boyer said he did not remember the actual crime, although he had given the Fullerton police a rather detailed account of stabbing the Harbitz couple. . . . With me, he concentrated on describing a headache in the temples spreading in the back of his head and being sharp and steady like 'being hit with a hammer' just as he was walking behind Mr. Harbitz. . . . He said he did not remember the actual killing until he got a towel because his leg was hurt."

BOYER EXPANDED THE COMPLAINT about headaches plaguing him regularly, especially while using drugs. He spoke of "throwing his life away" by using drugs and his difficulties in finding jobs. The Harbitz couple, he said, had been nice to him, "like godparents." He had gone to their home to ask for their son's address in hopes of asking him for a loan. Halfway back to El Monte, he had been surprised to find that he had wallets belonging to them, and "couldn't figure out how he got them."

In the hours prior to the crime, he had used drugs and alcohol. It had made him feel paranoid "like a SWAT team was after him." According to Boyer, the police had "weaseled" a confession out of him. Asked if he felt depressed, Boyer said he did, but not suicidal. "I ain't that brave," he said.

He added one more insight. When he walked down the hall in the Harbitz house, Boyer said, he saw a ghostly apparition of "a psychopath from a horror movie, 'Halloween II,' who stabbed everybody."

RICHARD BOYER WAITED MORE than a year in Orange County Jail to face a judge and jury. In the 1984 trial, the man who acted as chauffeur on the night of the killings, Vic Carter, was granted immunity in exchange for testimony. However, he reversed his statement that neither of them had used drugs on the day of the murders.

The prosecution introduced into evidence Boyer's bloodstained buck knife, the jeans he wore, and Ailene Harbitz's wallet recovered from a storm drain. The defendant's female roommate testified, also under immunity, that she knew Boyer had no money that morning because he had asked her for thirty dollars. When he returned home, he had forty dollars in small bills. She recalled that Boyer's knee had been injured by a stab wound. Before the police arrived to search her home, she had burned the blue jacket Boyer had worn. She also told jurors that he stopped wearing the buck knife on his belt after that awful night.

The defense argued that Boyer had been delusional due to heavy drug usage, therefore not responsible for his actions.

It stunned the general public when twelve jurors were unable to agree on a verdict. The judge was forced to declare a mistrial.

In a second trial one year later, another jury heard the same evidence, including the taped confession Boyer gave after detectives twice read the Miranda advisory to him.

In his own defense, Boyer testified that he had felt deep affection for Mr. and Mrs. Harbitz. He had borrowed money from them and they hadn't even pressed him for payment. He had no intention of hurting them, but had snorted and ingested heavy doses of drugs that day. He became paranoid and knew he was "in trouble." Inside their house, he said, he felt like someone was hitting the back of his head with a hard object. Just before he attacked Mrs. Harbitz, he had seen a foggy figure that looked like the killer in the movie "Halloween II."

His testimony landed on deaf ears in the jury box. This time, they convicted Boyer of two counts of first degree murder with special circumstances of multiple murder, robbery, and the use of a deadly weapon, which made him eligible for the death penalty. The same jury, after hearing aggravating versus mitigating circumstances in the penalty phase, recommended that he be executed for the murders.

It seemed that justice had won out at last. That was before the California Supreme Court reviewed the trial in 1989.

IN A CONFOUNDING DECISION, the justices stated, "We confront the rare but distressing case in which the outcome is determined by the constable's blunders. Defendant's inculpatory statement to the police was obtained in flagrant violation of the Fourth Amendment and Miranda v. Arizona. The courts . . . should have granted defendant's motion to suppress the statement. Its admission at his guilt trial was prejudicial by any applicable standard. . . . We cannot be satisfied beyond a reasonable doubt that the jurors would have convicted defendant of the charged crimes had they not heard his taped statement describing in detail his brutal stabbing of the Harbitzes, and taking of their property. Nor, of course, may we assume defendant would have testified conceding his identity as the killer had the extrajudicial statement not been admitted. We must therefore reverse the judgment in its entirety."

Fortunately, they decreed that all the other evidence was still admissible in any future trial. Once again, the taxpayers would be forced to spend a great deal of money to give Boyer a new trial, even in the absence of any doubt about his guilt.

Judge Donald A. McCartin presided over the third trial of Richard Boyer in June 1992. Chuck Middleton, one of the top prosecutors in the District Attorney's Office, presented the state's evidence, while attorney James Merwin defended. Without the taped confessions considered so important by the high court, Middleton convinced a new jury that Boyer had committed double murder with malice and aforethought. Regarding the defendant's rationalization that his mental processes were diminished by drug usage, and a horror movie, Middleton pointed out there was no reliable evidence that Boyer had taken mind-bending drugs on the day he slaughtered two victims. That excuse was nothing but a "transparent attempt" to evade responsibility. Boyer saw the couple's wallets, and "he had to kill what was between him and those wallets." He needed money, "and nothing was going to keep him from getting it."

The jury convicted Boyer and recommended that he suffer the death penalty. Judge McCartin, in handing down the sentence on October 23, said, "The thing that troubles me, Mr. Boyer, is that they trusted you. . . . You took advantage of this friendship. They were elderly and vulnerable."

Richard Delmer Boyer arrived on death row, for the second time, in November 1992. His new rounds of appeals are pending.

PART IV

TORTURED
JUSTICE

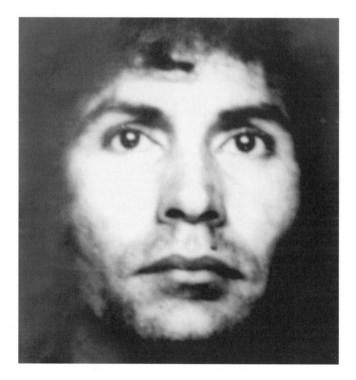

Rodney Alcala

16

The Second Alcala Trial
in Judge McCartin's Court

Before the start of jury selection for Rodney Alcala's second murder trial in the spring of 1986, prosecutor Thomas Goethals and defense attorney John Dolan met in court with McCartin to discuss how to screen jury candidates adamantly opposed to the death penalty.

"It's always troublesome," McCartin observed. "I usually find that if people say they absolutely cannot impose the death penalty, that about ninety-eight percent of the time, they refuse to back down even if an Adolf Hitler type killed a member of their own family." Goethals voiced his worry that an overwhelming number of prospective jurors might try to beg off due to the extraordinary nature of the Alcala case and its likelihood of consuming several months. McCartin didn't agree. "You know," he said to Goethals, "interestingly enough, you are one hundred percent wrong."

Goethals rolled his eyes. "Well, that's not unusual."

"Well, you are, because in my last death penalty case, when the panels found out it was a murder case with special circumstances, we retained more jurors than we usually do on a lesser case, such as fraud. . . . We ended up keeping forty or fifty percent instead of the usual twenty percent. Some people seem to prefer a case that holds their interest."

On Wednesday, April 23, 1986, Judge McCartin gave the prosecutor a signal to deliver his opening statements to a newly sworn-in jury.

THOMAS GOETHALS STOOD, buttoned his jacket, and made eye contact with individual jurors while greeting them. "During the next couple of weeks, I think you ladies and gentleman will relive through the evidence presented to you one of the most notorious and horrendous crimes in the history of this county."

Step-by-step, Goethals led the jury through events of seven years earlier when Robin Samsoe had vanished from Huntington Beach She had left on Bridgett Wilvert's yellow bike, ". . . a smile on her lips and a song in her heart . . . ready to start dancing again. Instead, she wound up forty miles away in the mountains with this defendant—and before long, she was dead." The prosecutor promised he would prove the case through forty to sixty witnesses and about two hundred pieces of evidence.

The opening statement was spellbinding, courteous, articulate, and just the right length to hook jurors. Tom Goethals had earned admiration from not only his direct audience, but from the full gallery as well. Even Judge McCartin admired it.

John Patrick Dolan stepped forward to present the defense story. "Ladies and gentlemen, it probably won't surprise you that I am going to suggest to you the evidence in this case will point to a much different conclusion as to what happened." He asked the jury to keep an eye on the evidence and not allow emotions to color their judgment. Hypnosis had tainted the testimony one witness would offer, he said. Other tainted testimony, he said, would come from jailhouse informants. "They take heroin addicts who are on withdrawal . . . puking all over the place . . . and put them in a position to get out of jail. . . . It's a little game called 'buy your way out of the jailhouse.'" Dolan concluded by imploring the jury to examine the evidence and find his client not guilty.

"Rodney Alcala is not the perpetrator in this case, ladies and gentlemen. He is the victim. . . ."

THE FIRST WITNESS to take the stand was Detective Art Droz from the Huntington Beach Police Department, followed by investigators and forensics specialists who described the crime, the search for evidence, and the discovery of a prime suspect. Bridgett Wilvert, now a young woman at age nineteen, told of her day at the beach with Robin, and of posing for Rodney Alcala. She pointed to the defendant, identifying him as the photographer. Jackelyn Young recalled interrupting the encounter and escorting the two children home. She, too, expressed certainty that Rodney Alcala was the man she had seen. Dance studio owner Beverly Fleming informed jurors that the bubbly, reliable little girl, Robin, would never have voluntarily missed her dance lesson on June 20, 1979.

Redoubtable HBPD Detective Richard Hooper testified about his work in the investigation and of his contacts with the U.S. Forest Service employee, Anita Craven.

Officer Thomas Rayl testified about his discovery of a Kane Kut-brand steel kitchen knife at the crime scene. Minuscule blood spots had been found on it. Photos of the knife were introduced as evidence exhibits.

Later, the jury would also see two complete sets of Kane Kut knives police had seized while executing a search warrant at the home of Alcala's mother, with whom the defendant lived at the time.

Judge McCartin waited until the second day before displaying his well-known impatience with superfluous testimony. Dr. Judy Suchey, a forensic anthropologist, had been called by the prosecutor to identify a skull found in the mountains as Robin Samsoe's. McCartin interrupted the proceedings and sent the jury into their conference room which also served as a lounge. He growled, "Why do we want to hear all this?

What's the bottom line? I assume it's the victim. There's no question about it. Why am I going through all of this? It doesn't do anything for me. It is not entertaining me, so why am I listening to it?"

Tom Goethals, who knew McCartin's reputation quite well, calmly explained, "It will only take ten minutes."

"Ten minutes! What do we need it for?"

"It goes to the identification."

"Is there any doubt?"

Defender Dolan didn't especially want to linger on the skull either. It could certainly do his client no good. He chimed in, "I am not raising any issue as far as identification."

Goethals persisted. "It's something I still have to prove. This is a major case and the jury wants to know the people have done everything they possibly could to investigate this case, examine it, and prove everything they have to prove. If that's not Robin Samsoe up there, this case is out of business."

Still unsettled, McCartin suggested the defense could stipulate identification of the skill, but finally relented and allowed the witness to continue. His point may have been nothing more than a wake-up call to both attorneys that he would not allow pointless testimony.

THE PITIFUL REMAINS of Robin Samsoe came under scrutiny again on Monday, April 28. Dr. Sharon Schnittker's words brought tears to the eyes of spectators and jurors. "Some of the bones were not attached to the main body of the skeleton. . . . Bones of the arms, as well as the ribs, part of the right foot and most of the left foot showed evidence of gnawing by small or large animals. They had been chewing on the ends of the bones as well as the shoulder blades. One of the arms was fractured due to animal activity. The hands were absent, probably due to animal life carting them away." She added that no signs could be found of tool marks, gunshot wounds, or fractures that might have occurred prior to death.

A tiny woman with a woebegone face hobbled up to the stand next. Rodney Alcala's mother testified that she owned a set of knives, Kane Kut brand. Goethals emphasized the name, making certain the jury realized it was the same brand as the knife found at the crime scene. On cross-examination, the anguished woman said the cutlery had been a gift and none of them were missing. Judge McCartin would notice her again. One morning he glanced out of his office window and saw her walking, all alone, toward the building's entry. A strong surge of sympathy engulfed him. She endured pain right along with other crime victims.

McCartin's hard-working clerk, Gail Carpenter, later spoke of her boss's compassion. She recalled, "Alcala was the first death case I worked on. The defendant had several relatives attending the trial. They truly believed he was innocent, and I was impressed at how kind the judge was to them, especially Alcala's mother. He took the added step of taking her down an elevator reserved for judges to keep the press away from her following the verdict. Alcala was always very polite in the courtroom. I truly believe he thought he was innocent. I always got the impression that he was a Dr. Jekyll / Mr. Hyde personality. As an example, when we began jury selection, and had qualified over one hundred candidates, we had a small card for each one. He sent me a little note and asked if he could shuffle the cards for luck. At that time, we used a rotating cylinder full of cards with jurors names on them." She would draw cards to select prospective jurors for individual screening, called voir dire. "Of course, what he asked wasn't allowed, or even considered, but I think it shows a little of the Jekyll-Hyde personality."

McCartin did feel sorry for Alcala's mother, who sat through every day of the trial. He could see her in the gallery. "She thought the justice system was doing her wrong or doing her son wrong. She was put into that mode of thinking by this horse's ass, Alcala. That was the hard part about it, seeing the pain she had to endure."

* * *

THE 1980 TRIAL had featured several jailhouse informants. Tom Goethals summoned an inmate who had not previously testified. David Jackson, escorted from the Orange County Jail, settled into the chair and stared at Rodney Alcala. In answer to the first few questions by Goethals, Jackson admitted that he had served time in prison for grand theft, robberies, and parole violations. At one time, he had been addicted to all kinds of drugs, but had been clean about four years. For the past two months, Jackson had been a trustee in the county jail.

Goethals established that Jackson had already been advised of his pending parole date before he agreed to testify about Rodney Alcala. There was no "deal" to give him an earlier release. His decision to reveal what he knew had taken place before Jackson's most recent arrest. He had heard of the charges against Alcala, and contacted a deputy district attorney with whom he was acquainted.

"Why did you come forward at that time?" Goethals asked.

"Because of the fact that it involved a child . . ." Even inside prison walls, child molesters are regarded as scum, and subject to mistreatment.

In jail, said Jackson, he had been in the protective custody unit with Carlos Cardenas and Rodney Alcala. Cardenas had testified in the 1979 preliminary hearing that determined Alcala should be tried for murder.

"Was there any conversation among the three of you?"

"Yes. There had apparently been bad blood between Mr. Cardenas and Alcala." Alcala evidently disliked Cardenas for ratting on him in that preliminary hearing. Harsh words were exchanged before Jackson had stepped between them to prevent a fight.

Apparently, Alcala appreciated Jackson's help, and began confiding in him. Over a period of time, said Jackson, Alcala admitted kidnapping and killing Robin Samsoe.

Jackson stated that Alcala had laughed about an incident that took place during his 1980 trial. There had been a demonstration for the jury of how the defendant might have placed the yellow bicycle inside his hatchback vehicle. "He was . . . making fun of the jury as if they were not too competent. Alcala told me, 'They were all acting like a bunch of ducks trying to get the bike in the car.' " In Jackson's recollection, Alcala had described the ease with which he had placed the bike in his vehicle.

One particular revelation had seared itself in Jackson's mind. During a hushed conversation, said the informant, "Alcala made a comment about some girlfriend who was staying in touch with him. He showed me a photograph of the young lady, and then made some other comments." Alcala had then spoken about "Robin," the girl he was accused of murdering. "He said that his girlfriend was nothing like Robin who was scratching, yelling, and acting like a little wild cat, and had a butt like a grapefruit." Jackson said he distinctly remembered that phrase.

Judge McCartin would later recall an eerie feeling he had during much of the trial. His chair and desk were elevated to allow a full view of the entire courtroom. Facing the lawyers and the defendant, he experienced an unfamiliar agitation. Not just from the constant back pain he suffered, but from a pair of eyes staring at him. "I never before had a defendant do this. When I glanced at Alcala, he stared me down with those intense brown eyes. Staring down the judge! I wasn't afraid, but it did give me an uneasy feeling."

INSIDERS HAD BEEN WAITING EAGERLY for the appearance of Anita Craven, who had testified in the first trial about seeing the defendant with a young blond girl in the mountains. Her demeanor on the stand had been odd. On Wednesday, April 30, the day she was scheduled to testify in the current trial, Craven made a jolting announcement to the prosecutor.

Goethals rushed into the courtroom, several minutes tardy, and apologized to the glowering judge. "Your honor, I am sorry. My next witness arrived a little late. . . . She is present outside in the hallway, under subpoena to testify. However, she has essentially informed me— well, I don't want to misstate what she said—that she is not going to testify because she doesn't have any recollection about the events in this case—essentially." But, said Goethals, he wasn't going to let that be the final answer.

McCartin proposed to bring her in and let her speak, outside the jury's presence, to see what could be done about the problem.

Craven at first seemed lively and responsive as she answered a series of questions from Goethals about her recent successful completion of classes for a new profession and about her health. She said she could recall working for the U.S. Forest Service, but didn't remember how long. She had no idea why her memory about the events in 1979 had failed. Judge McCartin asked, "Is there any other period you are having difficulty with?" Craven replied that the previous April and May, one year ago, had some blank spots in them. Her answers slowed and she seemed confused.

"Have you talked to any doctor about the problems you are having?" asked McCartin. Craven mentioned a psychiatrist, but couldn't recall his name.

Goethals next laid a foundation for a solution he had in mind. "Have you ever, to your knowledge, testified under oath or penalty of perjury and intentionally lied?"

"No, sir."

ANOTHER PAIR OF QUESTIONS from the prosecutor reinforced Craven's assertion that she had never given any false information to anyone about the case. After McCartin excused her to wait outside, he suggested to both lawyers that Craven was apparently "unavailable to testify within the meaning of the statutes." He decided that her testimony from the previous trial would be read aloud to the jury. After extensive discussion of the issue with the attorneys, they agreed to call Craven back to the stand on the and let the jury hear her assertion of memory failure.

McCartin stated, "We'll put her on and get that over with—unless she suddenly has a miraculous recollection. She just may—my warm, smiling face may cause her to recall everything."

It didn't. Craven answered a series of questions repeating the same declarations she had made to the judge and attorneys; she had no recollection of the events in 1979 nor could she even recall testifying about them in trial. She reasserted her belief that she would never have deliberately lied under oath.

LATER, DISCUSSING THE EPISODE, McCartin said, "When she took the stand, they started asking her questions. She seemed to hit the wall with some kind of amnesia, a post-trauma condition, that caused her to suddenly lock up, unable to answer questions. I didn't think it was phony by any means. The defense attorney was asking question after question and she just couldn't respond. Why would she suddenly have feigned memory failure? Such behavior wouldn't make any sense. She seemed to me a very fragile girl. Worked with the Forest Service, but didn't look the part at all; very frail physically. Something, some experience, had caused this and she couldn't shake it. We held a hearing, and decided that she simply couldn't respond to the questions. I made the determination that, according to law, she was unavailable to testify in this trial."

He ruled that Craven's testimony from the 1980 trial would be read to the jury.

First, though, a doctor explained to jurors that Craven had suffered posttraumatic stress disorder from seeing the body of Robin

Samsoe, which partially explained her memory loss. This prompted another hearing in which John Dolan, the defender, commented, "In our moving papers, I presented a request for independent examination of this witness and I assume your honor is considering that also."

McCartin replied, "I'm going to deny that request at this particular time. I don't think it would add or detract." It seemed like a routine decision at the time, but would eventually tilt the scales of justice.

When the jury returned from a long break created by hearings outside their presence, only eleven people filed into the box. Usually, McCartin's humor was directed at lawyers, but sometimes he liked to tease others as well. McCartin sent his bailiff, "Mitch" Miller, in search of the missing juror. Miller soon escorted him in and whispered something to the judge.

"Our man was fast asleep in the jury room," McCartin announced. Grinning, he spoke directly to the embarrassed fellow. "You look like you spent the weekend in there." He added, "Give him a blood alcohol reading." Laughter broke the pall of courtroom tension.

With everyone wide awake, court reporter Sandra Wingerd turned into a voice actress. The winsome, attractive redhead spoke Anita Craven's words, reading from a transcript of the 1980 trial. The testimony placed Robin Samsoe with Rodney Alcala in close proximity to where the little girl's savaged remains were found.

The prosecution's case had opened with Detective Art Droz and would close with him. Goethals called Droz to the stand again on May 12 to clear up a few details. He was the fifty–eighth witness. Afterward, Goethals announced, "The prosecution rests."

THE DEFENSE CASE OPENED with Edgar Allan Poe, literally. A former employee of the Forest Service by that name took the stand to share his recollections about Anita Craven. Before he said much, though, John Dolan put to rest any curiosity by asking the witness if he was related to the famous poet. No, he wasn't. Poe had studied hypnotism at one time, and had experimented with it on Craven, off duty. The hypnotism issue would be raised again.

A jailhouse snitch followed, claiming that he and David Jackson, the prosecution's informant, had discussed betraying another inmate at one time. Also, he said, Jackson was "desperate" to testify in a murder trial. At one point, he seemed to corroborate allegations that Alcala had confessed killing Samsoe.

Now, Dolan decided to attack the prosecution's case by playing the alibi card. He planned to show that his client had been at Knott's Berry Farm, a theme park twelve miles north of Huntington Beach, on the afternoon of June 20, in search of freelance photography work. Dolan questioned three witnesses, all employees of the theme park. Their testimony did establish that Alcala had been at Knott's, but failed to convincingly pin it down to June 20. One woman testified that she would have seen anyone who entered the office, and that she did not see Alcala. On a day that she "assumed" was June 20, she and other managers had left Knott's between 2:30 and 3 o'clock for a tour of another theme park.

According to the testimony of Alcala's sister, he was babysitting her children on the morning of June 20, and had left about 1:30 that afternoon.

The subject of earrings consumed the next couple of hours. Robin's mother had said she used fingernail clippers to alter the gold ball earrings worn by Robin. An "expert" said that his efforts to match the clippers with striation marks on the jewelry were inconclusive.

Dolan wanted to stress that Alcala had a pierced ear and often wore an earring. The next few witnesses stated that they had seen Alcala wearing one at various times, but couldn't recall any exact descriptions of it.

In the darkened courtroom, jurors watched the videotape of Rodney Alcala as bachelor number one on "The Dating Game." If

Dolan hoped the program would show Alcala actually wearing an ear-ring, his effort failed. In several close-ups of the defendant's face, his mane of thick, curly hair completely covered both ears.

On May 15, Dolan informed Judge McCartin that he planned to call only two more witnesses. In a hearing, outside the jury's presence, the defender stated that he wanted Gerald Crawford, a police officer who had already testified, to return to the stand. Then, Dolan would sum-mon a man named Juan Duarte.

Dolan explained. Two days after the crime, Crawford had seen Duarte in the mountains not far from the site where Robin's body had been found. Duarte had been acting suspiciously, so Crawford ques-tioned him. According to Duarte, he had just stopped to urinate. But because Duarte had once been convicted of murder, Dolan thought he might be a suspect in the Robin Samsoe case. The defense attorney said, "There's every reason to believe that Mr. Duarte, who has a prior homi-cide conviction, found at the scene of the crime on the twenty–second, is the person who is the perpetrator." The defense wanted jurors to hear this.

McCartin wasn't happy with the prospect. "It's my understanding that this isn't the way the system works. Knowing that there is probably a ten thousand-page investigation, we could spend the rest of our life bringing in people . . . I'd say the probative value versus the prejudicial effect and confusion of the jury, undue consumption of time. . . ." He complained that he did not want to enter into a "whodunit" game.

PROSECUTOR GOETHALS POINTED OUT that the issue had been aired in the 1980 trial. He cited several legal precedents in support of dis-allowing it, and quoted one. "Evidence which simply affords a possible ground of possible suspicion against another person should be inadmiss-able." Goethals argued that Duarte's previous conviction was a robbery-related homicide, which bore no resemblance to the Samsoe murder.

McCartin said, "This is getting into fantasyland. Seems to me the probative value of this type of evidence is zero and would do nothing but confuse the jury. . . . I'm going to rule it out. It's a waste of time."

In the previous trial, the defense had called a witness named Tim Nellis who testified that he had seen Robin Samsoe riding a bicycle in Huntington Beach on June 21, the day after she had been to the beach with Bridgett Wilvert. In May 1986, when John Dolan prepared to put Nellis on the stand, the prosecutor objected and asked for a hearing outside the jury's presence regarding the admissibility of Nellis as a witness. Tom Goethals argued that during cross-examination in the previous trial, Nellis had been shown a photograph of a different girl and had positively identified her as the one he had seen on June 21. In view of this inconsistency, said Goethals, the witness should be excluded. Judge McCartin agreed, expressing the opinion that whatever probative value Nellis' testimony might have had been destroyed by that error, and it would "confuse the issues." The defense would not be able to put Nellis on the stand.

Dolan had also been denied his request to have an independent psychiatric examination of Anita Craven. But the lawyer had not capitulated on the issue of bringing in "expert" testimony that might convince jurors to disregard Craven's testimony as unreliable. Outside the jury's presence, on May 20, a hearing was held to weigh the issue. It would turn out to be another round of ammunition for the appeals courts.

Judge McCartin examined a professional résumé by the proposed witness, a psychologist named Dr. George Paris.

Sitting in the witness chair, Dr. Paris said he had reviewed transcripts of numerous interviews conducted with Anita Craven and listened to a few tapes. He had evaluated the information, and concluded that "directive and non-directive techniques" of hypnosis had been used on her by interviewers. He defined those terms. "Most people expect or have a mind-set that hypnosis is like stage hypnosis. You do some magic ceremony and hocus-pocus and tell the person to quack like a duck, and that isn't what hypnosis is. Stage hypnotists use a lot of direct suggestions, however. Directive technique or suggestion is to tell a person to close their eyes or to move their arm or to be alert or to relax. A non-directive technique uses stories and metaphors and indirect kinds of suggestions like saying I have—in order to instill confidence, I have very special powers that can help you—help you deal with that. That's a non-directive kind of suggestion."

Observers glanced at one another and shook their heads. What was this guy talking about? Had he not personally interviewed Anita Craven? How could he make any conclusions without actually meeting her or speaking to her?

Referring the doctor to one particular police interview of Craven, Dolan asked, "Can you give us some examples in that interview of directive and non-directive interview techniques you detected?

Dr. Paris said he could. "The most obvious non-directive suggestions were when the person was talking about hypnosis and the mind being like a high fidelity video recorder and that you can go back and you can remember things and—in surgery—and that your mind is always recording. That's basically a non-directive kind of technique." Puzzled expressions appeared in the gallery. "A more directive approach would be the statement you can either do it by yourself with techniques, or if people, you know, who people can—I'm sorry—you know, assist. You put yourself into a state of hypnosis many times. That's a more directive kind of suggestion."

Dolan seemed to understand, even if no one else did, as he asked about the doctor's observations regarding a second interview. Paris said, "The subject was given indirect images of refreshing, like talking about having a Coke or something to drink . . . and images of flying, relaxation and to be cooler and more—more relaxed."

Even Dolan's voice sounded doubtful. "Okay—and what is the significance of those?"

The doctor spoke of "hypnotic induction procedures and suggestions." He said, "There were suggestions like putting two and two together, that seemed to be a prevalent theme throughout— throughout the sessions, adding things and taking this and putting that together and making sure you know what to do. There's a lot of suggestions—to remember things."

McCartin's face grew dark. He requested clarification of a few points, and asked, "What else do you have as far as suggestions of facts?"

"I'm not sure I understand what you mean, sir?"

"Tell me some other facts that you found in a particular statement that were suggested, and what response the interviewer had after making the suggestions."

"Oh! There was some specific suggestions that she would remember more and more and more, and that she would know those."

McCartin frowned and asked for more specific examples.

"There was direct suggestion by the interviewer, or hypnotist, depending on what you want to call them, to place the girl and the guy together." Some of the suggestions were followed by Craven, others were not, Dr. Paris acknowledged.

THE SESSION STUMBLED FORWARD like a scene from Alice in Wonderland. Dr. Paris answered a litany of questions, using terms such as "altered states of consciousness," "disassociating," and "confabulation." He implied that post-hypnotic suggestion may have colored Craven's statements.

Judge McCartin had another question. He rattled off the names of three officers who had interviewed Craven and asked, "You are indicating all these gentlemen hypnotized her? Is that what you are telling me?"

Dr. Paris didn't flinch. "I'm saying that there were hypnotic induction strategies and suggestions given . . . and that she was also hypnotized for fun. . . ."

"Well, you're shifting . . ."

"I'm trying to answer the question."

"All right. Why don't you answer it then?"

"Okay."

In an exchange that consumed the next half-hour, the doctor said that in his professional opinion, Craven had been hypnotized by investigators at least twice and subjected to hypnotic techniques other times. She had also been hypnotized in social situations.

Richard Farnell, the prosecutor in the 1980 trial had interviewed Craven before putting her on the stand. McCartin asked, "How about Mr. Farnell? Did he hypnotize her also?"

Dr. Paris equivocated a bit on this one. "I'm not sure there was a formal attempt to induce hypnosis at that time, based on what was on the tape. It's obvious that there was some things that weren't on the tape."

IF THE DOCTOR HADN'T ALREADY LOST credibility with McCartin, his next comments didn't help. "There was a telephone interview that involved some hypnotic phenomena, but I'm not sure it was directed on the part of the person who was talking to her."

McCartin sighed. "You mean they could have been doing it indirectly without knowing they were doing it? Is that what you're telling me?"

"Yes . . . I think on that telephone call . . . intentionally or unintentionally, purposely or nonpurposely, she . . . started exhibiting hypnotic behavior."

On cross-examination, Goethals asked how many crime victims Dr. Paris had interviewed. He said probably two hundred or more, in all kinds of crimes.

"And were they sometimes reluctant to talk about their experiences ?"

Paris agreed, but said Craven's behavior was not typical.

After a prolonged discussion, in which another hypnosis expert was named who might be summoned to testify for the prosecution, McCartin brought it to a sudden halt. "I'm a little bit distressed, gentlemen. These [hypnosis] cases have been coming up for the past thirty years. I've had the same problem before, and I've heard this hypnosis thing, and I've had many experts from the Stanford Dream Center . . . I've heard this. Fortunately or unfortunately, you're stuck with a judge who has gone through this hypnosis thing time and time again."

It had appeared to the judge that the case was nearing an end. "Now we have an expert, and I'll put that in quotes, comes in and brings up this whole issue of hypnosis. It makes me a little disenchanted to say the least. . . ." If he allowed Dr. Paris' testimony, then the prosecution would necessarily bring in an expert to oppose it. It would extend the trial, escalate the expenses, and end in a stalemate of "expert" opinions. "Why are we dancing through this at the last moment? It doesn't do much for my judicial demeanor. I want both sides to get a fair trial. That's the bottom line."

Dolan explained that the delay in summoning Dr. Paris had been due to scheduling problems.

MCCARTIN FELT NO LESS DISTRESSED as the verbal volleys continued with neither side scoring very well. The witness answered more questions related to the possibility that Craven was hypnotized without realizing it.

Huntington Beach Detective Art Droz was one of the men who allegedly hypnotized Craven. Goethals asked Dr. Paris, "Do you know that Detective Droz has testified, under oath, that he did not hypnotize her?"

"I didn't know that."

"So, if hypothetically you found that's true, then he's lying. Is that right?"

"No, I don't think he's lying. I don't think—he's not licensed, trained and qualified as a psychologist or psychiatrist to make those kinds of determinations.

"Which determinations are those?"

"That the person was hypnotized or not."

The same question about Droz deliberately lying was asked in several forms until Paris finally, with reluctance, said "Yes."

Goethals instantly posed the same inquiry about Rich Farnell? Was he lying too? The doctor modified his answer to, "He is gravely mistaken."

It took another half-hour to finally end the session with Dr. Paris.

McCartin said he would postpone a ruling on allowing the jury to hear Dr. Paris testify until Detective Droz and Deputy D.A. Farnell could respond to the doctor's statements.

In another closed hearing that afternoon, without the jury, Farnell was asked, "Did you personally hypnotize anyone in connection with this case?" He answered, "Absolutely not." Droz gave the same unequivocal answer about hypnotizing Anita Craven at any time.

JUDGE MCCARTIN ANNOUNCED HIS DECISION that the jury would not hear testimony from Dr. Paris regarding hypnosis. Defense attorney Dolan wasn't happy with the outcome, and challenged McCartin. "I am wondering if you are resolving the question of fact as opposed to the jury."

McCartin snapped, "I certainly am. That gentleman you had in here this morning ain't going to testify in this case. Is that clear?" He added, "It would confound, screw up, do nothing for this case as far as either side getting a fair trial. It would be fantasyland. And that's my ruling."

He looked and sounded exactly like Walter Brennan playing Judge Roy Bean in the old Gary Cooper classic film "The Westerner."

Said Dolan, "I think your position is clear, and so is mine."

McCartin concluded the exchange. "I sit here hopefully giving both sides a fair trial. That's what I am here for. If they want to reverse me, be my guest."

By the time Dolan rested the defense's case, forty–three witnesses had testified.

Tom Goethals called only four people in his short rebuttal of the defense's case. Now, each attorney would summarize in closing arguments to the jury what they believed the evidence had shown.

TOM GOETHALS HAD LOOKED WEARY in recent days. But he stood in front of the jury box with a new spring in his step, his face glowed with confidence.

"Ladies and gentlemen, I will take the suspense out of it right at the top. None of you is going to be the least bit surprised about what I am going to tell you. I told you this weeks ago and I've said it all along." He paused, then articulated each word of the next sentence. "This defendant is guilty of first degree murder."

He moved his gaze from face to face, as if speaking individually to each juror. "He is guilty of kidnapping. And it's true that he murdered little Robin Samsoe during the course of kidnapping. That's where I am going to end up. That's where I am starting.

"What evidence you have heard, from whatever source . . . should convince you beyond a reasonable doubt of each of those facts. I suggested to you during my opening statement . . . that the evidence in this case . . . could be broken up into four general categories: things that happened at the beach, things that happened in the mountains, things that happened in the Orange County Jail, and things that . . . indicated a consciousness of guilt on the defendant's part. And I labeled that 'flight.' "

First, he said, he wanted to review the law, then discuss the defense. Regarding the law, he defined first degree murder and said, "If you don't find it's first degree murder, you give the defendant an apology and you send him home because he's not guilty of anything."

Pointing an accusing finger at Alcala, the prosecutor said, "When this defendant took Robin Samsoe into that canyon with his knife, it wasn't any accident that Robin Samsoe ended up dead. What he did, he intended to do." Goethals orally underlined "intended."

Premeditation, he explained, must be shown as an integral part of first degree murder. What is premeditation? Goethals knew that jurors sometimes struggle with the question, wondering how long a killer must think of the act before he does it. Can premeditation be a minute or must it be hours, or days? The prosecutor read from a legal explanation. "The law does not attempt to measure units. . . . The true test is not the duration of time, but the rather the extent of the reflection. A cold, calculated judgement and decision may be arrived at in a short period of time."

Goethals wanted the jury to understand that if Robin's killer had planned her murder during the entire forty-mile drive from Huntington Beach to the mountains, or if he decided to kill her one minute beforehand, it could be regarded as premeditation.

Shifting gears, Goethals challenged the defense attorney's opening statements. He pointed out that sometimes lawyers promise to prove certain things, and then fail to deliver. He asked jurors to remember that each side's opening comments had been broken down into four areas. "Mine were the beach, the mountains, the jail, and evidence of consciousness of guilt, or flight. The defense said their areas were pathology, physical evidence, eyewitnesses and snitches. They went on a long time about informants from the jail."

Keeping personal eye contact, like a tactile connection with each juror, Goethals said, "The scientific evidence without question indicates that Robin Samsoe was brutally murdered . . . we agree on that. With respect to the second area . . . you were told there were only two pieces of physical evidence . . . the knife . . . and a couple of innocuous gold earrings. And you were told the knife wasn't even the murder weapon . . . and the earrings could not be linked to this defendant. . . . Obviously, we had a substantial difference on that.

"In the third area, of eyewitnesses, you were told about Anita Craven . . . . It was suggested that she was badgered, intimidated, cajoled, brainwashed—I don't know—there was a long list of words." No evidence had been offered to substantiate those allegations.

"If you will think back, there was no mention of other eyewitnesses." The defense hadn't provided anything to refute the testimony of several "very, very important" witnesses who had placed Alcala on the beach within a short time of Robin Samsoe's disappearance. They had unequivocally identified him in 1980 and in the current trial. They were not lying and they were not mistaken.

"Finally, and probably most interestingly, the defense went on and on . . . it was very good, very entertaining, very effective frankly . . . about things that went on in the Orange County Jail." Mister Dolan, he said, had indicated "a criminal conspiracy was hatched" in the jail.

Goethals produced a verbatim transcript of the defense's opening statement and read it to the jury. In summary, it said that desperate drug addicts embellished available facts from news reports and exchanged the fabricated stories for favorable treatment.

"What happened to that?" Goethals asked. "Two people came to court who had been in jail with the defendant, one called by the prosecution, one called by the defense. Ironically, both said the defendant made extremely damaging statements to them." The defense witness, said Goethals, mentioned that Alcala confessed to him, then retracted the story. The prosecution witness, David Jackson, didn't fit at all the charges made by Mr. Dolan. "Where is the criminal conspiracy hatched in jail, fostered by the police and the D.A. to get this defendant? Where is the evidence of that? There is zero, zero evidence of that."

Tackling the Knott's Berry Farm alibi, Goethals said, "There is no reliable evidence the defendant was at Knott's Berry Farm."

Admitting the case was primarily circumstantial, the prosecutor said, "It is not something to be a afraid of. Circumstantial evidence is equally valid with direct evidence."

The defense, he pointed out, had shrugged off much of the evidence as "coincidence." "Let's run through those coincidences."

He listed them:

–On June 19 and 20, there is a tall, thin, man with curly hair taking pictures at the beach

   –He is taking pictures only of young girls at several beach locations

   –In all cases, he is using the pictures in "a photo contest"

   –They all identify the photographer as Rodney Alcala

   –This same man approaches Robin Samsoe, and shortly afterward, she disappears. Goethals scoffed, "Now isn't that a coincidence?"

   –On "The Dating Game" videotape, made months earlier, he had long hair. Witnesses all say the "photographer" had long hair. Within days after Robin's death, he cuts his hair short.

   "What a coincidence."

   –He decides to leave town, but lies to everybody about where he is going.

   "Coincidence?"

   –He goes to Seattle, and keeps it secret. Pictures of girls and earrings turn up in his Seattle storage locker.

   "More coincidence?"

   –Alcala has previously photographed a girl close to the mountain crime scene. Yet another coincidence?

   –A yellow Schwinn bike mysteriously turns up at a thrift shop located on the route Alcala probably would use traveling home from the crime scene. Just another coincidence?

   –The earrings found in Alcala's locker match a description given by Robin's mother. More coincidence.

   –The Kane Kut knives. "The defense says the Kane Kut knife found in the mountains isn't even the murder weapon.

Goethals wore an expression of total disbelief. "Is that one of the most extraordinary coincidences you have ever heard in your life that lying there at the scene of a murder of a young child is a knife with human blood on it, and they want you to believe that's a coincidence?

–"The storage locker receipt. Now there's a really interesting coincidence. We know what was found in the storage locker. Tons of stuff including those gold earrings. . . . Why is he so concerned about that receipt after his arrest? Why does he ask a relative to go to the house and look for it? Why does he ask if the police have found it? What an interesting coincidence in light of what is found in the locker."

Focusing his attention on the earrings, Goethals pointed out that even a defense witness called them "little girl's earrings." Mr. Dolan had claimed they were modified and worn by Alcala, but Goethals scoffed at that notion. The little baubles were found inside a box of jewelry discovered in the Seattle locker. "Coincidentally," the only piece in there worn by Alcala were the earrings. Alcala only had one ear pierced. Why would he have clipped both of these? "It goes back to what Robin's mother told you. Those earrings belong to her daughter and the defendant took them when he murdered her up in that canyon."

Apologizing for overlapping the jurors' lunch break, Goethals spoke about the credibility of his jailhouse informant, about Anita Craven, and philosophized a bit. Winding down, he said, "I am about to sit down. Mr. Dolan will talk to you, then he will sit down and shut up, and it will be up to you all. This defendant has committed a monstrous crime. It's a crime against Robin Samsoe, it's a crime against her family, it's really a crime against the community. What crime affects us all and stays with us more than a brutal murder of a totally innocent young child? It affects every one of us. We can't get over it.

"Again, I underline it. Acquit the innocent but convict the guilty.

"I hope and I pray and I ask each one of you to have the courage and the common sense to hold this man accountable for what he did. And the only way you can do that is to convict him. Thank you."

At 12:45, Judge McCartin excused the jury for lunch, but limited it to one hour. "Please be back by 1:45," he admonished.

IT IS DIFFICULT TO MEASURE the impact of final arguments on juries. Certainly, powerful oratory has swayed crowds throughout the ages. Adolf Hitler used it to lead a nation into the bloodiest war in history. Winston Churchill and Franklin Roosevelt used it to avoid defeat and eventually emerge triumphant. Clarence Darrow applied it in courtrooms with incredible success.

Juries are legally bound, during deliberations, to weigh only the evidence presented during the trial and not the golden speeches made by attorneys. Common sense, though, suggests that a well-presented final argument may tilt the scales of justice one way or the other. In a system of "perfect" justice, that would not be the case.

TOM GOETHALS HAD MADE a rock-solid, persuasive presentation. John Dolan knew he faced a tough challenge.

As soon as he stood up, he took an apologetic stance. "Ladies and gentlemen, it's at this point I get to tell you what I think the evidence showed in this case. I told you what I thought the evidence was going to show in the beginning. It didn't show exactly what we thought. And I will talk to you about that in just a second.

"You heard the evidence, you heard the witnesses, and you are the ones who decides what the evidence was. . . ."

He explained that the prosecutor had, before the trial, supplied a witness list naming jailhouse informants who might be called. "I want to let you know that when Mr. Goethals doesn't call those witnesses, then you know why we didn't talk about snitches in this case."

Reminding jurors of the presumption of innocence requirements, Dolan said, "Rodney Alcala began this trial sitting in that chair not guilty." Jurors, he said, must abide by that. The police, he charged, had investigated the whole thing while working with a presumption of guilt.

Tackling the subject of circumstantial evidence, Dolan explained, "The problem is . . . things can have two interpretations." But in this case, there was only one. And "under that interpretation Mr. Alcala is still innocent." Dolan objected to Goethals' repeated use of the word "coincidence," pointing out that it had nothing to do with evidence, it was "just a little lawyer's trick. But you are not going to fall for that." Perhaps the litany had bothered Dolan more than he admitted. He added, "I am not obligated to tell you why coincidences took place."

One by one, he called out each juror's name, and stressed, "Each of you has the obligation to give us your opinion. You must decide the case for yourself."

Dolan expressed sympathy for the "horrible tragedy" suffered by the victim and her family, but asserted that it was not to be considered as evidence.

Attacking the prosecution's case, Dolan challenged the early identifications made by Bridgett Wilvert, Jackelyn Young, and Richard Sillett. He said the artist's sketch bore little resemblance to Alcala. It was reminiscent of Alcala's own protests during the very first police interview seven years earlier, "That doesn't even look like me."

The bike abandoned behind a thrift shop, according to Dolan, didn't resemble the one Robin Samsoe rode, either. It had yellow and white tape on the handlebars, but the thrift shop witness had seen a bike with black and white tape.

Several young women had testified about Alcala wanting to photograph them for a contest. Said Dolan, "If that proves the case, you know, beyond a reasonable doubt, I will tear up my law license and go to Montana and sell hamburgers."

Step by step, Dolan recounted Alcala's activities on June 20, according to family members, records of telephone calls, and testimony from

Knott's Berry Farm employees. In view of that, charged Dolan, "How could he possibly have been abducting Robin Samsoe a little after 3 p.m. all the way down in Huntington Beach, and be seen with her at sunset in the mountains, as testified by Anita Craven?"

Dolan tore into the testimony of Anita Craven that had been read into the record. He pointed to numerous elements of it he regarded as inconsistent, full of mistakes, or outright lies.

In regards to Alcala changing his appearance by getting his hair cut, Dolan reminded jurors that a female friend of the defendant had suggested prior to the death of Samsoe that he needed to change the styling. And the storage locker? "Do you think if he was trying to hide anything he would have rented it in his own name?"

Testimony from jailhouse informant David Jackson should not be trusted, said Dolan. Tracing the dates various informants were jailed, it didn't appear to Dolan that Jackson was even in the protective custody unit at the same time as Alcala.

Dolan recapitulated what he had covered so far. "After the area of identification, Mr. Alcala is still innocent. . . . After the so-called area of flight, Mr. Alcala is still innocent. . . . Now let's look at the physical evidence. The Kane Kut knife? You can buy them at any supermarket, for goodness sakes." Because Alcala's mother owned two sets, from which no knives were missing, that meant nothing, he said..

A SERIOUS QUESTION REMAINED regarding physical evidence, Dolan said. If Robin Samsoe had been in Alcala's car for more than half an hour, from the beach to the mountains, why was there "not a shred of evidence" in that vehicle to prove it? No hairs, no fibers, no prints, nothing. "Do you think that's even within the realm of reason?"

The earrings, Dolan asserted, belonged to Alcala. Furthermore, he pointed out, no witness testimony stated that Robin was even wearing earrings that day.

"That's it for physical evidence, ladies and gentlemen. Knife, earrings, lack of other physical evidence. . . . He's still sitting there innocent."

Once again, Dolan expressed sorrow for Robin's family, then added that Alcala's mother has also lost her son. "They put him in jail on the twenty-fifth of July, 1979, and for all those years, he has lost his life."

Standing at the lectern, Dolan checked his notes one last time to see if he had overlooked anything, then continued. "If you believe in proof beyond a reasonable doubt, if you believe in the presumption of innocence, then you have to find this innocent guy innocent. . . . And if you do what's right, you aren't voting against the people of the state of California, you uphold the law. The people of California win when justice is done. And that's all we're asking you to do. Just do justice. He's innocent and you should return a verdict that says that. Thank you."

At last, on May 22, 1986, after Judge McCartin performed the required reading of jury instructions, the dozen triers of fact filed into their room to begin deliberations. For the families of Robin Samsoe and Rodney Alcala, the torturous wait began.

AN IMAGE REMAINS ETCHED in McCartin's memory. While waiting for the jury's decision, he passed through the third-floor cafeteria and caught sight of a woman sitting by herself in a corner, weeping softly. It was Marianne Frazier, Robin's mother. The sight tugged at McCartin's heart. He had an impulse to walk over, pat her on the shoulder, and offer reassurance that everything would be okay. But, he would later say, "Judges aren't supposed to do that."

Four days later, the foreman sent word via bailiff Mitch Miller that a verdict had been reached.

With all one hundred forty-two gallery seats filled, and overflow spectators standing along walls in absolute silence, clerk Gail Carpenter read aloud the verdict.

In her high, crystal clear voice, Carpenter announced that Rodney Alcala, for the second time, had been found guilty of first degree murder with special circumstances.

Later, in the court hallway, the defense attorneys informed reporters that "overwhelming evidence" would be used in appealing the decision.

The penalty phase would begin in two weeks, on Friday, the sixth day of June.

ON D-DAY, THE FORTY–SECOND ANNIVERSARY of the WWII Normandy invasion, the battle began in Judge McCartin's court to determine if Alcala should spend the rest of his life in the general population of California's prisons, or on death row. But like any war, the combatants find ways to muddle things up. A postponement delayed proceedings until the following Monday.

It commenced with yet another problem. John Dolan announced, "I have been informed this morning . . . that Mr. Alcala wishes to relieve myself and Mr. Monroe and he wishes to make a statement on the record as to why he wishes to do that."

It is not uncommon for defendants in murder trials to fire their attorneys. Known as a "Marsden motion," the process is sometimes a valid expression of dissatisfaction with the defense lawyer's performance, but is often used as a delaying tactic simply to postpone the dreaded trip to a state prison. McCartin had no humorous comment. He simply nodded toward the defendant. "Surely. Mr. Alcala."

"Okay," the defendant said. In his years of listening to court proceedings and studying his own case while on death row, he had learned to sound like a practicing attorney. "I want to present a motion to the court under People versus Marsden—" he cited legal references "for substitution of counsel and also make a motion to declare a mistrial."

Alcala explained his reasoning. The attorneys, he said, hadn't implemented his plan for a defense. They hadn't "sufficiently" consulted with him or adequately investigated facts of the case. They were "unpre-pared" and made "unwise choices of trial tactics and strategy." He apologetically offered, "I am a rather quiet individual and I sincerely wanted to believe Mr. Dolan was acting in my best interests." His artic-ulation and intelligence impressed observers. "Mr. Dolan failed to pro-duce witnesses crucial to my defense." His lawyers, Alcala said, had also " failed to adequately investigate facts of the case."

Examples offered by Alcala included the lawyers' superficial han-dling of various issues Alcala wanted to discuss with them, and their omission of crucial evidence regarding jailhouse informants, one of whom "expected quid pro quo for his testimony." An especially impor-tant element involved inadequate exploration of the Knott's Berry Farm alibi. The defendant stated, "Mr. Dolan was not prepared to defend a death penalty case. His preparation regarding the facts was abysmal."

Alcala's barrage of criticism and appeal for redress lasted nearly thir-ty minutes.

Tom Goethals, invited by McCartin to comment, said, "Mr. Alcala can sit there and say anything he wants. . . . Basically what we have is a difference of opinion." The prosecutor believed that Dolan had made efforts to deal with most of the issues at the core of the defendant's complaints. Goethals added, "What's he got to lose by writing fifty pages and trying to muddle up the record? We oppose his motion."

Judge McCartin had listened to Alcala's speech with a certain admi-ration. "He's given a well thought-out argument and request." The defendant's position was certainly understandable, said McCartin. On the other hand, a great deal of time had been used in special hearings of issues brought forth by the defense attorneys. It was not uncommon, the judge noted, for defendants to think their lawyers could have done things differently.

In regard to Alcala's stated opinion that the court could "clearly see his attorneys' failures," McCartin said, "I don't, by a long way, feel that

is the case." Defendants are entitled to the services of reasonably competent attorneys and a diligent, vigorous defense by adequate evidence,
he explained, and stated that both Mr. Dolan and Mr. Monroe had met
those standards.

Alcala protested. He had "severed relations" with the defenders that
morning, so was "without counsel" at that moment, but wanted to proceed with the motion for a mistrial.

McCartin had a quick answer. "Well, my response to that is your
motion for mistrial is denied. . . . With regard to severing your relationship, I'm going to unsever it. . . . These gentlemen represented you
throughout and I'm ordering them to continue in the representation of
your case. . . . We will proceed to the penalty phase of this trial at
one–thirty this afternoon."

WITH THE SAME JURY RECONVENED, Tom Goethals called only
nine witnesses to present testimony of aggravating circumstances.
Among them were several women who had suffered at the hands of the
defendant when they were children. Jurors heard Mary Adams speak of
Alcala raping and almost killing her in 1968, when she was only eight
years old. Jennifer Carlson described the 1979 sexual assault and beating
she had endured in Riverside County. She was fifteen at the time.

For the defense, Tom Dolan elicited witness testimony that Alcala
was a model prisoner and a skilled typist who could be useful as a prison
clerk.

The defendant's mother told jurors her son had always been quiet,
studious and always kind to her. He had served in the Army. She didn't
want her son to be executed.

Dolan called Alcala to the stand. He began by profusely apologizing
to Mary Adams and followed with a similar expression of regret to
Jennifer Carlson.

Dolan asked questions about pictures Alcala had taken and about
having his ear pierced. He brought up the Knott's Berry Farm visit again

and the defendant's activities on June 19, 20, and 21, 1979. Observers wondered if the defense was still trying to establish an alibi.

Alcala acknowledged that on June 20, he drove from his Monterey Park residence to Seal Beach, which is about ten miles up the coast from Huntington Beach. He had planned to visit a friend, but she wasn't home. So he headed toward Costa Mesa to purchase picture frames from a specialty store. His route, on Pacific Coast Highway, would take him past the pier and the cliffs where Robin Samsoe and Bridgett Wilvert soaked up the sun on that afternoon.

Before reaching Huntington Beach, Alcala said, he spotted some pretty girls in tiny bikinis skating near a liquor store in Sunset Beach. He stopped and took pictures of Wanda Ford, at about 1 p.m. From there, he drove through Huntington Beach. In answer to Dolan's questions, Alcala absolutely denied stopping or taking any photos of Robin or Bridgett. He traveled about three or four miles past the pier to the Costa Mesa frame store. After completing his purchase, he drove back up the coast, through Huntington Beach, again without stopping, and arrived again in Seal Beach at about 2 p.m. His friend was still not home, so he headed north to Knott's Berry Farm and entered an office at about 3:30 p.m.

RESIDENTS OF NORTHERN ORANGE COUNTY know that a trip from Seal Beach to Knott's Berry Farm takes no more than thirty minutes. In Alcala's story, it took one and one-half hours. He didn't explain the odd discrepancy.

This penalty phase testimony, perhaps intended to create doubt in jurors' minds about the guilty verdict, may have had the reverse effect. Alcala now placed himself in Huntington Beach on the afternoon of June 20, within an hour or so of Robin Samsoe's disappearance.

Dolan brought up the gold-ball earrings again. Alcala insisted that he had bought them for himself and pinched off the lower balls with fingernail clippers. He had packed them away in his Seattle storage locker with other possessions. The reason he had rented the locker, he said, was because he planned to leave Southern California in order to flee from charges of assaulting Jennifer Carlson.

On cross-examination, Alcala testified that after his attack on Mary Adams in 1968, he eluded law enforcement officials, withdrew his life savings, and moved to New York, where he changed his name to John Berger. He worked at a camp in New England with teenage girls. When arrested on a fugitive warrant stemming from the Adams case, he lied to the FBI about his identity in an effort to avoid going to prison. In March 1972, he was convicted of child molestation.

Alcala's answers to Goethals took the jury along a winding path of numerous offenses involving young women and the defendant's prison terms.

Dolan used his final turn representing his reluctant client by allowing him to deliver a plea to the jury. Dolan asked him, "What would you want the jury to do?"

Facing them, Alcala said, "I would want you to give me life without the possibility of parole. You've heard a lot of really horrible things about me and you've heard that in prison I am absolutely no threat to anybody whatsoever. You've heard that in prison I provide a useful function, that I'm very good at what I do in prison. You know that life without the possibility of parole, I will never get out of prison. Prison is not a very easy life. It doesn't matter what prison you are at, when you have crimes like I have against [young girls], you are looked down upon by the people in prison. That's obvious. I feel the same way.

"I don't think of myself as that type of person." He would not be a threat to anyone while locked away, he said.

"I don't want to die. I don't want you to kill me. I'm not guilty of this crime and I don't know whether you believe me or not. I wanted to testify during the guilt phase but I wasn't allowed to do that. I thought you should know all these things and the decision was made without me, as to that. There was evidence I wanted you to see. I didn't kill Robin Samsoe and I don't think I should die for something that I didn't do.

"I think that you may well feel that someone who commits a crime like that should die. But I didn't do that, and I think if there's any doubt whatsoever in your minds as to whether I did that or not, that you should give me the slightest benefit of the doubt. I just—I don't want to die. And I didn't do the crime. I don't know what else I can say.

"I am absolutely harmless. . . . They are going to get years of work out of me, and good work. I provide a very useful function. I am no problem whatsoever. I don't know what else I can tell you except please don't kill me."

The jury filed slowly into their room on Wednesday afternoon to make one last difficult decision. They worked the remainder of that afternoon and all the following day. On Friday, June 20, 1986, exactly seventeen years since the day Robin Samsoe vanished, the jury delivered their verdict.

For the second time, Rodney Alcala would face the death penalty.

TWO MONTHS LATER, Judge McCartin conducted the official sentence hearing.

When Alcala and his attorneys again protested, the judge remarked, "Hogwash. He's as guilty as anybody who has ever come through my court."

He had learned the term "hogwash" decades earlier from his executive officer aboard the USS St. Paul, Commander Jack McCain.

Characterizing the murder of Robin Samsoe as "vicious and malevolent in every sense of the word," McCartin ordered Alcala returned to San Quentin's death row to await eventual execution.

Outside the courtroom, prosecutor Tom Goethals told reporters that the California Supreme Court is notorious for reversing death penalty cases, but "this was a good, clean trial and it should hold up under any objective review."

Alcala returned to death row, resumed his job as a clerk, and began filing motions for dismissal of the guilty verdict and penalty.

Agony of Defeat

In 1992 the California Supreme Court automatically reviewed Rodney Alcala's trial by Judge McCartin. After meticulous weighing of the facts the justices concluded "The judgment should be affirmed in its entirety."

In 2001, the federal court system galloped to Alcala's rescue. U.S. District Judge Stephen V. Wilson examined the condemned convict's appeal issues, and ruled:

1) Alcala's trial counsel had been ineffective in presenting the defendant's alibi,

2) The trial court, Judge McCartin, committed constitutional error in excluding the testimony of Dr. George Paris,

3) Judge McCartin's denial of an independent medical examination of witness Anita Craven violated the Sixth Amendment and,

4) Several "cumulative" non-constitutional errors had been made by the trial court. Wilson vacated the conviction and sentence.

ALL WAS NOT LOST, at least not yet. The district court's decision would be contested in the U.S. 9th Circuit Court of Appeals.

A three-member panel of that high court heard the case in February 2003. On June 28, the judges issued their findings.

"We conclude that Alcala's trial suffered from multiple constitutional errors that had a substantial and injurious effect on the jury's determination of guilt. Accordingly, we affirm the district court's ruling."

In making its decision, the 9th Circuit Court pointed accusing fingers directly at Judge Donald McCartin, and the defense attorneys as well. The key issues on which the court based its conclusions were:

1) The trial court (Judge McCartin) precluded Alcala from effectively challenging the testimony of the prosecution's key witness, Anita Craven. The exclusion of Dr. Paris' expert testimony deprived Alcala of an important opportunity to discredit the only eyewitness who allegedly could place Alcala with Robin Samsoe at the scene of the crime on the evening of June 20. Had Dr. Paris been permitted to testify, the jury may have discounted Craven's testimony as not credible in light of the fact that it was obtained through improper and dubious means, as well as the obvious and apparent instability of Craven's mental condition. Dr. Paris' expert testimony, combined with Craven's bizarre demeanor, would have seriously called into question her reliability as a witness. Had the credibility of the prosecution's star witness been effectively challenged, the case against Alcala would have been undoubtedly weaker.

2) Aside from Craven, the only eyewitness who could place Alcala with Samsoe was Jackelyn Young, who claimed to have seen Alcala with Samsoe at Huntington Beach on the afternoon of June 20 at 3 p.m. Had Alcala's counsel adequately presented his Knott's Berry Farm alibi, Alcala could have directly challenged the theory that he abducted Samsoe after she left Wilvert's house at 3:10 p.m.

3) Judge McCartin had made rulings that prevented testimony from Tim Nellis, a witness who claimed to have seen Robin Samsoe riding a bicycle in Huntington beach on June 21, the day after she disappeared. The judge had also prevented the jury from hearing about officer Crawford's encounter near the crime scene, several days later, with Juan Duarte who had served time for murder. The high court said that

Nellis', Crawford's, and Duarte's testimony would have further weakened the prosecution's theory of the case. The combined testimony of these witnesses would have challenged Craven's version of the events and presented a "colorable" third-party culpability theory for the jury.

4) The "erroneous" admission of the Kane Kutlery knives seized from Alcala's home permitted the jury to draw an impermissible connection between Alcala and the purported murder weapon—the key and only piece of physical evidence discovered at the crime scene that could be linked to Alcala. The prosecution's placement of undue emphasis on this "compels us to conclude the jury's verdict was tainted by the admission of this evidence."

5) Alcala's trial counsel presented a fatally impeachable witness, a jailhouse informant, without first assessing how he would respond on cross-examination to evidence that he had told police that Alcala confessed to him. As a result, this witness actually served to reinforce the informant's tale that Alcala confessed to murdering Samsoe.

6) Alcala's trial counsel completely failed to conduct any investigation of the crime scene. This failure likely resulted in loss of an opportunity to challenge Craven's purported observations as inconsistent with the objective evidence.

The 9th Circuit Court issued a fifty-seven page decision in the Alcala case. It ended with: "Therefore, we conclude that the cumulative impact of these errors is more than sufficient to demonstrate prejudice. The cumulative weight of the above errors deprived Alcala of a fundamentally fair trial. . . . We affirm the grant of Alcala's petition."

ON JUNE 28, 2003, Don McCartin sat in his retirement home on the shore of Bass Lake, and opened a copy of the Fresno Bee newspaper. "I saw the reversal story and I sat there in stunned disbelief. The more I read, the more it dumbfounded me. On one hand, I burned with anger. On the other, I felt extreme pity for the victim's family. Robin's mother had even received official permission to witness the execution. Now, she would have to face the entire process again. Actually, my compassion for her soon replaced the fury."

The Alcala case had lingered in McCartin's thoughts for years. "Because it's in front of me all the time. It's always here. You pick up the paper in 1990, and there it is. And now it's reversed again. It never goes away. Randy Kraft obviously lingers in my mind, too. He killed so many; probably fifteen or sixteen in one of the adjacent counties, and more in Oregon. And nobody else wanted to try him. It seems that his crimes were so mind-boggling, they just died away. But Alcala . . . it bothers you because you know how guilty he is and yet he keeps going forward for his own interest. He doesn't worry about the pain to his mother, his sister, or the victim's family. He doesn't care what he's doing to these people. I really get upset and angry. And I'm still furious about it."

Feeling that he needed to take some kind of action, McCartin said, "What could I do about all this? My thoughts turned to an Orange County author who had once autographed a book for me with the words, 'To the best judge ever . . .' "

One of the most bothersome elements of the reversal to McCartin was the decision-making process by the three 9th Circuit jurists, Senior Circuit Judge Dorothy W. Nelson, along with Circuit Judges Kim McLane Wardlaw and Raymond C. Fisher. How could they have arrived at their conclusions?

THEIR WRITTEN DECISION WAS LOADED with "may have" and "could have." Dr. Paris' "expert" testimony? To McCartin, it had been riddled with confusion and unsupportable theories about hypnosis. And what about the sworn testimony of the police officer and the prosecutor Paris accused of performing "induced hypnotism" on Craven? They had unequivocally denied hypnotizing her in any form. Why was that ignored? They had seemed more reliable than the hocus-pocus witness with his references to hypnotic influences. This "doctor" was a psychologist, not a licensed psychiatrist, said McCartin, a factor he considered in ruling out the testimony.

The Knott's Berry Farm alibi? No one had convincingly placed Alcala at that theme park during the hours in question.

Tim Nellis had probably believed he saw Robin on June 21, but it made no sense at all. He had seriously flawed his opinion by mistakenly identifying a photograph in the first trial. And why would this little girl be riding that bike around Huntington Beach, within a few blocks of her home, on the day after an intensive search had been launched for her and while her desperate mother worried?

Neither was there any reason to believe that Juan Duarte could have committed the crime. He had a perfect alibi in his employment records that indicated he had been at work on June 20 and 21. That issue would have just wasted more time. The jury would undoubtedly have rejected it.

The Kane Kut knife found at the crime scene was clearly the murder weapon. The high court seemed to have completely discounted the jury's intelligence by judging that their decision was "tainted." Jurors were smart enough to decide whether or not the Kane Kut knives in Alcala's home were of any probative value in the case.

And the defense's informant was "fatally impeachable"? That's what cross-examination allows. If every time a witness was shown to be unreliable through cross-examination, nearly all murder cases would be overturned.

Finally, the jurists' concern that defenders hadn't conducted an investigation of the crime scene? This appeared completely speculative. What could defense investigators possibly have found after the police had scoured every inch of turf in the region? This was heaping insult on injury.

The three justices who reached these conclusions, said McCartin, had never conducted a trial in their professional lives.

Senior Circuit Judge Dorothy Nelson, 74, appointed by President Jimmy Carter in 1979, had been a law professor and Dean at the University of Southern California. Judge Kim M. Wardlaw, 50, appointed by President Bill Clinton in 1998, had worked for a private law firm from 1980 to 1996, and gone directly to the U.S. District Court, California, in 1996 as an appellate judge. Judge Raymond Fisher, 62, appointed by President Bill Clinton, had clerked for a circuit court judge and for U.S. Supreme Court Justice William J. Brennan, known for his liberal, anti-death penalty decisions. Fisher had practiced with two private law firms between 1968 and 1997, and been an associate U.S. attorney general from 1997 to 1999.

Even the chief judge of the 9th Circuit Court, Judge Mary Schroeder, 63, had never tried a case directly. Appointed by President Carter, she had worked with the U.S. Department of Justice, had been a law clerk for the Arizona Supreme Court, and had practiced with a private law firm.

Wouldn't trial court experience provide a more balanced ability to decide these important issues in death penalty cases? The 9th Circuit Court had frequently been reversed by the U.S. Supreme Court on capital punishment issues, and openly chastised by the higher court on several occasions. Were 9th Circuit Court justices, indeed, biased against the death penalty?

Don McCartin thought so. He said, "You can check the record. They will find excuses to overturn any case they want to."

IN SEPTEMBER 2003, in one single eight-to-three ruling, the 9th Circuit Court overturned more than 100 death sentences, mostly in Arizona, Idaho, and Montana. The laws of these states had allowed judges, rather than juries, to decide, after guilt was established, if the defendant should serve life in prison or be executed.

The Los Angeles Times featured a cartoon in the Editorial section by Michael Ramirez. It pictured a flower-bedecked open casket, labeled "Murder Victim." A telephone cord stretches into it, and the unseen corpse is saying, "Hello, 9th Circuit? I was wondering if you could over-turn my death sentence too?" For a huge segment of the American population, it echoed their sentiments exactly.

Don McCartin called the Orange County author, and proposed that a book be written to inform the public about the Alcala case. He said, "Now, after all this, my goal is simply to outlive the men I sent to death row, but I don't think I'm going to make it."

RODNEY ALCALA WILL ONCE AGAIN sit in the same 11th floor Santa Ana courtroom to face a third murder trial. It must feel like home to him. He was returned to Orange County Jail in the summer of 2003 and is actively involved in the pretrial hearings conducted by Judge Francisco Briseno. By early 2004, Alcala had already filed a motion to represent him-self in court, but changed his mind and accepted appointment of attor-ney David Zimmerman as counsel. Zimmerman, 56, a well-respected Orange County criminal lawyer known by his peers for always wearing a fresh carnation in his lapel, worked feverishly to meet a trial date sched-uled for November, 2004. Tragically, he died of an apparent heart attack in June while snorkeling during a Caribbean vacation. As a result, the pending trial will probably be delayed another year or more.

The oft-passed baton of prosecuting Alcala has been handed to Matt Murphy, 36, a tall slim deputy district attorney who looks equally comfortable in a surfboarding wetsuit or a pin-striped Armani. Gregarious, athletic, quick-witted and disarmingly personable, Murphy can beguile juries. In nine homicide cases he has prosecuted, juries have returned with convictions in all nine.

This perfect Californian was born in Taiwan, while his father served as military doctor during the Vietnam conflict. The Murphys landed back in the Golden State where young Matt attended Loyola High

School in Los Angeles. Following graduation, he packed his surfboard and matriculated at the University of California, Santa Barbara. He recalls college life with a wide grin. "Disneyland may call itself the happiest place on Earth, but UCSB is right up there with them. Beautiful women, great waves, and an excellent school."

Matt Murphy

As vice president of his fraternity, Murphy was instrumental in founding a group called Greeks Against Rape, an organization of Greek-lettered frats vowing to make a stand against sexual assault. It stemmed from a particular sexual-assault case that infuriated him, and may have been the root of his interest in law. During his senior year, he participated in a "semester at sea." This inspired a seven-month post-graduation trot around the globe to Indonesia, Australia and other exotic meccas for surfers.

Murphy entered law school at the University of California, San Diego, in 1990. Earning superior marks, he won the American Jurisprudence Award for scholastic achievement. In Paris, he studied international law. Landing a job in with the Orange County D.A. was almost as difficult as riding a giant breaker on Hawaii's north shore. "I was the last person to get interviewed. A representative went to five schools in two days, screened hundreds of people, and put me on the alternate list. I barely squeaked in."

LUCKY FOR ORANGE COUNTY that he did. Murphy knew from the first moment he wanted to be a prosecutor. After a stint as a law clerk, he moved on to tackling juvenile gangs, working with the sexual assault unit, the felony trial panel, and finally to homicide trials in 2001. One of his proudest moments was his selection as Outstanding Felony Prosecutor, awarded by the Garden Grove Police Department.

In Murphy's first murder trial, he prosecuted Victor Miranda Guerrero, 24, for the rape-slaying of a Huntington Beach woman. His effective presentation of the evidence, in April 2003, was so convincing that jurors needed only four hours of deliberation to convict Guerrero, and a short time to recommend the death penalty. In January 2004, Murphy prosecuted multiple rapist Douglas Hopper and won a conviction that sent Hopper to prison for one hundred thirty–five years. When being congratulated, Murphy just smiled. Hopper acted as his own attorney and argued that he didn't do the crimes, but if he did do them, he must have been insane. The jury deliberated two hours in deciding guilt, and only twenty–nine minutes to declare Hopper sane. Murphy called it a slam-dunk case.

Homicide unit supervisor Lew Rosenblum, who had prosecuted Gregory Sturm, expresses confidence in Murphy's skills. "He hasn't lost a case yet," beamed Rosenblum, who understands what it's like to win. His record of sixty–six murder convictions out of sixty–six trials is one of the best in the nation.

The Alcala prosecution will be a giant challenge considering the staggering volume of evidence ruled out by the California Supreme Court and the U.S. 9th Circuit Court of Appeals.

EVEN IF MURPHY FINDS CONSTRICTIONS imposed by appeals courts impossible to overcome, and the next jury delivers a not guilty verdict for Rodney Alcala, the accused killer of Robin Samsoe is not likely to go free.

Fate intervened simultaneously with the 9th Circuit Court's decision in June 2003. In the same news reports, the district attorney of Los

Angeles County announced the filing of murder charges against Alcala in a "cold case" from 1977!

On December 16 of that year, Georgia Wixted, 27, was raped and murdered in her home on Pacific Coast Highway in Malibu Beach. The killer, apparently caught in the act of burglarizing Wixted's residence, sexually assaulted her, then savagely beat her to death. Fluid samples were taken from her body and saved. In 1977, DNA wasn't yet a viable forensic tool. But it certainly is in the twenty–first century. A recent law provides for taking DNA samples from California prison inmates. Los Angeles cold-case investigators compared DNA from the Wixted case to prisoners' computerized genetic profiles. They found that Alcala's DNA statistically matched the fluids left on Wixted's body.

When the third Orange County trial is completed, Alcala will be sent to L.A. County where he will face yet another murder charge. Perhaps there is such a thing as perfect justice.

Postscript

Capital punishment, in California and perhaps the whole nation, appears to be on its own death row. Public support of the death penalty seems to be gradually fading.

Voters in the Golden State twice marked ballots in strong majorities to re-establish capital punishment after it was struck down by the US Supreme Court in the 1970s. California residents were so firm on the issue, they waged a 1986 campaign against State Supreme Court Chief Justice Rose Bird along with Associate Justices Cruz Reynoso and Joseph Grodin. These three were the sparkplugs in overturning sixty-one death sentences. Robin Samsoe's mother, Marianne Frazier, worked feverishly to unseat them, and the electorate voted the trio out of office.

But in recent years, a sobering number of prison inmates, many of them awaiting execution, have been exonerated by DNA evidence. The possibility of convicting and killing an innocent person is horrifying. No one wants that.

AS A TRUE-CRIME WRITER, I have observed numerous trials and researched many more. I've seen a sickening array of photographs depicting savage slaughter of innocent victims. I frequently felt bitter hatred for these killers. All too often, I've heard endless excuses by defendants, but very little remorse. Judge McCartin has expressed his disappointment at convicted murderers who cannot bring themselves to show contrition or pity for victims and their families. In many cases, I've felt like I would like to throw the switch and personally watch these savage men pay the supreme penalty. What right do they have to continue living, with free medical care, education, entertainment, and food after the horrors they perpetrated? We all know that death row is not a vacation resort, but it is better than dying in bloody violence like their innocent victims did.

However, there are several good arguments against capital punishment, in addition to the grim specter of executing someone who is innocent.

In California, more than 650 condemned inmates occupy death row, including thirteen women. Since reinstatement of laws permitting capital punishment in 1978, ten men have been executed. (Some say eleven, but that includes one condemned in California but sent to Missouri to be executed for a murder he committed in that state.) That is not effective implementation of capital punishment. Each time the final hours approach for a convicted killer, a circus of last-minute demonstrations and appeals splash across television screens and headlines. And a high court nearly always issues a "temporary" stay, which lasts indefinitely.

Another factor against capital punishment might appeal to taxpayers. Vast amounts of money would be saved with the elimination of the death penalty. Each guilty verdict requires a penalty phase trial to determine life in prison without parole, or a death sentence. These trials last for weeks. An extraordinary number of them wind up with deadlocked, or hung, juries. Usually, this sets up the need for yet another trial. I have seen many cases that required three penalty phases. At each one, taxpayers foot the bill for highly paid psychiatrists or psychologists and other "expert" witnesses to travel, usually first class, lodge in expensive

Gail Carpenter, McCartin's now-retired clerk, a lovely person I've known since our meeting at the trial of David Arnold Brown in 1990.

Let me also note that this book is entirely nonfiction. To the best of my knowledge, the events depicted herein are factual. There are no fictionalized passages such as many other "true-crime" books contain. All dialogue was obtained either from interviews or from transcripts and recordings. To protect the privacy of certain individuals, I have changed their names in the text.

hotels, eat well, and collect big checks for their testimony. This is not only for the prosecution, but for the defense as well. The total expenses are staggering.

IT IS DIFFICULT TO PIN DOWN the exact cost of murder trials. Estimates range from $7,000 to $12,000 per day in California. Capital cases probably exceed that and they tend to run longer than other murder trials. The Randy Kraft case, which extended more than twelve months, is estimated to have cost more than ten million dollars, and this was back in the late 1980s. If capital punishment ended in California, penalty phases would become unnecessary, making trial expenses significantly lower.

The appellate process is also costly, and all 650-plus condemned inmates are guaranteed an automatic appeal to the California Supreme Court.

It has been argued that a great deal of money would be saved if the executions would just be carried out. Don McCartin had something to say about that. "There are death penalty advocates who believe it would be cheaper just to execute convicted killers. That's a myth. It is actually cheaper to sentence them to life without parole. So much more money is spent in capital cases. And the death penalty, as it is administered in this state, is not a deterrent because there are so few executions."

Whether it's cheaper or not, the death penalty is not being effectively implemented now nor is it likely to happen in the foreseeable future.

If James Gregory Marlow was right in saying "the fear of death is worse than death itself," maybe interminable residence on death row is apt punishment. But with such a low rate of executions, do the hundreds of condemned inmates really fear death? Not likely.

Perhaps it is time to reconsider death penalty laws in California, and maybe across the country. Whether or not this happens, one other measure should be put into motion as soon as possible. The records for all condemned convicts should be examined to see if DNA testing might be applicable. Where it applies, such testing should be implemented without delay to prevent undermining the entire system of justice with the execution of an innocent person.

Maybe perfect justice doesn't exist, but better justice is certainly an attainable goal.

—Don Lasseter, 2004

Acknowledgments

I would like to extend my deepest appreciation to several pe without whom this book would never been born or nurtured:

Jim Riordan of Seven Locks Press, who saw its potential and the go-ahead signal.

Barbara Chuck for her remarkable editing skills

Donald A. McCartin, a judge I first admired from his courtr gallery and ultimately counted as a buddy.

Matt Murphy, deputy district attorney, who generously gave time in the courtroom, then later in his office for discussions ar review more than sixty volumes of trial transcripts.

Lew Rosenblum, Matt's boss, who graciously agreed to my i sion.

Dennis McDougal, author and friend, who allowed me to c from his book, "Angel of Darkness."

Larry Welborn, reporter for *The Orange County Register*, for his tesy, help and good humor.

Bill Cook and Geoff Christison, keepers of the Orange C court archives whose efficient and cheerful assistance were inval to me.

hotels, eat well, and collect big checks for their testimony. This is not only for the prosecution, but for the defense as well. The total expenses are staggering.

IT IS DIFFICULT TO PIN DOWN the exact cost of murder trials. Estimates range from $7,000 to $12,000 per day in California. Capital cases probably exceed that and they tend to run longer than other murder trials. The Randy Kraft case, which extended more than twelve months, is estimated to have cost more than ten million dollars, and this was back in the late 1980s. If capital punishment ended in California, penalty phases would become unnecessary, making trial expenses significantly lower.

The appellate process is also costly, and all 650-plus condemned inmates are guaranteed an automatic appeal to the California Supreme Court.

It has been argued that a great deal of money would be saved if the executions would just be carried out. Don McCartin had something to say about that. "There are death penalty advocates who believe it would be cheaper just to execute convicted killers. That's a myth. It is actually cheaper to sentence them to life without parole. So much more money is spent in capital cases. And the death penalty, as it is administered in this state, is not a deterrent because there are so few executions."

Whether it's cheaper or not, the death penalty is not being effectively implemented now nor is it likely to happen in the foreseeable future.

If James Gregory Marlow was right in saying "the fear of death is worse than death itself," maybe interminable residence on death row is apt punishment. But with such a low rate of executions, do the hundreds of condemned inmates really fear death? Not likely.

Perhaps it is time to reconsider death penalty laws in California, and maybe across the country. Whether or not this happens, one other measure should be put into motion as soon as possible. The records for all condemned convicts should be examined to see if DNA testing might be applicable. Where it applies, such testing should be implemented without delay to prevent undermining the entire system of justice with the execution of an innocent person.

Maybe perfect justice doesn't exist, but better justice is certainly an attainable goal.

—Don Lasseter, 2004

Acknowledgments

I would like to extend my deepest appreciation to several people without whom this book would never been born or nurtured:

Jim Riordan of Seven Locks Press, who saw its potential and gave the go-ahead signal.

Barbara Chuck for her remarkable editing skills

Donald A. McCartin, a judge I first admired from his courtroom gallery and ultimately counted as a buddy.

Matt Murphy, deputy district attorney, who generously gave me time in the courtroom, then later in his office for discussions and to review more than sixty volumes of trial transcripts.

Lew Rosenblum, Matt's boss, who graciously agreed to my intrusion.

Dennis McDougal, author and friend, who allowed me to quote from his book, "Angel of Darkness."

Larry Welborn, reporter for *The Orange County Register*, for his courtesy, help and good humor.

Bill Cook and Geoff Christison, keepers of the Orange County court archives whose efficient and cheerful assistance were invaluable to me.

Gail Carpenter, McCartin's now-retired clerk, a lovely person I've known since our meeting at the trial of David Arnold Brown in1990.

Let me also note that this book is entirely nonfiction. To the best of my knowledge, the events depicted herein are factual. There are no fictionalized passages such as many other "true-crime" books contain. All dialogue was obtained either from interviews or from transcripts and recordings. To protect the privacy of certain individuals, I have changed their names in the text.